The *Gecekondu*:
rural migration and urbanization

The *Gecekondu*: rural migration and urbanization

Professor of History
Chairman, Middle East Studies Program
University of Wisconsin

CAMBRIDGE UNIVERSITY PRESS

Cambridge
London   New York   Melbourne

Published by the Syndics of the Cambridge University Press
The Pitt Building, Trumpington Street, Cambridge CB2 IRP
Bentley House, 200 Euston Road, London NW1 2DB
32 East 57th Street, New York, NY 10022, USA
296 Beaconsfield Parade, Middle Park, Melbourne 3206, Australia

First published 1976

Printed in the United States of America
Typeset, printed and bound by
Vail-Ballou Press, Inc., Binghamton, New York

Library of Congress Cataloging in Publication Data
Karpat, Kemal H.
The gecekondu.
Bibliography: p.
Includes index.
1. Urbanization – Turkey.   2. Rural-urban migration –
Turkey.   3. Squatters – Turkey.   I. Title.
HT147.T9K37   301.36′1   75–12159
ISBN   0 521 20954 4

HT
147
T9
K37

Contents

Acknowledgments

Special thanks goes to the sixteen members of the research team, whose tenacity, psychological understanding of the squatters, and rigorous work discipline have made possible this demanding research. I am gratified to know that some of these people have joined various institutions in Turkey and put to good use their research experience acquired in the *gecekondu* study. Thanks are due to the Department of Social Studies at the Middle East Technical University in Ankara and Bogaziçi University (formerly Roberts College) of Istanbul for supporting financially the original research; to the Comparative World History Program, and especially the Land Tenure Center, at the University of Wisconsin, Madison, for its research assistance. Finally, thanks go to the late Lloyd T. Fallers, to Janet Abu-Lughod, and to Joan Nelson for their suggestions and comments, and to the Department of History at the University of Wisconsin, Madison, for its clerical assistance.

K. H. K.

May 1976
Madison, Wisconsin

Introduction

The purpose of this study is to investigate the socioeconomic background of the migration and urbanization of a group of rural migrants living in three *gecekondus,* or squatter settlements, in the northern hills of Istanbul. The Nafibaba (Hisarüstü), Baltaliman, and Ahmet Celâleddin Paşa (or, more commonly, Celâlettin Paşa) settlements consisted, during the chief investigation conducted in 1968, of some five hundred dwellings of various sizes and shapes with a total population of about 3500. These settlements were chosen for study because they were inhabited almost exclusively by migrants from the countryside and better reflected the basic causes of internal migration, the continuous relations with the village, and the patterns of urbanization than did the settlements inhabited by refugees or migrants from abroad. The three settlements provided a basis for studying patterns of leadership and internal organization, urban adaptation, and related matters comparatively, although intragroup comparison was not the chief purpose of this study. In addition, a series of prior contacts and familiarity with these settlements provided intimate information on the settlements and facilitated the study of the impact of migration on the squatters' village of origin.

The *gecekondus* have been regarded in this study as being part of a total process of rural migration and urbanization, or modernization – that is, of the quantitative and qualitative transformation of the economic, social, political, and cultural order – in the third world nations. Consequently, the idea that the village and city are part of a continuum in time and space – that is, part of a nation and a national territory, affecting each other and in turn affected by macro developments at national and global levels – occupies a central place in this study. Moreover, the historical factors that undermined the traditional social structure in the third world countries and freed a large number of rural people for migration and settlement elsewhere are emphasized. The Turkish *gecekondu* has been compared with similar establishments in Latin America, North Africa, and Asia, and to a much lesser extent with those in subsaharan Africa, whose establishment and growth is similar but whose urban integration seems to differ slightly from the rest.

The approach in studying rural migration and urbanization as outlined above is warranted, I believe, by concrete developments in the third world. The disintegration of the traditional social and political structures in the nineteenth century and accelerated economic development in the form of industrialization and political independence, aided by high birth rates and low mortality after World War II, have caused a vast movement of rural migrants into cities in the developing nations of Asia, Africa, and South America. The urban population of the less developed areas has risen, according to the United Nations, from 220 million in 1940 to 490 million in 1960 and is expected to reach 1045 million in 1980. Most of this growth is due to rural migration.

A substantial part of these rural migrants, or these new urban dwellers, live on the outskirts of large urban centers in shacks built illegally on the property of the state, municipalities, or individuals. Thus, a considerable part of third world urban growth occurring after World War II consists of a series of uncontrolled settlements known as squattertowns or shantytowns in English. For instance, the United Nations has estimated that the uncontrolled, or squatter, settlements in 23 countries in Africa, Asia, and Latin America account for roughly 35 percent of their total urban population.

The basic role played by squatter settlements in the development and urbanization of the third world has remained, with a few notable exceptions, outside the mainstream of socioeconomic and cultural studies despite the fact that the squatter settlements are an inherent part of the process of development and structural transformation – of the urbanization-modernization – occurring in the third world. A substantial part, though not all, of the squatter settlements are inhabited by migrants from rural areas. According to a government study, 84 percent of the squatter settlements in Turkey are inhabited by migrants. Consequently, a deeper understanding of squatter settlements is essential not only for placing rural migration and urbanization in a new perspective, but also for devising the practical policies necessary to solve the problems caused by rapid urban growth and housing shortage. Squatter settlements, notwithstanding their poor reputation, must be seen as part of the process of occupational change and social mobility, demand making, political participation, and eventual urban-national integration that is transforming the rural society in much of the third world. Finally, squatter settlements throughout the world are rather similar to each other, making global policies to deal with the problems relatively easy to develop.

Views about squatter settlements have undergone rapid change since the phenomenon was signaled as a major development some 20 years ago. They were viewed first as an abnormal urban growth and then as self-help projects undertaken by low-income urban dwellers, mostly migrants attempting to build homes with their own skills and resources. Squatter settlements are now regarded as a by-product of the malfunctioning of the economic and social system in some third world countries, a malfunctioning that creates a relation of economic marginality between the city and the low-income groups and one of dependency between the national economy and other stronger systems. All these views, including the concept of marginality, which is very useful in analyzing the migrants' relations with the new urban environment and their integration into the city, have been used in this study in accordance with my own estimation of their relative value. While emphasizing the importance of macro factors involved in rural migration and urbanization, this study has also dealt with the squatters' individual relations with two larger social units – the village and the city – of which they are a part. The migrants' constantly changing relationship and reappraisal of their position toward the city and the village have been studied in this work to the extent possible, from the viewpoint of the migrants themselves, rather than from that of those not directly involved in the process.

The squatter begins his social metamorphosis as a village dweller, changes into a rural migrant and low-paid worker in the city, turns into a squatter, and, finally, if successful, integrates himself into the city to become an urban dweller. The migrants' changing relations and affinity with the village and the city have been analyzed throughout this study in the context of economic marginality rather than cultural or social alienation. A series of variables – such as planned economic development and rapid industrialization, the developing political culture, and its underlying populist participatory philosophy – make the rural migration and the urban growth in the third world rather different from a similar process that accompanied industrialization and urbanization in the West. I have attempted, while fully adhering to basic common concepts, to view matters related to migration and urbanization in Turkey also in the light of local conditions, as well as the values of the native culture, rather than to evaluate them entirely in accordance with the social experience and goals of other societies.

In accordance with the general approach outlined above, the three squatter settlements in Istanbul have been studied in an inter-disciplinary comparative framework as part of a broad process of historical and structural transformation affecting both the village and the city, and as a process of cultural, social, and political adaptation and personality change. The residents of these settle-ments have been interviewed in order to assess the reasons for their migration from villages, their problems of integration into the urban environment, and their continuing relations with the village, and their impact thereon. I have viewed communal solidarity and village attachments surviving in the settlement as factors providing for group cohesion and facilitating a relatively healthy integration into the city, while accepting the fact that village cultural attitudes and modes of organization were gradually changed and adapted to the requirements of urban existence. Social action and politics have been regarded as a major channel for the squatters' participation and integration into urban and national life, and also possibly af-fecting the emerging national political culture.

I believe that the plan of this study reflects the approach outlined above. In the first chapter I have attempted to place the three Turkish *gecekondus* in a comparative framework by using some of the published works on squattertowns in the world, notably in Latin America and North Africa. In the following five chapters I have attempted to deal with the historical background of migra-tion in Turkey, the establishment and growth and the structure and organization of the three settlements, and the integration of the migrants into the city. Finally, in the last two chapters I have dealt with the squatters' transforming impact on the village and with party politics and political behavior in the settlements.

The basic material for this study derived from 949 interviews, based on questionnaires, with individual squatters. I was assisted by a team of 16 trained researchers. At the end of each work day, the interviewers prepared an essay giving their most striking impressions or some relevant information not included in the questionnaire. This method brought forth a series of problems and issues that seemed important for the respondents. Since I planned to study the personality changes and the differentiated responses of men, women, and younger people to village and city conditions as fully as possible, I chose to interview individually each squatter above the age of 16 rather than limit the interview to household heads, the method followed by other researchers. This approach revealed the differences in the level of education, occupations, attitudes, and aspirations prevailing among men, women, and bachelor boys and girls. A total of 430 married women, 393 married men, 89 unmarried boys, and 37 unmarried girls – or roughly about 80 percent of the squatters above the age of 16 – were subjected to interviews lasting from one and a half to four hours. Possibly the often-heard expression "İçimizi de dışımızı da öğrendiniz gayri" (You have learned our inside and outside) stands as a testimony to the comprehensive scope of the interviews.

The reason for devising a third category – the "unmarried," or bachelor boys and girls – rather than using only age categories stemmed from considerations related to Turkish culture. In Turkey, sex and family status have greater impact than age alone in determining social behavior. The unmarried men are referred to in colloquial Turkish as *delikanlı* – literally "with mad blood" – and are recognized as having certain freedom of conduct usually not granted to the married. It was assumed, therefore, that, not having family responsibilities and enjoying a certain freedom of decision, the unmarried would feel freer than the married to express their personal preferences and aspirations when confronted with a multitude of choices of professions, life styles, and behavioral patterns in the city. (Age, of course, is implicitly taken into account since with a very few exceptions, probably only three or four, the "unmarried" were between 16 and 20 years of age.)

The questionnaire used during interviews included 88 major categorical questions followed by a series of explanatory open-end questions. The answers were index-scored according to frequency and rated in percentages. For married men and women, the answers were further broken down into four age groups and into settlements. Although only a few of the hundreds of tables compiled according to age groups or settlements appear in the text of this study, the essence of these tables has been duly incorporated in various analyses and conclusions. In a number of cases, direct quotations from the respondents' answers are included in the text or notes. I have worked – in 1968 and sporadically thereafter until the fall of 1974 – in the three *gecekondus* and other establishments of the same kind in Ankara, Izmir, Bursa, and Adana, as well as in the squatters' native villages. I have naturally developed a certain familiarity and insight into the squatter settlements that has been used to check, to supplement, and to complement the information obtained through questionnaires. Since the original survey was conducted in 1968, the three settlements have tripled in population and have integrated themselves in some measure into the city. Though frequent references are made to the transformation that has been taking place since the main survey was conducted, a detailed analysis of the growth and urbanization occurring since 1968 has not been attempted in this work; actually it should be the subject of another independent study.

The terminology used in this work needs some clarification. The terms *gecekondu, squatter settlement, shantytown,* and *uncontrolled settlement* (but not slum), and *squatter* and *migrant* have been used synonymously. The terms *men* and *women* apply to married men and women; the terms *unmarried* and *bachelors* apply to unmarried boys and girls. Turkish names are spelled as in the original. (A key to the pronunciation is below.) *

It is obvious that a study as comprehensive and as ambitious as this one may not satisfy the orthodox exigencies of all social science disciplines. Yet, in order to provide a comprehensive analysis of a social problem as complex as the squatter settlement, I found it necessary to combine various concepts and approaches utilized by economics, political sciences, anthropology, and sociology. An empirical rather than theoretical approach prevails throughout the work.

---

*   A short key to Turkish pronunciation: ş = sh in short; ç = ch in church; c = j in join; ı = o in seldom; i = i in machine; ü = u in the French tu; ö = the German ö; ğ is a soft g, much the same as the running together of the words *I am*.

1. The *gecekondu* in comparative perspective

Squatter settlements and their scope

The squatter settlements inhabited mostly by country people are part of a basic process of rural migration and urbanization in many nations in the third world. Population growth, economic development, industrialization, and mechanization of agriculture, changes in land tenure, and increased communication and transportation have all contributed to the unprecedented intensity and scope of rural migration and urbanization.[1] The problems deriving from the dislocation of rural people from their small towns and villages, their settlement in larger towns and cities, and their eventual urbanization – accompanied by occupational, sociocultural, and political change – are reflected in these squatter settlements. Thus, regardless of their cultural characteristics and history, the cities and the villages and towns in the third world today are economically and sociopolitically interdependent, more so than in the past. Urban forms of association and activity are extended to the people in the countryside, while rural people adopt new occupations and life styles by moving into cities, which in turn are altered structurally and functionally by the new economic and political forces represented in part at least by the migrants themselves. These cities still retain their role as centers of power and decision and as models of development by setting socioeconomic standards and goals; at the same time they are subjected to intensive socioeconomic change by the very forces they awakened in the countryside.

Thus, rural migration and urbanization and their by-product – the migrant, or squatter, settlements – are inextricably part of a more general process of structural change usually referred to as modernization. Yet most of the work on the modernization of new nations has been devoted to selected agents of change, such as the intelligentsia, the military, and the bureaucracy, and to the channels through which these elites reach higher social status and po-

7

litical consciousness, such as education and communication. Little attention has been paid to those people undergoing transformation. Emphasis has been placed on the "transformer" and the "leader," and much less on the "transformed" and the "follower." Consequently, knowledge about how ordinary people absorb the change and become "modernized" – that is, the steps through which they move from one form of societal existence to another – has remained rather scanty. This shortcoming has resulted partly from the elitist approach that has dominated the political-historical studies of the new nations and partly from the difficulty in locating and studying individuals and social groups in a transitional, acute phase of socioeconomic transformation or modernization. The rural migrants are such a group.

The shantytowns, squattertowns, uncontrolled settlements, or transitional settlements (as the United Nations named them) in the third world usually – though not exclusively – are inhabited by migrants from villages and rural towns, who represent one of the most strategically located groups to study the transformation of a rural group into an urban one. Even a century or two ago similar settlements could be found in a few fast-growing European cities. In the third world cities, however, they have become a general feature of urbanization chiefly since World War II. Probably because of the illegal manner of their establishment, their poor reputation among the old city residents, and their open contradiction to the idea of orderly development, shantytowns have been regarded as a social aberration, falling outside the scope of the normal processes of urbanization and modernization. Certainly, squatter settlements are not an inevitable step of urbanization and modernization; they could be avoided if housing skills and financial resources were available. But in the third world, squatter settlements have become an almost natural step for modernization in general and urbanization in particular. They have become a general feature of all the major and, in many cases, the minor cities of Asia, Africa, and Latin America. These settlements, therefore, should not be regarded as a deviation from but as part of the contemporary process of economic development and urbanization-modernization in the third world.

John F. C. Turner has viewed squatter settlements in the light of four hypotheses: as a manifestation of normal urban growth under historically abnormal conditions, as vehicles for social change, as the product of the difference between the popular demand for housing and that demanded and supplied by institutional society, and as a phenomenon that could be controlled by the encouragement of popular initiative through the government servicing of local resources.[2] Thus, it is clear that rural migration into cities in the third world results in squatter settlements that are as a whole part of a total process of social change, in the form of urbanization and modernization. They are mostly the product of internal migration and should not be confused with international population movements.[3]

The outstanding features of squatter settlements seem to be, first, that they are found in nearly all the cities of the third world nations and, second, that they are often similar to each other, in terms of their evolution and their relations with the city. One cannot easily find another world-wide social phenomenon whose structural and functional similarities greatly surpass their local, regional, and even cultural differences. Consequently, it would be desirable to test this hypothesis by regarding the three Turkish *gecekondus,* or squattertowns, studied in this work, and a few others surveyed by other scholars in Turkey, as part of a world-wide phenomenon and by comparing them with similar associations elsewhere in the world, especially in Latin America and North Africa. This comparison is not intended to be an exhaustive analysis but rather a tentative effort to establish some empirical bases for a more general theoretic endeavor.[4]

The United Nations Committee on Housing, Building and Planning reported in 1973 that a survey on world housing

has confirmed the view that those living in slum and squatter settlements now account for one quarter to one third of the urban populations of most rapidly urbanizing developing countries and that this proportion is itself growing rapidly. Clearly, it is the rapid growth of slums and squatter settlements that is the major factor determining the character of cities in the developing world.

Statistics from a variety of sources agree that world population is fast growing and this growth is reflected in rapid urbanization. Indeed, the world population has increased by 29.2, 37.3, and 49.3 percent, respectively, in every 50 years in the period 1800–1950.

During the same period the world population in agglomerations of 100,000 or more has increased by 76.3, 222.2, and 254.1 percent, respectively. But the increase of population in cities with more than 100,000 people reached 444 percent in Asia and 629 percent in Africa from 1900 to 1950.[5] Similar high rates of urbanization were evident in Latin America and the Middle East.[6]

A substantial part of this new urban population, mostly of rural origin, lives in dwellings rated as shantytowns and slums. (The two terms, which are often used synonymously, refer actually to two types of urban settlements substantially different from each other, as shall be discussed later.) In India, in the late 1950s and early 1960s, 24.1 percent of the population of Ahmedabad was reported to live in houses below standard, while 16.6 percent lived in huts or shantytowns. Half of the population of Bombay, or about 3 million people, lived in slums and shantytowns. The same may be said about Madras, Kanpur, and Bangalore where the hutment slum or shantytown prevailed. "Every city or town in India of any commercial or industrial importance," a report stated, "is now plagued by hutment slums causing many public health and sociological problems."[7]

In Brazil the population of Belo Horizonte grew by 68 percent in a matter of years; it reached 812,000 people in 1966. However, 15 percent of this population lived in *favelas*.[8] By 1960, more than 10 percent of Rio de Janeiro's population of 3,307,161 people were officially declared as *favelados* (shantytown dwellers), although some other studies considered to be more realistic placed the number of *favelados* in Rio between 700,000 and 1,000,000 people. Even Brasilia, the new capital, lived up to its second name (Capital de Esperança, "hope") and had already more than 15,000 *favelados* in 1959 – even before the city was officially inaugurated.[9]

In Turkey it has been estimated that the urban population of towns with 10,000 or more increased by 409 percent from 1927 to 1965. The rate of internal migration increased from 10.5 percent of the total population in 1955 to 11.8 percent in 1965.[10] The rate of increase in the Turkish cities with populations over 100,000, however, was greater than that in the smaller localities. Much of this urban growth was due to rural migration and consisted of a string of *gecekondus* surrounding the better city quarters. The Turkish Ministry of Reconstruction and Settlement estimated, according to a survey carried out in the early 1960s, that 64 percent of the dwellings in Ankara, 48 percent in Adana, about 40 percent in Istanbul, Iskenderun, and Erzurum, and 24 percent in Izmir qualified as *gecekondu* areas. Of the total city population, *gecekondu* inhabitants constituted 59.22 percent in Ankara, 45 percent in Istanbul, 44.95 percent in Adana, and 33.42 in Izmir.[11] It has increased steadily since (see Chapter 2). Squatter settlements occupy a high percentage in the total urban population in nearly all the developing countries in the world.

(It is interesting to note that shantytowns appeared also in some of the cities in the United States and the USSR during periods of intensive industrialization and urbanization. For instance, from 1848 to 1857, the growth of Chicago as a manufacturing center was accompanied by the mushrooming of "forty or fifty acres of shanties on the West Side near Halstead and Twenty-second Street." From 1862 to 1872, the West Side population went up from 57,000 to 214,000 people, mostly workers and their families who were "crowded into frame cottages on both the front and rear of lots, near the factories along the river, on streets that had few sewers and practically no pavements."[12] In 50 years, from 1850 to 1900, Chicago grew from a small town of 29,963 people to a metropolis of 1,698,575 people. The population density per acre grew from 5 to 14.)

The statistics supplied by the United Nations further supplement these points (Tables 1.1–1.3). Table 1.4 gives detailed statistics about cities in Peru.

Squatter or uncontrolled settlements appear under a variety of names reflecting the local culture and the specific circumstances of their establishment: *gecekondu*, "built overnight" (Turkey); *favela* (Brazil); *barriadas* (Peru); *villas miseria* (Argentina); *ciudades asilas* or *ciudades de refugio* (Colombia); *colonias proletarias* (Mexico); *corralones, pueblos jovenes* (Peru); *barriadas brujas* (Panama); *poblaciones callampas*, "mushroom population or settlements" (Chile); *cantegriles* (Uruguay); *rancheros* or *conqueros* (Venezuela); *barrios de los pobres* (Ecuador); and *barrios piratas* and *arrabales* elsewhere in Latin America; *bustee* or *basti* (Calcutta-Delhi); *chawls* (Bombay); *ahatas* (Kampar); *cheris* (Madras); *sarifa* (Baghdad-Iraq); *berraka* and *nouala* (Morocco); *bidonville* (Algeria-Morocco); *gourbivilles* (Tunisia).

Table I.I. *Estimated percentages of urban population (as nationally defined)*

	1920	1940	1960	1980	2000
World total	19	25	33	41	51
More developed regions					
Europe	46	53	58	68	77
Northern America	52	59	70	78	85
USSR	15	32	49	64	76
Oceania	47	53	65	70	72
Less developed regions					
Eastern Asia	9	13	23	35	51
Southern Asia	9	12	18	25	34
Latin America	22	31	48	63	76
Africa	7	11	18	27	39
More developed regions	39	47	60	71	81
Less developed regions	8	12	20	30	43

Source: Growth of the World's Urban and Rural Population, 1920–2000 (United Nations, E.69.XIII.3) and revised figures calculated by the Population Division of the United Nations Secretariat, Document E/C. 6/115 (1971).

Table I.2. *Urban and big-city population (in millions)*

	1920	1940	1960	1980	2000
Total	1,860	2,295	2,982	4,467	6,515
More developed regions	673	821	976	1,210	1,454
Less developed regions	1,187	1,474	2,006	3,257	5,061
Urban (as nationally defined)	360	570	985	1,854	3,329
More developed regions	260	385	582	864	1,174
Less developed regions	100	185	403	990	2,155
Big-city population (500,000 inhabitants and over)	107	180	352	665	
More developed regions	93	145	221	343	
Less developed regions	14	35	131	322	

Source: United Nations, Document E/C. 6/115 (1971).

Table 1.3. *Slums and uncontrolled settlements in various cities in developing countries*

Country	City	Year	City population[a]	Population in slums and uncontrolled settlements Total	Percentage of city population
Africa					
Senegal	Dakar	1969	500,000	150,000	30
United Republic of Tanzania	Dar-es-Salaam	1967	272,800	93,000	34
Zambia	Lusaka	1967	194,000	53,000	27
Asia					
Afghanistan	Kabul	1968	475,000	100,000	21
Ceylon	Colombo	1953		1,347 (d.u.)	
		1963	69,500 (d.u.)	30,500 (d.u.)	44
China (Taiwan)	Taipei	1966	1,300,000	325,000	25
India	Calcutta	1961	6,700,000	2,220,000	33
Indonesia	Jakarta	1961	2,906,000	725,000	25
Iraq	Baghdad	1965	1,745,000	500,000	29
Malaysia	Kuala Lumpur	1961	400,000	100,000	25
Pakistan	Karachi	1964	2,280,000	752,000	33
		1968	2,700,000	600,000	27
Philippines	Manila	1968	less than 3,000,000	1,100,000	35
Republic of Korea	Seoul	1970	440,000 (d.u.)	136,550 (d.u.)	30
Singapore	Singapore	1966	1,870,000	280,000	15
Europe					
Turkey	Total urban population	1965	10,800,000	2,365,000	21.8
	Ankara	1965	979,000	460,000	47
		1970	1,250,000	750,000	60
	Izmir	1970	640,000	416,000	65
North and South America					
Brazil	Rio de Janeiro	1947	2,050,000	400,000	20
		1957	2,940,000	650,000	22
		1961	3,326,000	900,000	27

Table 1.3. *Cont.*

Country	City	Year	City population[a]	Population in slums and uncontrolled settlements	
				Total	Percentage of city population
Brazil	Belo				
	Horizonte	1965	872,300	119,799	14
	Porto Alegre	1962	680,000	86,465	13
	Recife	1961	792,000	396,000	50
	Brasilia	1962	148,000	60,000	41
	State of				
	Guanabara	1950	2,240,000	159,000	7.1
		1960	3,300,000	337,000	10.2
Chile	Santiago	1964	2,184,000	546,000	25
Colombia	Cali	1964	812,810	243,840	30
	Buenaventura	1964	110,660	88,530	80
Ecuador	Guayaquil	1968	730,000	360,000	49
Mexico	Mexico City	1952	2,372,000	330,000	14
		1966	3,287,334	1,500,000	46
Panama	Panama City	1968	373,000	63,00	17
Peru	Lima	1957	1,260,729	114,000	9
		1961	1,715,971	360,000	21
		1969	2,800,000	1,000,000	36
	Arequipa	1957	117,208	10,500	9
		1961	135,358	54,143	40
	Chimbote	1957	33,000	6,600	20
Venezuela	Caracas	1961	1,330,000	280,000	21
		1964	1,590,000	556,300	35
	Maracaibo	1966	559,000	280,000	50
	Barquisimeto	1968	30,530 (d.u.)	12,518 (d.u.)	41
	Ciudad				
	Guayana	1966	86,000	34,000	40

[a] Where census or U.N. Yearbook figures were not available for city populations in years required to correspond with the data on slums and uncontrolled settlements, figures were derived using the most accurate base data
and growth rates.
Note: d.u. = dwelling units.
Source: United Nations, *Report by Secretary General to the United Nations
General Assembly 1970 A/8937.*

Table 1.4. *Population in squatter settlements in
Peruvian cities, 1961*

	Population	In settlements	Percentage
Chimbote	66,683	45,065	67.5
Iquitos	58,110	36,000	61.9
Arequipa	162,195	63,200	39.0
Sullana	28,709	10,200	35.5
Chiclayo	90,726	31,500	34.7
Piura	81,405	28,200	34.6
Trujillo	104,198	34,500	33.1
Lima (Metro)	1,640,000	404,225	24.6
Pucallpa	27,238	6,000	22.0
Tacna	27,139	4,000	14.7
Cuzco	81,057	5,010	6.2

Source: Laquian, ed., *Rural-Urban Migrants*, p. 117.

Shantytowns appear in general as a conglomeration of hastily built shacks on the outskirts of cities; they range from one-room dwellings to full-size houses with or without a small yard, depending on the availability of land. Most post-World War II shantytowns were established in the vicinity of work places. Invasion was a frequent but not exclusive method for establishing a settlement. It has not been unusual to see empty hills covered in a single night with a great number of shacks in which tens of thousands of people moved with their belongings in a matter of hours. The population of shantytowns may range from a few dozen to over a hundred thousand people. The larger squattertowns often emerge after small settlements, each one bearing its own name, combine to form a single body, or the existing ones spread out and incorporate existing villages into their own body.

The squatter settlements have been defined in a variety of ways, chiefly according to their physical appearance or legal status. The United Nations refers to them simply as "non-legal or illegal occupation of land or construction of buildings by low-income people." The third world governments appear to define squattertowns chiefly in legal terms and regard them as an infringement on

private property rights. Thus, in Lima, Peru, shantytowns are defined as established with or without municipal authorization on the
"territorial zone of fiscal, municipal, communal or private property
. . . found on the outskirts of the populated centers . . . [and
occupied] by invasion and in spite of legal dispositions on property."[13] In Kuala Lumpur the squatter is defined as "a person who
settles on land without a legal title or right to it."[14] The Brazilian
Institute of Geography and Statistics defines the *favela* as an urbanized area consisting of a minimum number of 50 dwellings of
huts and barracks of rustic appearance and unlicensed and unin-
spected buildings erected on the land of the third or unknown
owners and without general city services.[15] In Turkey, law 775 of
July 20, 1966, defines the *gecekondus* as "dwellings erected, on
the land and lots which do not belong to the builder, without the
consent of the owner, and without observing the laws and regulations concerning construction and building." The *bastis* of India
are defined as "kucha-hut, with a single door, made out of mud,
bamboo, stones and tin sheeting."[16]

In the next sections shantytowns will be viewed comparatively
within the framework of two basic social phenomena – rural migration and urbanization – and their underlying causes.

Rural migration

Historical causes of migration

Rural migration, which feeds the population growth and squatter
settlements in the third world cities, was preceded and prepared
historically by basic changes in the economy and social structure
of the third world in the nineteenth and early twentieth centuries.
These changes undermined the traditional land tenure, the system
of production and exchange, and the social system that supported
them. The fluctuations in the world markets occurring toward the
end of the nineteenth century tended to further aggravate this
trend, while the national economies of third world countries became dependent on industrial and financial centers in the West. As
Max Weber noted, fluctuations in the world market stimulated migration even from eastern Germany into industrialized areas.

The disintegration of the traditional social structures that began in the nineteenth century – caused by the expansion of trade, the introduction of a cash economy and the adaptation of agricultural production to markets, and the rise of urban centers serving as exchange places and export outlets – may be cited as the first major historical factor preparing the ground for migration. In Turkey, the Black Sea region developed an active trade – small food-processing plants – and geared its local economy for export, largely as a consequence of expansion of the Tabriz-Trabzon (Trebizond) trade route and the subsequent opening of the southern Black Sea shores to the British, French, Austrian, and Russian trade during the nineteenth century. Consequently, agricultural methods, as well as the entire pattern of production and the traditional social organization, were changed. A new type of middle class rose in cities and towns. All this came to an abrupt end toward the end of the century as the Tabriz-Trabzon route lost its economic importance and trade slackened. Deprived of measures likely to continue economic development, the middle class began to disintegrate because many of their professions were no longer in demand. Unemployment began to rise in towns among the working population. Since many agricultural products found no buyers, agriculture, which had been geared to produce raw material for the market, reverted to subsistence farming, but without being able to feed the rapidly growing population.

Some trace the beginning of massive rural migration and hence the rise of *favelas* in Brazil to the technological changes introduced in agriculture and to the abolition of slavery in 1888.[17] The economic crisis of 1929–31 further affected the agriculture of Brazil and increased unemployment, as it did in nearly all the countries whose main source of foreign currency were the agricultural commodities exported to the West. Some of the affected governments tried to fight the agricultural unemployment by supporting industrialization, which in turn stimulated the growth of population and eventual migration into the city. For instance, as early as 1910 the efforts of Diaz in Mexico to industrialize the country was considered a major factor of social dislocation, population growth, and migration. In Algeria the major cause for migration was the disintegration of the traditional structure as a consequence of the French colonial policy. Indeed, the French administration introduced in 1863 and 1873 laws that destroyed the age-old communal type of property in the countryside by dividing it among the *douars* (tribal segments) and by subjecting it to the provisions of private property, whereas forests, wooded areas, and *beylik* lands (fiefs of the old administrators) became state property.[18] Some of the best arable lands in Algeria – some 3 million hectares (one hectare is just over two acres) – passed into the hands of the Europeans. Muslims, who were deprived of prime lands and continued to enforce the liberal Shariat principles with respect to inheritance, saw their holdings diminishing further in size and productivity.[19] The tribal leaders also relinquished their authority to *caids* (government agents). Thus, the tribe and its supporting economic basis disintegrated and impoverished the population, indirectly compelling it to move elsewhere.

In Morocco, the drought in the southern provinces, the European colonization, the deterioration of the arable soils, the usurpation of the land by notables, the French administrative measures, coupled with a historical tendency of the southern people to go to the more humid and greener sections in the north,[20] stand as the main historical and economic causes of migration and settlement in the cities.[21] Elsewhere in Africa, as E. P. Skinner pointed out, migration was a modern phenomenon, stimulated by the presence of the Europeans and sustained by changing socioeconomic conditions. The current pattern of migration among the Mossi was set after their traditional routes to the north were destroyed, the French began to build railways in the south, and manpower needs in the Gold Coast increased.[22]

Similar historical causes of social disintegration and migration can be cited ad infinitum. Nevertheless, it must be noted that the economic crisis of 1929–30 was a turning point in the economy of the third world and in the history of migration. These countries seem to have developed their agriculture largely according to the food and raw material needs of the industrial centers in the West, while cities were established primarily for trade, communication, administrative, and military purposes. Later some industries were located in these cities and stimulated their growth and occupational differentiation. In colonial regimes, the ruling power used the capital and provincial cities to maintain its integrated administration and as an economic basis for its power and for the collection of taxes. The city in Africa was a place where many natives took menial jobs and received wages which they often spent on imported goods. It was also a place for the upper groups to educate their children, who often subsequently became alienated from their native culture and joined the colonial administrative bureaucracy. The economic development in the third world, dependent on outside centers of financial and economic power, nevertheless brought about a limited degree of mechanization and improvement in agriculture, which began to alter the rural structure in some of these countries. All this came to a halt in 1929–31, as farm prices fell and the agricultural employment dropped considerably. Large numbers of people were ready to migrate wherever employment opportunities became available.

The mechanization of agriculture after World War II, which left jobless the agricultural workers and eliminated the marginal farmers, coupled with a population explosion were other recent causes that aggravated further the social dislocation and increased the pressure for migration in rural areas.[23] Indeed, the population explosion in the third world after World War II was caused, in part at least, by the same economic and social factors stemming from the disintegration of the traditional socioeconomic order and the consequent breakdown of the natural birth control methods inherent within it. Better medical facilities and other factors helped further the population growth. It is not the purpose of this study to deal with the causes of population growth but merely to stress the point that structural differentiation, economic development, and population are closely interrelated and form the macro framework in which village-city relations develop. That villages and cities are part of the same socioeconomic whole is a concept central to this work.[24]

An understanding of the historical causes of migration is also useful in evaluating the pattern of migrants' movement, settlement, and integration into the city. For instance, in Latin America the Spanish Catholic – Indian cultural duality, consisting of the original Indian – Quecho and Cholos of Peru – the meztee, and the Spanish colonial stratum, was occasionally evident in the settlement patterns, in the associations formed by migrants in the city, and in their spoken language and cultural attitudes.[25] In Turkey, for instance, the Alevi, an unorthodox sect, tend to settle in one area and try to maintain some of their traditions, thus reflecting in rather faint fashion the old conflict between orthodoxy and unorthodoxy in Islam. As a whole, however, whether in Turkey, Latin America, or even Asia, squatter settlements tend to be homogeneous; especially if they are small[26]

Population growth and economic development

The main "push" factor in rural migration is poverty and low income and all it entails, such as lack of educational and medical facilities. The "pull" factor in the cities is the opportunity for employment and higher income and the availability of educational, medical, and other facilities. However, population growth in many third world countries is above or equal to economic growth, thus providing limited or no room for an increase in living standards. Moreover, a large number of these countries, especially in Asia, are faced with unemployment or marginal employment. It is this aspect of the problem that has given rise to a series of views that urbanization in the third world is taking place without industrialization, hence the terms *urban peasants* and *pseudourbanization*. Consequently, many of these nations appear overurbanized in relation to their size and resources.[27] There is no question that there is overcrowding and insufficient economic development, yet new forces are at work. These third world cities perform a variety of new functions and should not be judged according to elitist or Western concepts of urbanism. Actually, the rate of employment among recent rural migrants in the city is relatively high, their living standard – at least in comparison with that in the village – is up, and their future expectations are optimistic.

The contradiction between high birth rate and slow economic development and the relative well being of the rural migrants can be explained partially by the nature of the economic development in some of the third world nations. These countries have freed themselves to some extent from dependency on the industrially developed nations as suppliers of raw materials and foodstuffs and have begun to industrialize and develop their economies through central planning and the exploitation of their domestic resources.[28] Industrialization and the distribution of manufactured items including consumer goods led to the development of domestic centers of production and consumption. The development of domestic industries and markets provided an outlet for employment to a large number of semiemployed villagers and to those who had been dislocated by more efficient farming methods and by mechanization. Consequently, migration and urbanization should be regarded as a consequence of economic development in general and of agricultural conditions in particular. Thus, the transfer of workers from agriculture to industry appears as a movement of manpower from village to town and has the indirect effect of easing the pressure on land and permitting agriculture to move – if favorable conditions are provided – from subsistence farming to production for market. In turn, all this stimulates consumption of farm commodities in the city and of manufactured goods in villages and integrates the rural areas into the national economy.[29]

As a result of these changes, inland cities in the third world that were closer to consumer centers began to develop fast, sometimes even faster than the old seaports that had been used as outlets for exports and imports. Moreover, the increasing demand for consumer goods, both domestic and imported, that was stimulated by the auspicious climate created by international trade and favorable monetary conditions prevailing from 1950 to 1970 further aided the growth of cities. Thus, the basic shift in the direction and goals of production, from agriculture to manufactured goods and from export to domestic consumption, dramatically showed the cities to be the most efficient units of production and consumption and intensified labor division. The rapid growth of urban centers stimulated in turn the demand for goods, especially food stuffs. Lack of demand for agricultural commodities, incidentally, was considered an impediment to the development of agriculture in the third world. The demand for food stuffs in turn helped improve farm efficiency by allowing the introduction of large mechanized agricultural units, which led to further dislocation of marginal farmers and eventually to their migration into cities.

However, all this does not explain fully the paradox of high unemployment and slow economic development at the national level and the relative development and satisfaction among the migrants in squatter settlements in the cities. The explanation lies in the fact that the newly established industries were located in cities and that industrialization created jobs in the tertiary (service) sector of the economy and spurred the growth of small enterprises employing

5 to 25 men in the lower segments of the secondary (industrial) sector. These depended not on efficient and expensive machinery but on cheap manpower. In Turkey, the new arrivals worked mostly in small enterprises or had a variety of low-paying jobs including peddling food stuffs. In an area surveyed in Bogotá, Colombia, 82 percent of the new arrivals worked in enterprises employing fewer than 20 workers. The older arrivals formed 74 percent, whereas those born in Bogotá made up 67 percent, of the workers in such enterprises.[30] Small individual enterprises are also found in the shantytowns.[31]

The enterprises employing the rural migrants usually pay low wages, use traditional technology, and have low productivity and inefficient marketing. Because they are small and median enterprises, and rely on a mode of organization similar to traditional craftsmen organizations, they have a major capacity to absorb extra manpower.[32] These types, and the low-paying enterprises may prefer to employ unskilled migrants, who may feel more at ease working in such jobs rather than in modern enterprises using high technology. Jorge Balan has made the point that if one knew certain structural characteristics of the migrants' communities of origin and of destination, one could predict the degree of success of migrants in competing for jobs with all city dwellers. If the rate of job creation is low and skill or credential requirements are high the migrant will be at a disadvantage. Now, however, in the cities it seems that the rate of job creation is high and skill or credential requirements are low, all of which favors the migrant.[33]

Thus, one arrives inevitably at the conclusion that the rate and nature of economic development in the third world cities favor the employment of unskilled and low-paid workers. It is the presence of these workers and their economy that made T. G. McGee speak of an "upper" system and a "lower" system of economy in southeast Asia, the latter consisting of squatters and migrants in the city.[34] The other dimension of the same economic development is that rural migration is making available to small enterprises cheap manpower, cheap even by the standards of the third world. Moreover, by easing the rent pressure indirectly the squattertown assists in the accumulation of capital and the growth of a middle class. Most of the privately owned industrial enterprises do not provide housing for their employees. This situation, coupled with the rise in rents, placed the marginal workers – most migrants and shantytown dwellers fall into this category – in a rather difficult financial position. Because of a lack of trade union membership and support, the migrants employed in small enterprises are unable to engage in collective bargaining and costly strikes to force the employers to raise their wages in accordance with the rise in living and housing costs.

When the opportunity presents itself, the worker-migrant builds his own dwelling (usually on the land of the government, municipality, or absentee private landowners), saves on house rent, and thus is less pressured to ask his employer for higher wages. One may assume therefore that the shantytowns have an indirect role in keeping wages down in some enterprises and services. Moreover, the location of the shantytowns on the outskirts of cities is an indirect boost to investment since such location is determined largely by its proximity to the work place. Many new plants are established on the outskirts of cities in order to avoid the high prices for land or rentals in the city proper. In sum, it seems that a series of general economic conditions related to capital formation and industrialization favors rural migration and the establishment of shantytowns.

Shantytowns and slums

Shantytowns appear as the by-product of rapid economic development and industrialization, of changes in agriculture and shortage of housing. In other words, it is not the result of communal or psychological disintegration in the village or in the city. Consequently, despite some resemblance in outward appearance, shantytowns should not be confused with the slums in the industrially developed nations, notably in the United States, and similar ones (usually located in the oldest quarters of the city) in the third world cities. The differences between slums and shantytowns are so vast as to deserve special attention. Slums, according to one view, represent "the end product of forces in American society that are divisive and destructive";[35] the dictionary defines a slum as a thickly populated street or alley marked by wretched living conditions. Some scholars regard the slum, mostly following the characteristics of the American model, as a source of poverty, run-down housing, crowded concentration of lower-class people, high rate of crime and divorce, violence and alienation, isolation, strife with the conventional world, detachment from the city people, low literacy, family disintegration, loss of identity, child neglect, sexual indecency, racial discrimination, gangsterism, hatred of police, and, lately, urban guerrillas. Some regard the slum as a social necessity for the elite, providing them with services (call girls, gambling, underworld connections); others see it also as a place of fulfill-ment, giving to its residents a sense of identity, independence, and satisfaction.[36] These views may, in fact, reflect the observers' own class values since some areas classified as slums, when subjected to close scrutiny, appear as a healthy and integrated community with a life of its own – for example, the West End in Boston,[37] which was demolished because an interest group wanted the land to build high-rent apartments.

In any case, slums can be separated into several categories. J. R. Seeley has divided them into "slums of despair," or the place for "permanent necessitarians," a last resort for people who have suffered total defeat in life, and "slums of hope," or the place for the "temporary opportunists," who used its low-cost facilities in making their way upward on the social ladder.[38] Finally, others have looked on the slum as an aggregate of groups and cultures that do not ignore the outside world but use it only to the extent it is applicable to the situations prevailing in the area.[39]

Few of the features ascribed to the slum are applicable to the shantytown. Indeed, aside from low income, drab-looking houses, and lack of the normal city facilities, few squattertowns show any symptoms of social or psychological disintegration, moral de-pravity, and crime. Those who look at the exterior of a shantytown usually transfer to it all their stereotyped images connected with a slum. But those who have had personal contact with the shanty-town dwellers "agree," as Mangin stated it in his outstanding study, "sometimes to their own surprise that it is difficult to describe squatter settlements as slums."[40] In the squatter settlements there is poverty but no culture of poverty. On the basis of my own in-vestigations in Turkey, I fully concur that the squatter settlements, with due exceptions, are not centers of crime, prostitution, juvenile delinquency, economic drain, and radicalism, but associations of optimistic people aspiring to reach a higher living standard and a more satisfactory mode of existence. Mangin views the squatter settlement not as a problem but as a solution to a problem.

There are, on the other hand, in every major city in the developing nations, usually within the ancient city walls, groups of lower-class dwellings that closely resemble the slums in the industrial nations and occasionally create concern for law enforcement agencies. Known as *callejones, corralones, jacals,* and *tugurios* (alleys, shackyards) in Latin America (some of the *katras* and *abadis* and *ahatas* in India may be included in this category),[41] *kaledibi* (bottom of fortress) districts in Turkish cities, and *casbas* and *fondouks*[42] in North Africa, these settlements usually harbor low-income people. Having arrived in the city as migrants and workers one or two generations ago, these people eventually became alienated from their original communities, but without forming a new community of their own and without integrating themselves fully into the city. These older settlements were established around railroad stations and yards, in old caravansaries (inns) in the Middle East, and factories usually close to the center of town. This development occurred mostly during the limited economic development and industrialization of 1880–1930, under the impact of the dominating Western powers. In comparison with the shantytown, these old-type slums make up a rather small percentage of the total city population. The shantytown may be regarded as the hopeful beginning of the migrant's effort to integrate himself into urban life, whereas the slum may symbolize his failure to achieve it.

Migration patterns and causes

The literature on migration in Turkey and elsewhere in the world stresses the fact that the building of roads and the availability of transportation in the third world was a technical factor facilitating the villagers' movement into cities. A substantial part of the traffic between major cities and smaller towns, where the roads usable by motor vehicles usually end, is made up of villagers moving to cities or going to visit their relatives there or migrants returning to see their relatives in rural areas.

The migratory movement at the foundation of the squatter settlements seem to fall in one of the following patterns:[43]

1   From village or tribal area to the city (direct migration)
2   From village or tribal area to a smaller town and then to city (indirect migration)
3   From one or more smaller towns to a city (semidirect migration)
4   From one city district (usually poor and overcrowded) to the squatter settlement (direct migration)
5   From city back to a town or village, either to retire or live there (return migration); this rare occurrence will not be dealt with

The rural migrants in the 1950s and before usually followed patterns (2) and (3), whereas those migrating later followed pattern (1). The founders of the squattertowns usually followed pattern (4). The evidence in hand suggests that, contrary to an appearance of disorganization and hastiness, migration to the city and to the squatter settlement follows a rational plan involving decision making and information about job availability and housing facilities. Usually the first settlers in the city who are relatives or village friends of the would-be migrants provide the strategy for migration and settlement.[44] Again, the information culled from a variety of sources shows that throughout the world, the first migrants are younger men (unmarried or recently married) and are followed eventually by their young male close relatives (usually brothers), wives and children, and occasionally by their parents. The studies on squatter settlements surveyed in this work indicate that on the average about 75 to 80 percent of the squatters are below 40 years of age – that is, in their prime working age. In Rabat in 1965 56.5 percent were less than 20 years old. The rate of literacy among migrants is usually much higher than the literacy rate in the village. Indeed, the literacy rate among men in Turkey was 84 percent (much above the national average of 65 percent); in Lima, Peru, 86 percent; in Caracas, 75 percent; and in India (Delhi), 42 percent. The literacy rate was even higher among the younger generation, who consider education necessary to compete for jobs in the city.

The size of squatter families in various countries appears also to be smaller when compared with those in rural areas, though it is higher than the size of an average urban family.[45] Migration and life in the squatter settlement provides, through economic hardships and self-awareness, a form of check on population growth, which could become even more effective if the information and the means of birth control were made more readily available to the shantytown residents. Many of the women interviewed in Turkey blame their parents for raising too many children to be able to educate them properly. While the first migrants are younger and better educated, as migration advances the quality deteriorates: the ratio of older, unskilled, and uneducated increases, and people from remote areas, such as mountainous regions, and isolated tribes with limited exposure to communication begin to arrive in the city.

Shantytown dwellers throughout the world usually express their reasons for migrating in economic terms, such as poverty in the village, stemming from lack of land, unproductive soil, excessive population ("too little land, too many people"), and low wages (or, expressed differently, desire to earn more money). Other reasons for migration often cited by migrants include lack of educational and medical facilities in the village, desire to join family (usually husbands and parents), yearning to be away from in-laws and live within a nuclear family, search for a freer and more active life In Colombia fear of violence and in Turkey the *kan davası* (vendetta) appear as incidental causes of migration from village to city.

The actual move to the squatter settlement, if occurring after migration to the city, is usually attributed to high rentals, the hope of acquiring a house and becoming a "proprietor," better housing (since many shantytowns are more sanitary and spacious than the dilapidated buildings in the city), desire to join relatives, and other reasons.[46]

There are other cultural and historical reasons conditioning rural-urban migration. In Turkey, besides economic and personal reasons, the choice of a city of settlement was also conditioned by "social gravity," that is, historical precedents, a sense of cultural and historical identification with the city, and other related factors.[47]

The establishment of the squattertown

The manner in which squatters in all third world countries take possession of the land, plan and build their dwellings, and eventually expand them is strikingly similar. The immediate cause prompting such action is the shortage of housing coupled with high rentals in the city. This situation is aggravated by lack of a proper government housing policy stemming either from lack of social concern and planning experience or, most often, from investment priorities that favor industrialization and defense rather than social welfare. Moreover, as mentioned before, the location of employment places often determines the site of the *gecekondu*. (For instance, in socialist Yugoslavia, which underwent rapid industrialization, rural migration was prompted by the same causes as elsewhere in the world. However, shantytowns were not established there not only because of stern government measures, but also because of the availability of modest but very inexpensive rooms rented to factory workers that cost 2 to 5 percent of their monthly earnings.)[48]

The specific ways that shantytowns are established, a spectacular affair indeed, follow a precise and planned course in which housing and building skills, community spirit, entrepreneurship, and profit motives play their part.[49] In some cases a few individuals may establish a few dwellings on a large, vacant, and rather inaccessible piece of land and then parcel and sell it to relatives and friends.[50] In Turkey there are specialized *gecekondu* dealers who have built and sold dwellings to migrants and have become rich and prominent in the process. In some other cases the settlement may be established as the consequence of an organized mass invasion by dwellers living in the overpopulated city quarters or older squatter settlements; election time is preferred for such action. There are very few cases in which the incoming villagers established a settlement directly before spending some time in the city. The decision to invade a vacant lot is made after it has been surveyed in advance. Then thousands of people move overnight onto it, divide and name it (usually giving it a name that sounds patriotic or is associated with a famous national or religious figure), and begin to build shacks on it with the assistance of friends and relatives. Paper boards, tin plates, and other usable materials are used to erect the "houses" in a matter of hours. By morning the previously empty land appears dotted with one-room shacks that, if successfully defended against the police, may be gradually expanded to become permanent houses. Observers agree that if it were not for this form of house building, the housing authorities could not meet the housing demand.[51] Moreover, the mere act of invasion is actually a community action that forms a basis for solidarity and cohesion in the shantytown. The investment in this form of housing in terms of labor, material, and land improvement adds considerable value to the city properties and subsequently increases the urban tax revenues.

Equally important is the fact that if the shantytown dwellers eventually become the owners of the shack-houses they turn into champions of private property, free enterprise, and democratic politics. The rate of house owners in shantytowns is high. In Turkey, 84 percent of the squatters interviewed in this study owned their houses. In Latin America (Caracas) the percentage of house owners ranged between 93 and 96 percent. In India between 81 and 93 percent of the total number of inhabitants interviewed in one study owned their houses. In Rabat's shantytowns 75 to 90 percent of dwellers owned their *baraques.* (In contrast, the slum dweller does not own the apartment or the house that he inhabits.) In some cases, as in Rabat and Kuala Lumpur, the shack owners pay a rent to the land owner.

It seems that shantytown dwellings everywhere expand in a more or less similar manner. Usually new units are added to the original room, especially after the deed to the land has been legally acquired, and thus shacks often become true houses. The physical shape of squatter dwellings and the materials used show great variation from country to country; however, a thorough study of this technical matter is beyond the scope of this comparative survey.[52]

The shack is an anchor point in the squatter's existence. One is struck by the tenderness and devotion (especially after the legal title to the land is safely secured) with which the squatter, at least in Turkey, tends to his shack, turning it into a real house. Many have small gardens and a variety of flowers seldom seen in city slums. Most squatters regard their shack both as a shelter in which to recuperate their energy for the next day's arduous work and as a means to be with their own families and to integrate themselves into the community at large. Consequently, it is easy to understand why the crime rate is very low. Even those students who had misconceptions about the squatters agree that crime, prostitution, gambling, and drugs present little problem in most of the shantytowns.[53]

The urbanization of rural migrants

The city and the third world

There are two disparate views about migrants' relations with the city – that is, their urbanization. One school of thought, led by Louis Wirth and accepted as the leading one for more than two decades, defines urbanization as a totally transforming process that leads to the disappearance of the neighborhood and to the disintegration of kinship bonds, to the decline of the social significance of the family and of the traditional attachments and solidarity.[54] In this view, urbanization is a process of assimilation whereby the migrants discard their folk culture, the faster the better, and acquire urban habits and values. According to this view, the city and the associations prevailing there are so different from the rural ones as to make impossible their adoption by villagers without a complete break with their own background. Eventually the new urban and national identity emerging in the city would not only supersede the migrants' local, tribal, village, and communal loyalties but actually replace and obliterate them.

A second school of thought defines urbanization in the context of rural migration as a process of ruralization, or "peasantization," of the city. In other words, this school regards the squatter settlements as an extension of the rural zone into the city, or as the continuation of the natural environment within the urban technological one, where the migrants reproduce and maintain an almost exact replica of their village culture and the rural mode of life.[55] If pushed to extremes, the first view, which adopts the elite middle-class view of urbanism, would lead to a total dichotomy between village and the city, whereas the second would end in a total rejection of the urban environment and its transforming effect. These seemingly exclusive views will be dealt with after a third problem that seems quite relevant to the urbanization of the shantytown is briefly mentioned. The problem concerns the nature and function of the city in the third world.

It is essential to note that the traditional city in the third world, especially the Muslim, had little in common with the "ideal" Western city of Max Weber. Its political and economic life was different from that of the countryside, although its cultural and religious life was not. With the expansion of European political and economic domination in the nineteenth century, many cities in the third world became centers for the economic and political power of the colonial powers and of the native classes associated with them in various administrative or educational roles. Throughout this period the native "modern," or urbanized, class preserved its formal cultural ties with the lower classes, often by speaking the same language and by maintaining, outwardly at least, the same religious affiliation. It acted so since peaceful, friendly relations with the lower classes was essential for performing its intermediary economic role. In those cases in which the native middle urban class became alienated from its own group, it either disintegrated, as with the Levantines, or tried to rejoin its original group by initiating revolutionary action against the outsiders or by striving for an ethnic-cultural revival.

The Muslim cities discussed in various places in this study are probably the most striking example of this transformation. These cities have flourished, with ups and downs, since the inception of Islam, which looked on the city as a special environment where absolute perfection and virtue could be reached. Consequently, Muslim city planners strove to create in the city all the material and moral conditions necessary for the *umma* (community of God) to attain perfect virtue.[56] Thus, the Muslim city and its culture flourished and dominated, but also it integrated the countryside culturally into the system, through a centralized political administration. Intensive upward social mobility from the village into the city occurred mostly within the large religious establishment and was facilitated by the *vaqf* system (pious foundations performing social services, usually in the city, based on revenue derived largely from agriculture).

The Muslim city fell under the political and economic influence of the industrial, market-oriented economics of the West in the nineteenth century and collapsed rapidly, chiefly because its sustaining economic foundation – that is, its crafts – and market organization proved unable to compete with Western goods. However, simultaneous with the collapse of the traditional city, a new urban development occurred in the Muslim countries of the Middle East and North Africa. The new urban growth took place around the old city, if the latter had a central position and possessed good land or sea routes to be used as outlets for export, as was the case with Istanbul and other cities.[57]

This urban development created a new dichotomy between village and city in the Islamic countries by giving priority to economic interests conceived not as part of a cultural-religious system, but strictly as market relations. Thus, the old cultural and social harmony between village and city was broken. The break was aggravated further by the emergence of an urban secular educational system and a political elite oriented toward the West. Eventually, the cities in the third world, both Islamic and non-Islamic, came to resemble each other largely because of their economic role as outlets for the export of food and raw materials and as importing and marketing centers for goods coming from the industrial nations. These cities were not manufacturing centers, did not possess industry and high technology, communication, and fixed capital, and could not provide outlets for specialized education and scientific investigation; in comparison with Western cities, they were not centers of innovation and of high concentration of skills. All this changed rapidly as political independence, at least in some cases, combined with economic development and industrialization forced the third world cities after World War II to acquire rapidly the technological and the cultural and scientific features associated with industrially advanced countries. In other words, the third world "city" was compelled to become a new or a modern city by following a special evolutionary path of its own, and eventually by acquiring some technology. (This seemed to support in some ways Sjoberg's view that technology distinguishes the modern, industrial, from the premodern, preindustrial, city, the latter to be found in old or preliterate and feudal societies.) Consequently, the cities in the third world are undergoing profound transformation through industrialization or acquisition of technology. As noted by other scholars, the primate and parasitic and orthogenetic cities (a single, large city in a country where most cultural, political activities are concentrated and perpetuated and investment monopolized) that were dominant in the third world are being replaced by generative and heterogenetic cities – that is, the modern multifunctional cities.[58]

As a whole, urban transformation and the peculiarities embodied in it call for a new view in appraising the squatters' impact on the cities in the third world. If the current migration were caused by temporary social and political factors, rather than basic permanent structural changes, and if the number of migrants were limited (as happened repeatedly in the past, notably in Turkey), the city might have assimilated the newcomers by absorbing them into its prevailing structure and rigid urban culture. Obviously this is not the case with the present migration. The newcomers have imposed on the city their own outlook on society and the world, often to the outraged dismay of old urbanites.

The massive influx of a rural or semirural population into the old cities of the third world coupled with industrialization had also changed drastically both the urban environment and its culture. The folk culture and the various forms of religion often bordering on animism brought in by the migrants have altered the traditional forms of elite culture prevailing in the old cities. In the Muslim world, in particular, the rural migrants have shattered the idea that cities are the symbols of cultural refinement and religious orthodoxy and have undermined profoundly the sharply differentiated social arrangement that had made the city appear as permanently superior to the village.

I believe that the new city emerging, at least in some Muslim countries, comprises to a degree both the features of the traditional Islamic and European cities, along with the folk culture, community feeling, natural attitudes, pragmatism, and materialism of the countryside. Muslim cities had long developed a special form, culture, and personality of their own on which Europe grafted its own version of urbanity in the nineteenth century. But recent massive migration from the countryside has changed all this. Descloitres and his associates have noted that the Algerian inhabitant of the *bidonville* was an uprooted man whom the Europeans and his own native city bourgeoisie and craftsmen, both of whom represented the two established city traditions of Europe and Islam, were powerless to absorb.[59] The Algerian and Morroccan *bidon-villes,* which grew as a third distinct type of urban settlement in Muslim North Africa, eventually overwhelmed the traditional Islamic and European urban traditions and created a separate identity through political revolution. Nearly all the Muslim cities in the Middle East are rapidly losing their traditional elitist features as they are opening up to the influences of the countryside through the migrant-squatters.

The emphasis placed on the role played by rural migration on urbanization in the third world should be balanced by another view – namely, the transforming impact of the city on the migrant.

The city has a profound changing effect on the migrant, especially in occupational habits, organizations for social and political actions, family size and relations, levels of aspiration, and values related to communication. This change occurs in large measure because the city itself is being transformed by industrialization, technology, and political action. This situation can be described as "modernization" for the city and "urbanization" for the rural migrant.

Rural migrants' concept of the coexistence of urban and village culture

This study adopts the hypothesis that urbanization can assume different meanings and forms depending on the prevailing historical, economic, and cultural factors. Consequently, it is assumed that the migrant in the city changes not in a predetermined ideal direction, but rather according to the conditions prevailing in his environment.[60] The comparative study of various migrant settlements in the world shows the existence of basic similarities among them, stemming from the same set of objective conditions governing rural migration and urban adaptation.

The view that the rural migrants move into the city without a prior knowledge about urban life and conditions and that the squatter settlement is the consequence of this ignorance and unpreparedness is not borne by the facts. On the contrary, migrants have a rather clear concept of the city, its facilities, and their chances of fulfilling their own expectations in the urban environment. The city is regarded as a place of comfort, where people are better educated, have good manners, and control power and wealth. Once in the city, the migrant strives to acquire first those material characteristics that he regards as inherent aspects of urban life, such as better living conditions, better clothing, and the speech and manners of city dwellers.[61] Migrants describe the differences between village and city in impressionistic terms: The village is considered materially backward, without culture (actually educationally underdeveloped), full of boredom and frustration, whereas the city is regarded as representing possibilities for material advancement and potentials for personal achievement and development. Migrants attribute their lack of skills and education generally to the fact of their being born and raised in the village. The villager regards the movement into the city as an opportunity and a necessity – as did the lower-class urban dwellers moving into the shantytown – to acquire a higher living standard and to set new goals beyond just living and reproducing.[62] These views coupled with the occupational change that is the most direct and tangible consequence of the movement into the city induce the migrant to believe that his situation is rapidly improving.

The studies on rural migrants throughout the world tend to agree that the newcomers in the city consider their migration a sound decision. The overwhelming majority appear to be satisfied with their life in the city, especially in comparison with their former village existence. The squatters, usually the village migrants rather than those who came from old city districts, express in general a feeling of satisfaction and optimism. They seem very confident that their situation will improve in the future, and that their children, in view of the opportunities for advancement offered by the city, will have a better life than their parents. In Turkey, about 92 percent of the married men and women interviewed believe that their children will have a better life; in Venezuela (Caracas) one study mentioned that 56.9 percent of the squatters feel that their situation will improve within the next three years; another study places the optimists at 69 percent.[63] In Brazil, between 43 and 73 percent of the *favelados* feel that their children can become high government officials, owners of a large business, university professors, lawyers, and deputies. Thus, the *favelado,* "however unrealistically does not feel hopelessly trapped in the *favela.*"[64] The same feeling is shared by Rabat's squatters: "One doesn't have money but has hope."[65]

This positive picture of the squatter settlement, which may not be shared by all outside observers, or even by some of its inhabitants, is in large measure not only the consequence of a relative material betterment felt by migrants, but also the result of a sense of community and belongingness developed within the settlement. The questions of what kind of community and what kind of belongingness are at the core of the squatter settlements and their integration into the city.

It has been mentioned before that the rural migrants retain elements of their village culture, especially communal-village forms of association, and that their settlement, according to some views, is a "rural" enclave in the city. The literature on the subject abounds in examples of squatter settlements retaining close communal and kinship ties similar to those prevailing in traditional villages and maintaining relations with their kin and village mates. Even in marriage matters migrants seem to have a special preference for girls from their original village. In fact, some researchers claim that the range of kinship is extended and the sense of ethnic similarity becomes stronger in the city.[66] (This is actually a rather transitional stage occurring during the initial period of stay in the city.) The settlement may retain village customs, and organize fiestas, in which some special drinks – Tiltantongo's residents in Mexico City drink pulque, fermented juice of the maquey plant, but mostly when entertaining visitors from the native villages – may be consumed, and rituals, such as *compadrazzo* (coparenthood), may be practiced.[67] Interestingly enough, even in Turkey the migrants coming from areas practicing *kirvelik* (ritual parenthood established usually during circumcision) though using it less than in original villages, still retain the custom.[68]

The maintenance of village customs can be attributed to the compact settlement of people from the same village or the same kinship or culture group in one area and to the close ties maintained with the village of origin through visits, marriage, and a variety of other activities, as seen nearly everywhere in the Middle East, North Africa, Latin America, and even in Yugoslavia, as one study indicates.[69] There is no question, as William Mangin notes, that "many peasants in cities carry with them much of their rural culture and pass some of it on to their children."[70] Yet, as shall be explained later, this village culture is changed and adapted to a new political culture, while new identities are created in the transition to a new form of social and political existence. The migrants constantly express their attachment to the *tierra,* in Latin America, to the *ocak* (hearth) or *memleket* (land of origin), in Turkey, and to the *douar* (tribal segment), in Morocco. Yet, aside from short visits, few of them sincerely plan to return to the village, except for retirement. Even the Nigerians, who dream and talk constantly about returning to their original village, do not do it.[71]

The original sense of community, the kinship ties, and other elements of the traditional village culture are partially retained and incorporated into the city culture and partially abandoned. This village culture, if it can be called that, is maintained because it is useful and provides the migrants with a basis for achieving psychological and physical security through identification with a culture and values deemed good and reliable, primarily because they had been tested repeatedly in the past by their parents and the village as a whole. It is interesting that the same migrants who denounce the material backwardness of the village become the most ardent defenders of its social cohesion and communal solidarity. The neighborhood and community ties and the solidarity prevailing in the squatter settlements are also powerful means for assuring the survival of the settlement, and together with it the squatters' investment in dwellings and land. The act of land invasion, and the subsequent development of the settlement, creates certain powerful bonds of solidarity in the community because, if maintained, it assures the participants ownership of a house and because it is a positive act of self-affirmation in a new environment.[72] The invasion and occupation of the land is socially, politically, economically, and psychologically a creative act, though legally it is considered an offense or even a crime.[73]

The attachment to a basic village culture and to a traditional communal solidarity derived actually from the migrants' marginal position in the city. The key question did not arise in the settlement but in the relations between the settlement and the city and the rest of the society. The squatter identified himself gradually with the city only after securing for himself a safe place and a role in the settlement community. The shantytowns, remarks Chene, "are the crossroads where the peasants are initiated gradually into the urban life, though it must be underlined, this is a life quite dif-

ferent from European urban life."[74] The migrant begins his urbanization by undergoing the most basic transformation – namely,
the occupational change. The squatter community is a strong and
safe basis for starting the integration into the urban environment.

Occupational change and employment

Urbanization for the migrant means a move from the village to the
city and occupational change. Through the move to the city the
villager's "determination of his social status shifts from its basis in
a kin group, to an occupational group."[75] Indeed, the migrants'
most profound break with the village and the first major step toward urbanization is caused by occupational change. There is no
other single field of activity that seems to affect the migrant's personal and social life as much as occupational change. Whether a
hawker or factory worker, the migrant performs not agricultural
work but a more or less specialized function requiring some skills
acquired on the job, or in a special place. He keeps regular work
hours, receives his pay in cash, and spends it on the market. The
relatively low skills required for services and the traditional environment in which the migrants work, as well as their willingness
to take any jobs, work to their advantage. Moreover, rural migrants in Turkey and in Latin America tend to be upwardly mobile
usually through occupational mobility, rurality being no impediment to their advance. The most important reason for the mobility
is the amount of time spent in the city, which usually is used for
the purpose of specialization and socialization. Some exception to
this situation has been noted earlier.[76]

   The rate of employment is very high in nearly all the shantytowns of Turkey, Latin America, India, and North Africa surveyed
in this study. In the Turkish shantytowns 93 percent of the men
and only 30 percent of the women were employed. In Lima, Peru,
a *barriada* had 99 percent employment among the men; an official
survey of 154 shantytowns in the same city showed that only 4.7
percent of the economically active members were unemployed. In
Caracas, Venezuela, 72.5 percent of the men were employed. In
India (Delhi), which is known for its high rate of unemployment,
81.2 percent of the *busti* dwellers had jobs. Algerian *bidonville*
dwellers had 92 to 94 percent employment. In Buenos Aires, Ger-

mani found almost no unemployment among squatters. The same high rate of employment prevailed in the *favelas* of Brazil.[77] (Unemployment was generally high among women, but this must be attributed to the same social and cultural factors affecting higher class women, too.) Nearly all shantytowns seem to harbor a fairly large number of small entrepreneurs, self-employed cab drivers, hawkers and peddlers, and so on, whose economic ambitions and innovative spirit is enhanced by a powerful drive to achieve higher social status through the only channel of mobility open to them: economic achievement. Consequently, the squatters' occupations show such a great variation as to defy a meaningful classification; in Rabat, for instance, Chene found 22 categories. Squatters may be found in any sector of the economy that offers employment usually in lower-paying jobs. In Turkey 56 percent of the employed males interviewed for this study held jobs in construction, technical occupations, trade, crafts, and agriculture, while the rest were employed in a score of privately or publicly owned enterprises.

In Algeria and Morocco (about 74 percent employed) the squatters work in sugar, cement, and tobacco factories, but also clean and maintain parks; in India (Delhi) they appear as textile workers, masons, clerks, mechanics, hawkers, cobblers, petty shopkeepers, tailors, and carpenters.[78] On the other hand, many squatters, even those who have relatively high-paying jobs, seem eager to open their own businesses and work for themselves: "for one's own account," *kendi hesab'ma* (Turkey) or *por su cuento* (Latin America), as they put it. In fact, when the opportunity arises, many squatters open, wherever possible, small repair and grocery shops, raise chickens in the backyard and sell eggs, or engage in some other small-scale trade. In some exceptional cases, they have devised their own sewing machines or brought important innovations to the existing ones and become large-scale manufacturers. (In Delhi some huts were used for industrial purposes. An area holding 13,158 families had 92 such industrial establishments.)

The earnings of squatters, which cannot be accurately ascertained, are in general lower than those of skilled workers. In a way this is natural and expected because the squatters' position in the labor market is marginal and they must adapt to an intensive job mobility according to the market demand. In Turkey the squatters' wages were at least 30 percent below the average monthly earnings of regular industrial workers. In India, in one settlement of Delhi, 71 percent of the workers earned between 25 and 99 rupees a month, whereas the aspired earning was 70 to 160 a month.[79] A more complete earning figure is available for Rabat.[80] Yet, these low earnings, although compensated in part by the fact that most squatters do not pay house rent, does not cause moral disintegration and pessimism in the settlement.

There was also among squatters interviewed in this study an imperceptible but sure change, not only in dress but also manners, family habits, culture, and attitudes. Change in the traditional culture among migrants seems to occur not as a sudden break with the past, but as a slow assimilation of the urban influence, and also adjustment of the folk culture to it. It seems that the city in the third world, with its incipient technological, industrial, and scientific orientation, stimulates innovation and creativity and gradually increases the migrant's capacity for emotional detachment, abstract thought, and empathy and his ability to create broader ties with individual and corporate entities.[81] The extended family and kinship relations, although surviving in squatter settlements, nevertheless have been gradually replaced by the nuclear family, which has decreased in size. Some women in the Turkish settlements stated that they wanted to settle in the city in order to escape the traditional authority and the restricted life with the in-laws in the village. The desire to marry with least formality prevails among squatters of Algeria and Morocco, while in Turkey the bachelors have definite individual ideas about the choice and qualifications of their future consorts.[82] Polygamy is practically nonexistent in the Turkish squatter families – only one case in all three of the settlements studied in Istanbul and 2 to 3 percent in Morocco in the late 1940s. At the same time in the town of Rabat, Morocco, family ties have loosened considerably,[83] whereas in Latin America such ties remain quite strong. One report claims, however, that religion among Latin American migrants is losing its power. The migrants in Mexico City claimed to be good Catholics but none went to church except for *compadrazzo* since they lost their fear in finding security in the city.[84] In the Turkish case, one could argue both that religion is strong and weak, according to the settlers' claim to be good Muslims or their disregard for Islamic rituals (see Chapters 7 and 8). As for Morocco, Chene reports the existence among squatter dwellers of a strong religious attachment and belief in invisible forces and in saints.[85] Indeed, an area of major differences among migrants studied in various countries was the attitude toward religion. The differences were so great and contradictory as to demand another careful study dedicated entirely to this problem.

Politics: a method of integration into urban and national life

The rural migrant in squatter settlements appears to maintain his village culture while at the same time changing and adapting himself to the city culture. The contradiction between rural continuity and urban change can be reconciled if one regards both processes as occurring within the framework of two broader social and political phenomena specific to the third world nations: (1) the emergence of a new type of city, which embodies some of the technological and industrial features of the Western city but also the culture and communal spirit of the countryside; and (2) the emergence of a new national political culture that embodies both the spirit of the new city and the folk culture of the countryside. It also reflects the profound contemporary cultural, social, and political currents and the populist ideologies shaping the regime of the third world countries. For example, Istanbul and other large Turkish cities abound with festivals where local or regional songs and dances are played and with restaurants that advertise regional cuisine and dishes. Today, folklore and the countryside culture are finding their way slowly but steadily into the national Turkish culture through radio and television. Much of this folk culture had penetrated the city and the national culture via the migrants and their settlements. (See also Chapter 6.)

Similar developments are found elsewhere, too. Buechler found that "Folklore festivals add national dimension to the fiesta system . . . increasing in popularity since the Bolivian Revolution of 1952, they reflect the new national interest in peasantry."[86] Doughty notes that in Lima, Peru, since 1964 a radio station has played 14 hours daily of highland, or provincial, music; and clubs have organized fiestas in order to help their hometowns. Though living and working and becoming attached to the city, the residents are also related to their original place, which is a "kind of totemic homeland."[87] The ability to develop attachments to several different entities is the foundation of modern political culture and of nationhood, if the nation, indeed, encompasses and supersedes local and regional attachments. The acceptance of both the village and the city as part of one's national political culture has been facilitated, in my view, by the mass influx of rural migrants, by their ability to maintain themselves culturally in the city through the establishment of squattertowns, and by a give-and-take process that results in cultural-political identification with the city and nation. The identification with the nation and national political culture is unusually strong in the migrant towns since they help create it and thus become part of the new political environment and the life that goes with it.[88]

The end of the colonial, or imperial, rule, true economic and political independence, economic development, science and technology, new methods of social and political inquiry and organization, intensive social mobility, and powerful populist and nationalist ideologies are some of the forces at the foundation of the urban change and of the political culture in the third world. This emerging political culture with its populist, democratic, and national dimensions unites and supersedes both the city dweller and the migrant whose village culture is recognized now as part of the national culture. A series of historical and cultural factors, such as common religion, language, and administration, in some third world nations, especially in Latin America, facilitates the acceptance of a broadly based national political culture that supersedes ethnic, religious, and linguistic differences, at least for the time being.[89] Moreover, the emphasis on economic development, social justice, and even class consciousness, often in the form of anti-imperialism and anticolonialism, helps supersede some regional, religious, and linguistic differences. All this has a profound effect on the migrant's relations with the city and his urbanization. It reduces his absolute marginality in the city to a relative marginality,[90] which appears to stem solely from economic conditions. In other words, the relative absence of political and cultural barriers shortens the time necessary for the migrant to adapt himself to city life.

Urbanization among rural migrants in the squattertowns appears to them mainly as a process of economic and occupational integration rather than strictly a matter of culture change. The emphasis in this process is on *integration,* which is the response to *marginality,* rather than on *assimilation,* which is one remedy for *alienation.* It is in the context of integration into the city, which is so vital to the survival of the settlement and the urbanization of its residents, that politics and political action in the squattertowns acquire their true significance.

The squattertowns in Turkey and in Latin America have a variety of associations or clubs established either for social and sport activities within the settlement (these usually consist of people with common backgrounds, such as the Comunidades Campesinas representing the Cholo Indians in a settlement in Lima)[91] or for contact with the city authorities, political parties, and the government. The *barriada* associations in Latin America and the *Gecekonduyu Güzelleştirme Derneği* (Society for Settlement Improvement) in Turkey are essentially pressure groups designated to protect the property, develop the community, and secure the basic urban facilities such as water, electricity, and bus service from the city authority.[92]

Political organization and action in the squatter settlements are by far the most dynamic form of interaction with city and national governments; they are a vehicle for making the squatter settlements thrive, usually in the political systems that possess direct universal suffrage and compete for the votes of the electorate. Hence, the squatters attach great importance to the political parties and the right to vote, not only as channels of communication and pressure on authorities but also as mechanisms for integration into the city.[93]

The squatters in Turkey and elsewhere in the world have been rather subjectively criticized for organizing themselves politically, for using every available means to secure benefits to themselves, and for heavily taxing the transportation, electricity, water, and sanitary facilities without contributing much to their cost and maintenance. True, the squatters have a pragmatic outlook and do not hesitate to use every opportunity to convert objective needs into political demands,[94] but in large measure this is derived from hostile attitudes on the part of the police, city residents, and occasionally the press. The squatters respond by uniting and rapidly developing organizational skills and a sophisticated, pragmatic view of politics. Their struggle for survival as a community and as individuals in the city eventually creates habits of collective action, a sense of communal and civic responsibility. Political groupings and associations became also inadvertantly channels of communication through which the squatters gradually define their new urban identity and relate themselves to the outside world, on the basis not only of tradition but also of rational decision and interest.

The view the political parties are used by squatters for securing material benefits is shared by other students of shantytowns. Ray, Mangin, Cornelius, Medina, and others who have studied the political behavior of Latin American squatters have pointed to the close identification of the *barrios* with party politics, usually the party in power, to their shrewd exploitation on behalf of the settlement of politically ambitious landlords and other office-seeking candidates, and to a variety of other activities.[95] Yet the association with the political parties, in addition to securing the squatters' participation in city and national politics, helps them to develop vested interests in the existing social and political systems. (See Chapter 9 for a more extensive treatment of politics in the Turkish *gecekondu*.)

Indeed, democratic party politics as a means of education, participation, and full integration into the urban-national system is also a channel for building confidence in the future. Consequently, politics, and all it entails, becomes a positive factor in stimulating the squatter's interest and drive to become full-fledged members of the system in the shortest possible time.

Thus, the prevailing political ideology in the shantytown is not hate and aversion toward the system, as romantic revolutionaries had speculated and hoped for.[96] Attempts by radical groups to organize the squatters for violent and radical action have generally ended in failure.[97] One would agree with Mangin that the "dominant ideology of most of the active *barriada* people appeared to be very similar to the beliefs of the operator of a small business in 19th century England or the United States."[98]

The urbanization of squatter settlements has been presented so far in a positive spirit largely because general economic and political conditions favor their development. Indeed, optimism for betterment seems to prevail among migrants, the rate of employment is relatively high, and their living conditions, however modest by accepted city standards, appear to be far better than those in their original villages and towns. The city holds for them chances for advancement, which were conspicuously lacking in their original localities. Moreover, the squatters' family and communal life in the settlement is reconstituted, at least for the time being, in good measure according to their village and town culture. Thus, the settlement provides a continuity for familiar cultural relations that minimize the danger of alienation and prepare the squatters' gradual transition to urban living in a relatively well-integrated fashion. Now, one can visualize the opposite when these favorable conditions disappear, and the marginality of the squatters turns into cultural and political alienation and they are subjected to economic hardship and their families to social disintegration. Indeed, if the squatters' integration into the city is delayed their economic situation worsens, and their sense of alienation deepens, they may turn into a formidable radical political force. A very good example was supplied by Algeria and Morocco immediately after World War II.

Some of the traditional village and tribal structure of those two countries was destroyed, as mentioned before, by the French colonial administrative and economic policies. The natives were deprived of their traditional ways of life and social organization without being integrated into the emerging modern economic system. Meanwhile, the European settlers, established in luxurious quarters in coastal cities, began to exploit the resources of the country, often in alliance with a Muslim middle class. The latter abandoned "in large measure the usual concern of the fortunate Muslim for the humble and took over the rudeness all too common in Western businessmen."[99] After World War II, the French invested heavily in industry. The ensuing need for manpower rapidly attracted large numbers of the already landless and impoverished tribesmen and villagers residing in the interior. Meanwhile, the industrial development destroyed the handicrafts that had employed a substantial part of the Muslim population. The result was social dichotomy. The upper urban population was represented by the French and other Europeans, as well as by a Muslim group of enterpreneurs. The working class laboring in the low-paid industrial jobs and services were Muslim. A large number of them lived in the *bidonvilles*. This was, in fact, a recently formed proletariat of rural and tribal origin employed in its own land mostly by a religiously and ethnically different urban minority.[100]

In Algeria, the European Christian urban population amounted to about 295,000 people as against 282,000 Muslims in 1926. The Muslim urban population swelled to 889,000 people in 1954 and continued to climb steadily; it had grown from 8.5 percent in 1906 to 18.5 percent in 1954. In 1954 the city of Algiers already had 276,621 Europeans and 293,465 Muslims. Of the latter, 86,500 were living in 15,560 barracks in the *bidonvilles*. Eventually the *bidonville* population of Oran, Bon, and Algiers grew to constitute 30 percent of the total Muslim urban population. In Morocco the situation, although not as acute as in Algeria, was not very dissimilar. It was estimated in the late 1950s that the arrival of one European in Oudja and Agadir brought five rural Muslims into the city. The ratio in Casablanca was three or four Muslims to one European.[101]

The North African squatters felt alien to both the European settlers and the Muslim parvenus. In fact, the latter's highly intellectualized orthodox Islam clashed with the migrants' mystical beliefs and predisposition toward miracles. Few efforts, if any, were made to integrate the migrants into the city, to allow them to defend their own interests, or to pay attention to their labor demands. The government in Morocco created a labor office to control, rather than protect, the workers. The *bidonville* lived uneasily for a while on the margin of the two systems, consisting of the European and Muslim upper classes, largely on the strength of the traditional family ties and the social and moral resources brought from the tribe. The economic and social situation worsened as the very low wages in industry forced the wives to take outside work in factories or in the houses of the wealthy.

Thus, the mixed urban upper groups and the working class, composed largely of migrant villagers and tribesmen, came to be separated by a profound economic, cultural, and social gap. As early as 1955, Le Tourneau felt that the "North African proletariat, new but already numerous, is, then, unhappy not only because of the material conditions of its life are hard but also because it is psychologically disoriented and very far from finding its balance."[102] Robert Montagne, witnessing the rapidly changing character of North African cities because of the influx of a rural population that was not assimilated, asked in anguish, "But who is going to make the synthesis of these nascent cities? What is going to come out of this alluvial soil?"[103]

The synthesis came out in the form of an ideology and mobilization of the *bidonville,* especially in Algeria, for the struggle against the French and the sociopolitical system they represented. The rise of nationalism, the changes in the philosophy of the existing parties (*Hizb al Watani,* which affiliated itself with the trade unions in Morocco), the struggle against the feudal lords in the interior, the shift in the attitude of the Muslim craftsmen and the trade groups, the role played by migrants in the city to mobilize their relatives and friends in the villages, the leadership assumed by the intelligentsia, the emergence of GPRA and FLN, the use of the folk Islam as a revolutionary ideology, and all other elements that entered into the making of the Algerian and Moroccan revolutions were germinated largely in the *bidonville.* "It is within this mass of humanity," wrote Frantz Fanon, the prophet of revolution in the colonial world, "this people of the shantytowns, at the core of the lumpenproletariat, that the rebellion will find its urban spearhead. For the lumpenproletariat, that horde of starving men, uprooted from their tribe and from their clan, constitutes one of the most spontaneous and the most radically revolutionary forces of a colonized people."[104]

The unique conditions that prevailed in Algeria and Morocco may not repeat themselves identically elsewhere in the world. But the potential is there. The squatters, who form 10 to 40 percent of the urban population in the third world, if properly understood and cultivated may become part of the urban environment in an orderly, humane, and democratic fashion. If not, they have the power to change it on their own. The shantytown born as a consequence of the unique condition of our times represents a universal social problem that must be understood and solved.

2. Historical roots of migration and the *gecekondu* in Turkey

Social and economic changes

Turkey and her predecessor, the Ottoman State, have been subject to intensive population movements since their inception. One can, in fact, claim that the history of Turkey and the Ottoman State is a history of migration.[1] From the fifteenth through the seventeenth centuries the Ottoman government settled tribes in the Balkans and Anatolia in order to colonize the newly conquered lands or in order to cultivate the land and increase tax revenues. After the Ottoman State began losing territories, notably to Russia and Austria in the eighteenth century and to the newly formed Balkan states in the nineteenth century, large numbers of Muslims and Turks moved to and settled in the territory occupied today by modern Turkey. Roughly 6 million people, Turks and Muslims, moved or were forced to move into the Ottoman State from 1783 to 1913. After the establishment of the Turkish Republic in 1923, about 1.5 million additional people came to settle in Turkey from Greece, Bulgaria, Yugoslavia, and Romania, either as a result of agreed exchange of populations or as refugees or immigrants.[2] Though deprived of well-organized settlement plans and even suitable administrative organizations, nevertheless Turkey was able to absorb this massive inflow of refugees and immigrants through a process of self-accommodation and mutual help.[3] Kinship and religious ties, linguistic and cultural similarities, a shared sense of history, community, and charitable obligation were instrumental in facilitating the assimilation of the newcomers from abroad. The assimilation was also enhanced by the fact that from 1915 to 1928, the newcomers were settled mostly in rural areas, usually in the villages of the outgoing Greeks and Armenians, and thus did not pose a direct challenge to the established social and political order represented by the city.

In the second half of the nineteenth century the Ottoman State – which covered at that time the Balkans, the Middle East, and North Africa – underwent profound structural changes caused by a series of new socioeconomic and political factors. Actually, the Ottoman State was the first non-Western country to feel fully the impact of industrialization and the expansion of the market economy in the West. Eventually the traditional Ottoman system of agricultural production, which was based on a mixture of small individual farms, landholdings by *wakfs,* or *vaqfs* (religious foundations), and government-owned estates and which had been changing constantly since the end of the sixteenth century, collapsed. This evolution culminated in the emergence, after the acceptance of the Swiss Civil Code in 1926, of a new system based on private ownership of lands – that is, a true capitalist system of land ownership and production. The traditional crafts and the organization for supplying food to cities, supported in part by a corresponding traditional agricultural basis and by a rather complex government controlled system of prices, also disintegrated, especially after 1829 and 1838. (In 1829 the ban was lifted on Wallachia and Moldavia to supply the Ottoman State with certain amounts of food at advantageous prices; the Commercial Treaty of 1838 gave England trading and tariff privileges, which undermined and destroyed the Ottoman crafts industry.)

These changes were followed by a massive break in whatever was left from the ancient traditional social organization. This arrangement had placed the nomad and the peasant in the food producers' category. The groups that acquired, finished, and distributed the produce were the craftsmen and the merchants in town. The military–bureaucratic group and the religious men formed the other two upper social estates. All these changes in the nineteenth century freed the groups from their predetermined occupational categories and allowed them to move and reorganize in new professions according to the internal and international forces of a market economy.

The nineteenth century witnessed the rise of a series of ports in Turkey along the Black Sea and the Mediterranean serving as outlets for exports or transit, similar to the cities-ports of Asia, Africa, and Latin America. This urbanization had profound demographic impact on Turkish villages and towns. W. D. Hütteroth has shown in a detailed study that there began in central Anatolia about 1830 a massive movement of population – including nomads – from mountain villages to small towns in the valleys and lower elevation sites. This migration coupled with the flow of people from abroad produced a string of district towns and villages established on fertile agricultural lands and geared for the production of foods[4] to be exported through port cities. This sociodemographic transformation in the nineteenth century profoundly affected the northeastern part of Turkey, especially the Trabzon (Trebizond) area of the Black Sea – the area from which most of the migration studied in this book came.

The expansion of commercial relations after Russia broke the Ottoman trade monopoly in the Black Sea through the Küçük Kaynarca treaty of 1774 and after the British intensified their commercial relations with Persia in the nineteenth century were major factors stimulating the economic development of the southern Black Sea shores. Consequently, the ports of Trabzon (which was the terminal point of the trade route to Persia[5]) and Giresun (the old Cerasus, the original place from where the cherry tree was brought by Romans to the West) became important commercial centers. While in the past the internal manufacturing centers, small as they were, determined the economy of their surrounding areas, now the ports, geared to export foodstuff and import manufactured goods according to the needs of the foreign markets, set the pace of economic life. Consequently, the town of Şebinkarahisar (located south and southwest of Giresun and Trabzon), which was a commercial and handicraft center manufacturing goods and distributing them to a large area through a guild system, lost its economic importance. A beautiful town, it remained of secondary importance, despite a resurgence of some economic and political activity early in the twentieth century.[6]

The intensification of trade and the increased communication in the nineteenth century in the Black Sea regions stimulated the cultivation and the export of a series of local produces, such as wood and its derivatives, dried fruit, fruit brandy, dyes, and construction materials, including cut stone and lumber. These were the normal products of a forested mountainous area and were exchanged for items, including wheat, that were in short supply and were imported either from southern Anatolia or directly from Russia and the Balkans. Thus, through expanded trade a series of local products found wider markets, and production and population increased. All this in turn produced a certain division of labor according to ethnic and religious affiliations. For instance, villages producing livestock and raw materials were located in the mountainous areas and were inhabited mostly by Muslim (Shiite and Sunni) Turks. Armenians and Greeks, especially the first, were found in rural areas but tended to settle in the newly developing towns and engage in manufacture and food-processing occupations.[7] A report by the British consul in the area describes the situation rather eloquently:

The Mahometan population whether Turkoman or Laz furnishes excellent husbandmen, sailors, fishers and carpenters. The Kurds, also Mahometan, are exclusively shepherds. The "Greeks," or Byzantines, are good stone cutters, tolerable tradesmen, and frequently shop and public-house keepers. They invariably gravitate coastwards or townwards. The Armenians are tolerable agriculturists, good tailors and jewellers, and, above all, great usurers; they are also shoemakers, porters, and servants. As a rule, the Turkomans are the steadiest, the Laz the most enterprising, the "Greeks" the most restless, the Armenians the most industrious; and in general the Mahometan are the most dependable, the Christians the more ingenious.[8]

Thus, the Greeks and Armenians, definitely not a majority in the area, concentrated in towns and seaports and in the trade and crafts.[9] Though most numerous, the Turks (Turkoman refers to newly settled people of nomad origin) stood at the bottom of the social scale as producers and workers. The old people in the area still recall that the Armenians and Greeks kept to themselves the secrets of their craft (making dye, mulberry brandy) and dismissed their Turkish employees who learned the secrets.

The flourishing trade in the area received the first setback when the British abandoned the Black Sea route over Trabzon for trade with Persia and began to use the ports in the Persian Gulf in their trade with Iran.[10] Furthermore, the expansion of the French trade in the Mediterranean, the Ottoman wars with Russia in 1853 and 1877, and the opening of new trade routes through Georgia (Tiflis) by Russia moved the center of international trade to the south and north and harmed the economy of the area. Unemployment increased and forced Turks and non-Turks to seek work in bigger centers as far away as Istanbul, Odessa, and even Moscow. The British reports give an excellent description of the situation:

The Persian traffic, one of historical antiquity, has always been the best resource of Trebizond, which derives from it three fourths of its commercial consequence. . . . The heaviest and, it seems, the fatal blow was dealt to Trebizond by the opening of the new and rival Perso-transit route through Russian Georgia. To this important line of communication with Central Asia the Russians first paid serious attention in 1867, and have since then shown the greatest diligence in perfecting both the line itself and the means of transport. The progressively increasing gains of the new route have been the proportionate losses of the old one; and the completion of the railway from the coast to Tiflis has accelerated the process. Should the Russian administration continue the line on to Persian frontier, as it intends doing, the Persian transit via Trebizond will be reduced to utter insignificance."[11]

Meanwhile the war of 1877, which disrupted the trade in the Black Sea and resulted in loss of territory for the Ottoman State, dealt additional blows to the economy of the area.

British trade in this part of Asia Minor, states a report, cannot be what it was hitherto. The territory annexed to Russia, may be expected to be provided henceforth, as the Caucasus is now, with cotton goods of Russian manufacture. . . . The transit by way of Trebizond is decreasing . . . if no means are adopted now to revive the transit through Trebizond, the Erzeroom route may gradually sink into insignificance, and, perhaps be even completely abandoned.[12]

The war, moreover, stimulated the growth of Samsun, which was already competing with Trabzon chiefly in order to become the major port for exporting the products of northern Anatolia. "Samsun," states another report,

is in fact the point of arrival and departure for merchandise to and from Marsivan, Amasia, Tokat, Sivas, Yozgat, Kara-Hisar, Keysareck, Kharpoot, Keer-Shahr, Diar-Bekir, and even more distant localities. To sum-up, Samsoon commands a more active trade than any other single part on the Turkish coast of Black Sea . . . from the year 1860 to 1866 there was no fluctuation in the trade of Samsoon. . . . But in 1867 and 1868 the demand for corn raised the exportation to an equivalent value of 28,000,000 francs (or 1,120,000 £ English) while by indirect result the importation rose, though not equally, and obtained a total value of 21,000,000 francs (or 840,000 £ English).[13]

The disruption of the lucrative trade in northern Anatolia affected the entire economic life in the area. It created unemployment and forced the inhabitants to seek work wherever it was available. A British report alludes to the situation in the following terms:

> On rough calculation the population of this province amounts to about 1,000,000 inhabitants, more than four-fifths of whom are Mussulmans. The proportion of the Christians between themselves is one Armenian to three and a half Greeks. The population of the inland districts addict themselves exclusively to agriculture and are content with producing just enough to satisfy the want of their families. Many Christians, Greeks especially, emigrate to Russia where they find more remunerative employment and return at the end of one or more years. Musselmans proceed to Constantinople, where they find work as boatmen, porters, etc.[14]

The Armenian uprising (one occurred in Şebinkarahisar and was led by local intellectuals and merchants),[15] the Soviet revolution in 1917, which curtailed further the trade with Russia, and, finally, the Turkish War of Liberation of 1919–22 (and the subsequent departure of the Greeks and Armenians) destroyed the new economic and commercial life, and its social basis, as it emerged in the nineteenth century. The fierce reaction of the Turks, mostly peasants and workers, to the Greek and Armenian middle classes – involved as intermediaries in the foreign trade with the French, Austrians, Russians, and English – was the result of economic development and the subsequent social-political dichotomy shaped by religious-ethnic differences. A minority enjoyed the benefit of development while the Turkish and Muslim majority were left out. In a way this was similar to the socioethnic-religious differentiation created by economic developments and the political aftermath in Algeria and Morocco, as mentioned in the preceding chapter. Incidentally, this area south of the Black Sea coast was also the center of intensive leftist movements, including the creation of a number of local soviets in 1919.[16]

"Gurbetçilik": the beginning of migration

The Turkish element in the area, though it was superior in numbers, did not possess the capital, the entrepreneurial leadership, and the skill to galvanize the stagnant economy. Consequently, the local rural population, which in the nineteenth century had begun to specialize in the production of specific items for export, was forced to return to a subsistence agriculture. Moreover, the local forests that were exploited rationally in the past (the Tahtacı, timbermen, who were mostly Alevi or Kızılbaş, used them for centuries without destroying them) were simply cut out entirely so that the population could use the soil to raise corn and vegetables to feed itself. Deprived of trees and vegetation the steep hills could no longer hold the thin layer of soil (only about 10 to 25 inches thick). It was soon washed down into valleys and then into the sea. Since without vegetation the soil could not hold humidity for long, it often remained barren and dry. Eventually in the Republic, the government imposed severe restrictions on wood cutting and many villagers who earned a living by exploiting the remaining forests or by grazing sheep were left without a means of subsistence. Consequently, many left their native areas in search of a living. The ecological tragedy followed its course further. The starving population began to raise more goats, the only animals that could climb the rocks and steep hills and move rapidly over large distances in search of scarce food. In the process the goats ate the buds and the small trees and rendered the land even more desolate and unproductive. Finally, a series of severe earthquakes from 1938 to 1959 caused massive land slides that destroyed villages and covered with stone debris some of the arable land.

Thus, *gurbetçilik,* an institution of great importance for this study, was born. *Gurbetçilik,* which means literally "in strange lands" or "outside of one's home," is a form of seasonal migration.[17] The men from the Black Sea region left the village every year seeking jobs as chefs, drivers, porters, menial workers, and so on, first in nearby towns and then further away. (Some old people in the region told me that they still remembered the jobs held in Russia during the czarist regime.) *Gurbetçilik* was also an indirect stimulus for early marriages and large families since men unsure of their future wanted to have a large family as soon as possible.[18] In the Republic the people from the Black Sea area hard-pressed for jobs supplied a major part of the manpower that built the railroads in the eastern part of Turkey. Many eventually reached Istanbul and held there jobs for generations.

Contemporary migration seems to have historical precedents. For instance, Zihni Yilmaz, the late *muhtar* (head man) of the village of Yeniyol (Anna), claimed that *gurbetçilik* began in the region some 100 to 120 years ago. He recalled that two of his grandparents went to Istanbul and found jobs there at the Sultan's court, one as a boatman and another as a porter. The job was left to their sons and grandsons. Zihni recalled also that his father periodically replaced one of his brothers to allow him to return to his village for a while, and thus kept the jobs in the family. The villagers excelled in hard work, and their reputation for honesty had assured them permanent jobs as porters and guards in Istanbul. Meanwhile, their wives and children remained in the village. Sometimes the father would take with him his son or brother if jobs became available to them. *Gurbetçilik* thus became a permanent way of life and created its own values and customs. Men would work several months a year in some town or city in order to earn enough money to feed their families in the village. They would return to the village to rest and to reproduce and would receive there special respect and care as breadwinners and as hardship sufferers. However, many did not return home at all, for without care they became ill and died. Indeed, many of the squatters whom I interviewed in their settlements in Istanbul grew up as orphans and had to take care of their families at an early age because their parents had died while working away from home as *gurbetçis* (migrants). The educational social effects of *gurbetçilik* are self-evident. First, it gave the villager, at least in northern Turkey, the possibility for communication with the outside world and enabled him to interpret the conditions affecting his village and his life. Second, it exposed the villagers through their own kin working in cities to national events and ideas and fostered a sense of shared values with the outside world.[19] Third, job-seeking wanderers assured of continuous employment in the city would not hesitate to settle there and bring their families and thus put an end to their *gurbet*. In fact, this is what has happened since 1954.

In sum it is essential to stress the point that the *gurbetçis* became *gecekondu* dwellers, not in a haphazard fashion, but with a thorough knowledge of the employment and housing conditions in the city. The move into the city was prompted by social disintegration in the countryside, economic hardship, traditions of migration, and some knowledge of the urban environment. Thus, the employment opportunities that emerged in cities after 1950, due to increase in economic activity, created a mass migration that partly ended the century-old *gurbetçilik,* at least in our area of research.

Causes of recent migration

The preceding pages have provided the historical background for the migration of the squatters interviewed in this study. However, the massive population shift from village to cities in Turkey after World War II was triggered by a series of new social, demographic, economic, and political factors that brought to a climax and gave a new direction to the social and economic dislocation in the nineteenth century. In the first place, there was a steady increase in the rural population from 1923 to 1946, which outstripped the rate of increase in agricultural production. Moreover, conditions in many rural areas deteriorated not only because of lack of investment and modernization in agriculture, but also because the ruling elite sought to improve a few cities as models of progress and modernity through heavy taxation of the peasants. Eventually the peasants turned against the ruling Republican party and – benefiting from direct suffrage, opposition parties, and free elections – voted it out of power in 1950. Partly in order to increase the agricultural production and partly to comply with the demands of the upper agrarian groups, the incoming Democratic party government of Adnan Menderes engaged in a massive mechanization of agriculture, largely through the assistance provided by the United States from 1951 to 1953.[20] About 1 million farmers were dislocated by some 40,000 tractors introduced in this period. The pace of mechanization of agriculture let up considerably from 1953 to 1957 and intensified gradually afterward; in fact, the modernization of Turkish agriculture from 1961 to 1972 was much more substantial and widespread than during the traumatic period from 1951 to 1953.[21] The slow but steady mechanization of agriculture, especially after 1960, coupled with the adjustment of the village economy to regional and national markets resulted in cost accounting, efficiency, and increase in production. This development eliminated the marginal farms and left no justification for surplus manpower to stay in the village and live off the labor of the actual producers, regardless of their intimate family ties.[22] The pressure of some landlords and tribal chiefs and the *kan davası* (vendetta) cases were other rather insignificant factors that stimulated rural migration.[23] Thus, after 1955 rural migration intensified as a series of new technological, economic, and political factors affected the peasantry economically and psychologically.

The general direction of rural migration was from the mountainous, poor, and less developed sections in the east and northeast toward the more developed, industrializing, and fertile areas in the west. (See also chapter 7.) The Black Sea region was the largest migrant-sending area; the Marmara and west-central Anatolian regions were the largest migrant-receiving areas, containing 63 percent of all the *gecekondus* in Turkey.

The new arrivals in the city faced an acute shortage of suitable low-cost housing. Rampant inflation lowered the real income of the wage earners and government officials, making them unable to meet the rising cost of rents, which was further stimulated by the growing demand for housing. At the same time, a boom in construction business, which was entirely in the hands of private entrepreneurs, created land speculation of gigantic proportion: Some lots around Ankara and Istanbul that sold for 50 liras in 1949 went up to 50,000 liras in 1965 and permitted a rapidly growing class of urban entrepreneurs to accumulate capital. This class, in turn, instead of investing in industry, built luxurious dwellings in order to assure themselves a steady income and safeguard the value of their money. The construction boom increased the need for workers, most of whom came from villages. The newcomers into the cities from 1952 to 1956, working mostly in the construction industry, lived first in low-quality houses, often crowding 7 or 8 people in single rooms or even on construction sites. Originally, the construction workers, most of whom were not unionized, received low salaries. But as the construction boom continued, and later industrialization got underway, manpower became somewhat scarce and consequently wages in the private sector, including those paid to the workers in the construction industry, rose faster than those employed in the public sector, although the latter had better insurance and fringe benefits. All this in turn attracted additional people from villages. Only after the revolution of 1960 a state planning organization was established and indirectly was instrumental in persuading the Turkish capitalists to invest in some manufacturing ventures.

The construction boom was helped also by the government's house credit policies. Salaried personnel employed by the government or by private enterprises received loans at low interest rates (1.5 to 4 percent) to build houses. Eventually this group, similar to all other house owners, benefited from the increase in real estate values, thus becoming less susceptible to inflation, despite their outward vehement protest against the rise in living costs. On the other hand, the low-paid government and municipal officials, often policemen and clerks, who could not form cooperatives and become house owners were the hardest hit by inflation and high rents. These were among the first to move out to the outskirts, especially in the capital, and build the *gecekondus*. A survey of one of the *gecekondus* in Ankara shows that 9.82 percent of the squatters were government officials.[24] The self-interest of these officials as well as their knowledge of the bureaucratic apparatus and government policies helped the *gecekondus* in some measure to assure their survival. However, Ankara is an exception since the overwhelming majority of squatters elsewhere were made up of various working groups of rural origin.

Industrialization emerged after 1963 as the chief factor creating structural changes and giving further stimulus and a new direction to rural migration. The net national production of Turkey went up from 9 billion Turkish liras (only round figures are given) in 1950, to 16 billion in 1960, and to nearly 21 billion in 1965, and doubled by 1972. Meanwhile, agricultural production, which was about 80 percent of the GNP in 1950, fell to about 55 percent in 1970. The working male population engaged in industry and services grew from 17.5 percent in 1950 to 23 percent in 1955, and then rose to 25.3 and 29 percent in 1960 and 1965, respectively. Those employed in agriculture decreased from 69.3 to 57.8 percent from 1950 to 1965.[25] The effects of this development was evident in population growth, migration, and urbanization. The total population of Turkey rose from 20,934,670 people in 1950, 31,391,307 in 1965, 35,666,549 in 1970, to approximately 39,000,000 in 1974. The urban population, which was 24.9 percent of the total in 1950, rose to 34.5 percent in 1965 and to 38.9 percent in 1970. In terms of the total population the rural population increased yearly by an average of 1.8 percent from 1950 to 1965; the urban population growth was slightly over 5 percent during the same period. In 1965, Turkey had 14 cities with a population over 100,000, and 10 cities with a population of 50,000 to 100,000. In 1970, there were 20 cities with a population over 100,000, 20 cities with a population of 50,000 to 100,000, and 58 towns with a population of 25,000 to 50,000.[26]

Much of this urban growth was due to migration. According

to the censuses of 1950, 1955, 1960, and 1965, the total cumulative number of migrants in these years amounted to 1,692,933, 2,507,454, 3,186,166, and 4,018,770 people, respectively, rising from 8.1 percent of the total population in 1950 to 11.8 percent in 1965.[27] In other words, over 11 percent of the Turkish population were migrants of one kind or another in 1965. Therefore, migration provides a key to understanding not only the changes in the Turkish demography, but also the basic transformation in the quality of the population. The rise of the *gecekondu* in these conditions appears as a foregone conclusion.[28]

The *gecekondus* found around almost all major Turkish cities, notably the developing industrial and commercial centers, were created mostly after 1950. Although Table 2.1 leaves out some important industrial and commercial centers such as Eskişehir, Kayseri, and Konya, it gives a fair idea of the extent of the squatter settlements in Turkey. Table 2.2 and Map 1 in turn indicate in a general way the national geographical distribution of the *gece-*

Table 2.1. Gecekondu *population in thirteen Turkish cities* (*early 1960s*)

	Number of gecekondu dwellings	Total gecekondu population	Total city population	Percentage of city population
Adana	18,925	104,088	231,548	44.95
Ankara	70,000	385,000	650,067	59.22
Antakya	2,635	14,493	45,674	31.73
Bursa	8,713	47,922	153,886	31.14
Diyarbakır	1,400	7,700	79,888	9.64
Erzincan	3,500	19,250	36,420	52.86
Erzurum	5,750	31,625	90,069	35.11
İskenderun	4,275	23,513	62,061	37.89
İstanbul	120,000	660,000	1,466,535	45
İzmir	18,025	99,138	296,635	33.42
Mersin	896	4,928	68,485	7.19
Samsun	5,700	31,350	87,688	35.75
Zonguldak[a]	14,000	77,000	54,010	

Source: Adapted from Ministry of Reconstruction and Settlement, *13 Büyük Şehirde Gecekondu.* Completed with figures taken from the official statistical yearbook of 1959, the census of 1960, and other sources.
[a] The *gecekondus* of Zonguldak are outside the city, around the mines.

Table 2.2. Gecekondus (*1966–70*)

	Number of dwellings (1966)		Number of dwellings (1966)
Major Towns		Burdur	39
Adana	19,489	Çanakkale	728
Ankara	101,073	Çankırı	156
Antakya	7,512	Çorum	273
(Hatay)		Denizli	0
Antalya	2,051	Edirne	679
Balıkesir	3,463	Eskişehir	4,290
Bursa	14,300	Giresun	0
Diyarbakır	6,491	Gümüşhane	0
Elaziğ	462	Hakkari	0
Erzincan	1,862	Kastamonu	0
Erzurum	2,470	Kayseri	2,819
Gaziantep	10,509	Kırklareli	123
Isparta	1,385	Kırşehir	200
Istanbul	131,904	Kütahya	287
Izmir	40,392	Malatya	4,074
Kars	1,879	Manisa	1,578
Kocaeli	5,979	Maraş	1,704
(Izmit)		Mardin	295
Konya	5,042	Muş	0
Mersin	2,061	Niğde	779
(Içel)		Ordu	130
Muğla	1,090	Rize	0
Nevşehir	22	Sakarya	0
Samsun	2,960	(Adapazarı)	
Tokat	2,053	Siirt	0
Other Towns		Sinop	6
Adıyaman	599	Sivas	2,603
Afyon	421	Tekirdağ	1,020
Ağrı	56	Trabzon	28
Amasya	282	Tunceli	619
Artvin	0	Urfa	4,716
Aydın	179	Uşak	534
Bilecik	306	Van	0
Bingöl	1,168	Yozgat	2,393
Bitlis	43	Zonguldak	10,619
Bolu	0	Total	408,375

Source: United Nations, Request by the Turkish Government, in Accordance with ECOSOC Resolution 1224 (XLII Session).

Note: 0 = No information.

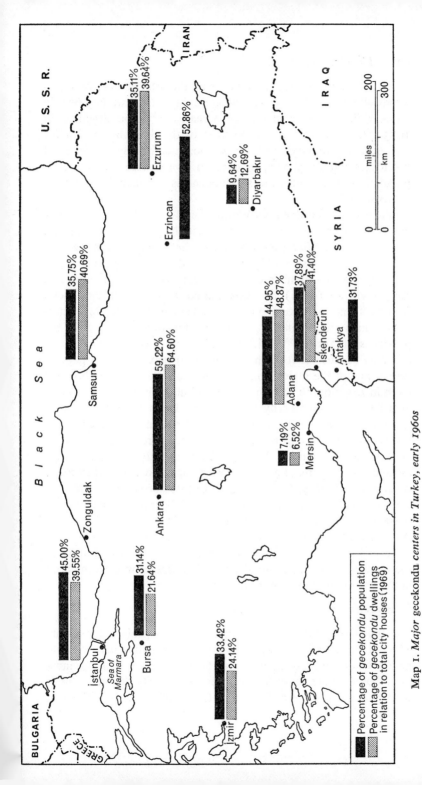

Map 1. *Major gecekondu centers in Turkey, early 1960s*

Source: Adapted from a map prepared by the Turkish Ministry of Reconstruction and Settlement.

kondus. The government estimated that the total number of squatter dwellings in Turkey was 500,000 in 1969 and 693,694 in 1972, with an estimated annual increase of 70,000 dwellings in 1973–74. By 1974 the total number of dwellings in *gecekondus* was estimated to have reached 709,000, inhabited by an estimated 3.5 to 4.5 million people, or about 9 to 12 percent of the total population. The figures are so eloquent as to make further comments superfluous.

Migration in Turkey until World War II consisted chiefly of migrants from abroad and was motivated largely by political and cultural factors. After 1950 it was overwhelmingly internal (except for 154,000 Turkish immigrants expelled from Bulgaria in 1951 and 1952, and a number who came from Greece, Romania, and Yugoslavia afterward) and was caused by economic and social factors. Thus, in Ankara only 1.3 percent of the squatters interviewed in a study came from abroad; the rest originated in the provinces of Turkey.[29] In Izmir, which had special attraction for migrants because of its climate, only 12.9 percent of the population in one of the major squatter settlements came from abroad.[30] Even in Zeytinburnu settlement in Istanbul, known as a *gecekondu* area densely populated by the *göçmen* (Turks from abroad who came to Turkey in the 1930s, settled originally in villages and towns, and then moved to cities), only 51.8 percent of the inhabitants were born outside Turkey.[31] Consequently, one may safely assume that 90 percent of the squatter population of Turkey today was born in Turkey; in fact, many of those abroad who settled in various *gecekondus,* mostly in Izmir and Istanbul, came to their present location after a prolonged stay in the villages and towns of Anatolia. Their migration to the city was the consequence of the same economic conditions that stimulated the mass migration of the natives. Table 2.3 shows the relative ratios between those born in the country and those born abroad.

Urban reaction to rural migration

The influx of rural migrants naturally causes profound reaction. The old city inhabitants – that is, the established families with old middle-class values – regarded the migration as a peasant invasion. Complaining about the disappearance of city manners and of privacy and accepting at face value the rumors of rising crimes in

Table 2.3. *Division of population according to birthplace* (*census of 1965*)

	Born in the same province	Born in a different province	Born in another country[a]
Migrant-receiving provinces from interior and abroad			
Istanbul[b]	940,570	1,123,010	227,867
Ankara	1,019,673	586,918	37,511
İzmir	800,601	295,754	137,696
Adana	737,500	147,004	18,039
Migrant-sending provinces[c]			
Sivas	670,292	31,842	3,024
Trabzon	575,202	20,080	490
Giresun	418,185	9,339	481
Gümüşhane	256,020	6,640	69

[a] Bulgaria, Greece, Romania, Yugoslavia.
[b] The census figures cover the entire province population. But in the case of the first four provinces the overwhelming majority of the population lived in the city proper. Consequently, the point that the majority of newcomers were born outside the province but within the boundaries of Turkey is well illustrated.
[c] These four provinces were chosen because the majority of the squatters interviewed in this study came from there. Unfortunately statistics concerning only the metropolitan population were not available.

squatter settlements, they hoped to prevent this migration by every possible means. Staunch defenders of the old elite order and its values, they continued to live in their select quarters while being gradually overwhelmed by this rising tide from countryside. A venerable female descendant of one of the Ottoman aristocratic families told me:

The regression of Turkey began with the downfall of Abdulhamid II [1909]. It has accelerated with Atatürk. The end came in 1950, with the introduction of democracy which spoiled the scum of the towns and the ignorant and hungry peasants. And it is a disgrace that learned men devote their time to studying these wretches, instead of fighting to preserve what is left of the civilization of our great peers.

Intellectuals and newspapermen who disdained the first group either as conservative bourgeois or decadent Osmanlı aristocracy looked on the squatter settlements as the spawning ground for the revolution they wanted to lead; but they seldom, if ever, left their comfortable houses and secure offices to visit the *gecekondus*. The politician who sensed the vote potential of the *gecekondus* was quick to establish a foothold there from the very beginning. He promised titles to the land on which the squatter houses were established, city water, electricity, and transportation, and the squatter offered his vote in exchange. A number of candidates for the Parliament who ventured into the *gecekondus* perceived that this was a new situation and when the squatter bill came up for debate in the legislature, they had the courage and the foresight to claim that the *"gecekondu* is in fact the expression of a dynamic spirit, a creative miracle which must be understood and channelled properly."[32] Some deputies regarded the *gecekondus* as a solution to the housing situation: In Ankara they claimed that the squatters built 5,000 to 15,000 dwellings in a year, whereas the state, with all the technical and financial means at its disposal, built only 700 dwellings in three years in order to improve an old *gecekondu* area.[33] The first comprehensive bill concerning the *gecekondu* was prepared by a coalition government headed by Ismet Inönü in 1963 and 1964. It reached the floor of the Assembly on March 24, 1966, and was enacted as *Gecekondu Kanunu* (number 775, July 20, 1966).[34] This legislation was enacted only after a series of other minor laws proved ineffective to prevent the establishment of the *gecekondu* or safeguard the municipal property against the invasions of the rural migrants.[35] According to one sponsor of the bill:

The gecekondu started in Turkey after the Second World War as a consequence of the changes in the social and economic conditions. The development of industrial centers in cities, the lure of city living attracted the population of towns and villages. The housing in cities was insufficient to satisfy the demand and consequently the gecekondu was born by itself. Yes, if you look at our so-called large cities, Izmir, Istanbul, Ankara, you can see that they do not look like the big cities of the West but as large villages . . . other cities such as Zonguldak, Samsun, Gaziantep, Adana, Bursa are engaged in a gecekondu competition with the three large cities and are just about ready to catch up with them. . . . [But] the birth of the gecekondu is actually a race for civilization. The peasant wants to become civilized, but unable to find the means to achieve civilization in the village he comes to the city. It is a question of the availability of civilization.[36]

The official Turkish view on the *gecekondu* is clearly expressed in the request for assistance to rehabilitate the dwellings addressed by the Turkish government to the United Nations:

Urbanization and its accompanying "gecekondus" are not considered today as undesirable phenomenon in Turkey. Instead, the rapid growth of cities and the existence of gecekondu areas – planned or unplanned – are considered positive factors in national development, for, from them are to come the workers for the proposed massive industrialization programme of the decade of the 1970's. In Turkey, urbanization, even as a singularly demographic phenomenon, becomes a "vehicle of economic and social development." The approach is realistic in the sense that under the present economic and social conditions of Turkey, there is probably no other alternative to this proposal of allowing massive migrations to urban areas; for, agricultural land appears to be at, or near, its maximum utilization, and "urbanization precedes industrialization" according to the Development Plan. At the same time, and as a balancing economic-social force, extra efforts are being made by the Government to improve agriculture production, to modernize village life, and to distribute "inevitable" urbanization as equitably as possible – and feasible – over the entire Nation. This total process of rural modernization-urbanization-industrialization is being developed through regional planning.

The government of Bülent Ecevit – that is, the Republican People's party, which accumulated a plurality of votes in the national elections of 1973, thanks to the *gecekondu* votes – promised to issue land deeds to all dwellings built until the end of 1973. This clarified the issue – legally, at least – although the actual issuance of deeds proceeded very slowly.

The origin of three "gecekondus"

The preceding pages have provided a general background for the study of the three squatter settlements that are the subject of this work – the *gecekondus* of Nafibaba (Hisarüstü), Baltaliman (the two are combined today), and Celâlettin Paşa in Istanbul. (See Map 2.) The population of the three squatter communities came from the 36 provinces of Turkey (Table 2.4 and Map 3); however, 597 people of 950 interviewed came from the provinces of Gümüşhane, Sivas, Giresun, and Trabzon – in other words, from northeastern Anatolia or the Black Sea. (See Map 3.) A further scrutiny of the data (Table 2.5) indicates, for instance, that the *kazas* (districts) of Şiran in Gümüşhane province, Alucra and

Table 2.4. *Origin of migrants by province in Nafibaba, Baltalimanı, and Celâlettin Paşa*

	From villages	From towns	Total
Gümüşhane	234	5	239
Sivas	126	27	153
Giresun	135	13	148
Trabzon	54	3	57
Kastamonu	54	2	56
Istanbul			40
Bolu	29	1	30
Sinop	24	2	26
Ordu	18	8	26
Çankırı	17	2	19
Rize	16	1	17
Sakarya	15	0	15
Balıkesir	6	5	11
Erzincan	10	1	11
Isparta	8	3	11
Tekirdağ	6	4	10
Çorum	7	1	8
Other provinces[a] and places[b]			73
Total			950

[a] These provinces and the number of migrants are Adana (1), Afyon (1), Amasya (4), Artvin (1), Bilecik (2), Bingöl (6), Bursa (6), Çanakkale (1), Edirne (3), Elaziğ (3), Eskişehir (1), Kırklareli (2), Kocaeli (2), Konya (3), Nevşehir (6), Samsun (6), Tokat (5), Yozgat (7), Zonguldak (1), province origin unknown (1). An overwhelming majority of these people are of village origin.
[b] Foreign immigrants from Bulgaria, Greece, and Yugoslavia totaled 8.

Şebinkarahisar in Giresun province, and Suşehri and Hafik in Sivas province account for about 463 migrants. If considered further, it appears that the villages of Kırıntı and Yeniköy (Gümüşhane-Şiran), Kayacık (Giresun-Alucra), Gökçekent (Sivas-Suşehri), and Düzyayla (Sivas-Hafik) supplied 355 migrants. Thus, approximately 37.3 percent of the population in the three *gecekondus* came from five villages located in the same region. Many of these villages were the *gurbetçi* type – that is, senders of seasonal workers to wherever employment was available (see Table 2.5). On

Map 2. Gecekondu *settlements in the Istanbul area*

Source: Adapted from map prepared by the Turkish Ministry of Reconstruction and Settlement.

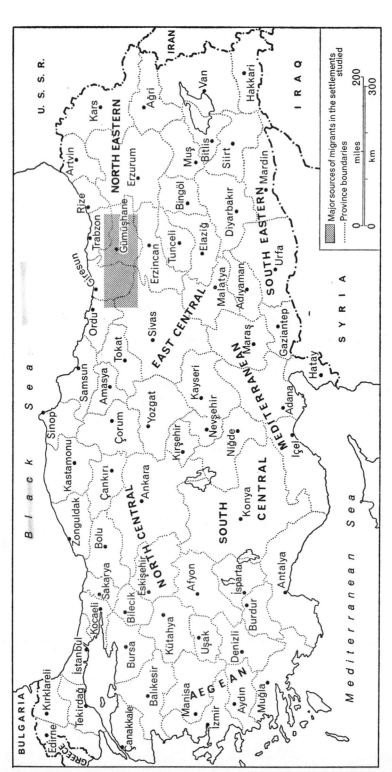

Map 3. *Turkish provinces*

Table 2.5. *Distribution of migrants according to district town and village of origin in four provinces*

Province	Towns[a]		Villages	
Gümüşhane	Şiran	5	Kırıntı	159
			Yeniköy	55
			Two other villages	4
	Bayburt		Various villages	16
	Total	5		234
Sivas	Sivas City	3	Various villages	2
	Suşehri	3	Yukari Göréde[b]	24
			Akıncı	15
			Tatar	8
			Günlüce	5
			Other villages	26
	Hafik		Düzyayla	22
			Other villages	4
	Koyulhisar	19	Various villages	12
	Other towns	2	Various villages	8
	Total	27		126
Giresun	Giresun City	6	Various villages	1
	Alucra	4	Kayacık	67
			Mindeval	7
			Other villages	10
	Şebinkarahisar	3	Yeniyol	14
			Gölve	6
			Other villages	22
	Other towns		Various villages	8
	Total	13		135
Trabzon	Trabzon city		Various villages	2
	Araklı	1	Tosunlu	21
			Other villages	1
			Koyuncular	9
	Sürmene	2	Kahraman	6
			Yağmurlu	5
			Other villages	5
	Other towns		Various villages	5
	Total	3		54
Total		48		549

[a] The first town indicated at the top of each one of the four sections is the provincial center (*vilayet merkezi*); other towns are district centers (*kaza merkezi*). "Other villages" and "various villages" refer to localities attached administratively to the cities or the towns shown in the second column.

[b] Yukarı Göréde, Tatar, Günlüce, and Akıncı are very close to each other and are all part of the same subdistrict (*nahiye*) called Gökçekent. The village of Yukarı Göréde is the subdistrict center.

Table 2.6. *Squatters' location in three* gecekondus *according to province of origin*

	Nafibaba	Baltaliman	Celâlettin Paşa	Total
Gümüşhane	224	15		239
Sivas	104	8	41	153
Giresun	139	4	5	148
Trabzon	30	26	1	57
Kastamonu	36	11	9	56
Istanbul	22	7	11	40
Bolu	29		1	30
Sinop	21	3	2	26
Ordu	6	6	14	26
Çankırı	1	17	1	19
Rize	12	1	4	17
Sakarya	14	1		15
Balıkesir	7		4	11
Erzincan	9		2	11
Isparta	11			11
Tekirdağ	3	1	6	10
Çorum		6	2	8
Other provinces and places	(21)	(14)	(38)	73
Total	689	120	141	950

investigation it turned out that the villages of Kayacık and Yeniköy were settled by people from the village of Kırıntı about half a century ago.[37] Thus, it appears that the village of Kırıntı had a key role in the establishment of the Nafibaba settlement. Common birthplace and lineage played a role in giving to the Nafibaba settlement a certain internal cohesion and cultural continuity. (See chapter 7.) The squatters from Kırıntı and sister villages formed an important enclave in Nafibaba *gecekondu* but were not in the majority – that is, approximately 281 people of 682 people interviewed in this settlement came from the same village stock. (The interviews covered about 80 percent of the inhabitants above the age of 16.) The role of this enclave as a self-perpetuating rural community will be discussed later.[38]

It appears from the foregoing that the majority of people in the three settlements surveyed (Table 2.6) came from northeastern Anatolia and notably from an area of about 100 miles long and 20 miles wide between Şiran in the east, Koyulhisar in the west, the Kelkit river in the south, and Balaban mountains (with peaks rising to 10,000 feet) in the north. The main source of migration consisted of a string of villages at the base of the Kelkit river. These villages were attached to the towns of Şiran, Alucra, Şebinkarahisar, Suşehri, and Koyulhisar, all of which had populations of less than 20,000.[39] These towns are part of a much larger region about 400 miles long and 120 miles wide stretching along the Black Sea mountains. It is considered one of the poorest and overly populated areas of Turkey. The economic backwardness of the area is rather paradoxical since the soil, though poor, receives abundant rainfall and the population is hard-working, alert, and displays an unusual spirit of enterprise. (Much of the building industry in Istanbul is in the hands of Karadenizliler, or people from the Black Sea region.)

The economic backwardness of the area, which was the prime cause of migration, resulted as the consequence of a series of changes in the political, economic, and social order of the area in the past 150 years. (Information indicates that the area was well to do in the earlier centuries. The Turkish traveler Evliya Çelebi, who visited Şiran, Şebinkarahisar, and Koyulhisar in the seventeenth century, describes the area as prosperous and well built. He speaks of local notables who met him and honored him with gifts and food.)[40] A brief history of one of the migrants' villages shows a rather intricate interplay of economic forces, migration, and politics.

Some of the squatters, and residents of the villages of Kırıntı, Kayacık, and Yeniköy, notably members of the established families in Kırıntı, claimed that their ancestors had come as part of a large wave of migrants from Central Asia some four centuries earlier and established themselves in the area after receiving permission from Karaca Bey, the ruler in Şiran (see Chapter 7). The bulk of the group continued their westward movement and settled in Giresun and other places along the Black Sea mountains. The four families that claim to have been the leaders of the established group retain the same position today and have strong representation both in the squatter settlements in Istanbul and in the village itself.[41] The inhabitants of Kırıntı were or became later *kızılbaş,* that is, Shiites (Alevi). They still retain their Alevi identity, as shown by their acceptance of the leadership of a *şıh,* or sheikh. The present *dede,* or sheikh, in the village was Ibrahim Günel. The people do not recall the name of the original *kabile* (clan). They were probably part of the Çepni (*aşiret*) tribe of the Uçok branch of the large Oghuz groups that settled in northern Anatolia. The original group raised livestock and dealt in lumber and wood derivatives, hence one could consider them part of the Tahtacı (timbermen) group of Kızılbaş.

According to the villagers, they established their first village on a high plateau in order to escape the attacks by Sunnite (Orthodox) Muslims. However, the location of their original village at a site that today is called Harmancık seemed to have been dictated by economic and strategic reasons. Harmancık has a controlling position over the Tarhana pass on a route connecting the inland villages with the commercial centers of Alucra and Şebinkarahisar. This road was connected, in turn, to the old trade route linking Persia to the Black Sea part of Trabzon. Though secondary in importance, this was nevertheless a vital route for the local trade, as indicated by the ruins of some caravansaries (travel inns) stretching along it. Possibly the original village was a *derbend* settlement (charged with the maintenance and protection of roads, passes, and bridges) and thus enjoyed a special status as a tax-exempt village. The present site of Kırıntı, which is located at some distance from Harmancık, was originally a Greek village called Munadich. The Greeks left it during the economic boom in the nineteenth century and went to settle and engage in trade in the towns along the Black Sea shores. Subsequently the inhabitants of Harmancık and other groups from mountains, together with army deserters, including Janissaries, came and settled in the village. Another group not related to the original settlers was formed by the family of Gündoğans, who apparently were permitted to settle in the village by the leader of the community and eventually became part of it. Yet, even today all evil doing in the village is attributed to the Gündoğans since they are still considered somewhat inferior to the original stock.

Push factors of migration

The purpose of this background information has been to emphasize the fact that rural migration in Turkey was prepared and
nurtured by a series of internal historical, economic, social, and
technological factors. It is this force of the "push" factors that
has compelled many Turkish scholars to look on rural migration
and urbanization as a "fast depeasantization" phenomenon without
a corresponding industrialization movement.[42] Consequently, as
expected, the migrants in the squatter settlements surveyed in this
study indicated their situation in the village as the chief cause for
their move from village to city. Economic hardship or poverty in
the village was cited as a chief reason of migration. An overwhelming majority of the men and women and the unmarried interviewed
said that they left the villages because of poverty and living difficulties. Many cited also the lack of land and low soil productivity
as the chief cause of poverty and the immediate cause of migration
into the city (Table 2.7). Yet interestingly enough an overwhelming majority of migrant men, women, and even the unmarried (the
latter usually referring to their parents' property) responded that
they had owned some land and houses in the villages (Table 2.8).

The actual amount of land owned by squatters in their village of
origin varied. Many estimated the size of their land according to
the local traditional measures rather than the metric system adopted
by the government. Thus, some 69 percent of the men use as the
measure of land the *dönüm* (the legally accepted measurement
equivalent to 100 square meters, or 10 dönüms per hectare); another 20 percent used the *teneke* (pail full of seeds necessary to
sow a field, and in some cases the total number of pails of crops
harvested) and *kile* (about 40 pounds weight); and 2 percent gave
tarla (field) as the measure of their land areas. Some even responded that their land was so fragmented because of inheritance
and they owned so little land that no measurement could be applied, whereas others did not even remember the exact surface of
the land they owned. It was calculated on the basis of total *dönüms*
that each family head owned 18.9 *dönüms* (median) or 36.7
dönüms (mean), or about 3.9 and 7.5 acres of land. But the
quality of the land in this area was very poor. The best soil could

Table 2.7. *Reasons for leaving village (in percentages)*

	Men	Women	Unmarried
Material hardship (poverty)	47	52	49
Lack of land	30	13	16
Search for a better future	8	7	15
In order to join husband		14	
Others (to end *gurbetçilik*)	15	14	20
Total	100	100	100

Table 2.8. *Ownership of house and land in place of origin (in percentages)*

	Men	Women	Unmarried
Houseowners[a]	90	81	93
Landowners[b]	82	68	68

[a] Five percent of the women said that in the village they had lived in their in-laws' house.

[b] One percent of the men and 6 percent of the women did not remember whether they had land in the village.

produce in good years about 300 pounds and the poorest 70 pounds of wheat per *dönüm*.

In general, lack of good cultivable land, irrigation, water, and the low productivity of the soil,[43] the division of properties into small parcels, and, to a lesser extent, the mechanization of agriculture, feuds over land, the pressure of landlords, and the use of land for reforestation by the government were cited as the chief shortcomings of the local agriculture.[44] In many places the need for food was so strong that land that should have stayed fallow one or two years had to be cultivated every year, which further exhausted its productivity. Another cause that prompted the villagers to migrate to Istanbul was the desire to end *gurbetçilik* (seasonal migration). It must be emphasized that inhabitants of villages where *gurbetçilik* was intensive migrated because of established traditions of migration and knowledge of the city. A squatter's statement best describes the situation:

I wandered with my quilt on my back through two thirds of Turkey and settled when I found good opportunities. As long as I know, my people went to work elsewhere. We lived with money sent from other places. Our people migrated to Istanbul, Ankara, to Adana, and now to Germany. Now I would like to go to Germany. Nine months a year I worked out of the village. Since I could not stay permanently in my village it was better to settle in Istanbul. We worked out of the village while the older and the younger ones stayed home and worked the land. We gathered some money and thus made a living. Actually one single man could do all the work in my family. I and my brothers left because we were not needed. We worked in towns and then consumed all we earned in the village. It was better to work and live in one and the same place. Most of our people were working out of the village. If a home had 10 people certainly 5–6 were working elsewhere out of the village. We came to Istanbul because we got used to coming here, our feet became used to walking this way.

There were other reasons for leaving the village, such as the better educational facilities, desire to make money either to pay debts or to buy land, or to acquire education to catch up with relatives who seemed to be prospering in the city, better medical care, and so on.[45]

Women, on the other hand, though generally concurring with men's opinion about the reasons for leaving the village, had a much more concrete view of the living difficulties in a rural area, where they did most of the work in fields and homes – especially in the *gurbetçi* families, where men left their village in the summers. They were attracted to the city by the desire to escape the hardship of field work and to find better opportunities for their children. Some women migrated because they wanted to keep up with their neighbors who had migrated to the city earlier. The unmarried, usually 16 to 20 years of age, said that they migrated to follow their parents or were attracted by the opportunity for a secure and better future in the city. This last group, because of its limited experience in the rural area, seemed less aware of the hardship in villages and more prone to take the city facilities for granted.

The small size of some of the squatters' original villages, especially those located in mountainous areas, was another indirect cause for migration. (See Chapter 7.) The per capita cost of education, electrification, and road building in such villages was so prohibitive that often nothing was done. Indeed, 20.7 percent of all squatters interviewed came from villages with 51 to 150 people, 13.0 percent from villages with 151 to 250 people, and the rest from larger villages. Obviously few of these people had chances of advancement in their original village. Moreover, a large number of the people living in small villages were related to each other. This kept the village closed to outsiders in every respect. Eventually migration broke up the isolation and forced the inhabitants to mix with other families, although there are still some isolated villages. Some of those who stayed in the village were in most cases relatively well-to-do families. Often the rich who stayed in the village criticized and belittled the parvenu squatters out of malice and envy because they had destroyed the village traditions and customs by bringing outside ideas and marrying "foreigners."

The immediate decision to leave the village was taken most individually by the men, whereas the women followed their husbands' or relatives' advice (Table 2.9). Decision making in migration appears to be largely a personal choice of changing a rural form of occupation and style of life for another, whatever that may be. This decision, besides showing a degree of individualization, expressed dissatisfaction with one's birthplace as well as a certain readiness to adapt to an urban existence. The decision to migrate

Table 2.9. *Decision to leave village* (*in percentages*)

	Men	Women	Unmarried
Own decision	59	39	34
Husband's decision		30	
Followed advice of relatives			
(own family included)	27	25	63
Followed advice of friends			
and fellow villagers	11	5	1
Other	3	1	2
Total	100	100	100

Note: The table shows a high degree of individualism and independence of decision. It is difficult to determine precisely whether or not this was a *post facto* reconsideration of the event after a period of residence in the city. Nevertheless, I am inclined to think that the decision was made individually.

places the migrant in a position of marginality, not alienation, toward his village, and also forces him to seek adjustment to other forms of organization and occupation. The villagers in turn strive to retain strong ties with the migrant for practical and family reasons, despite the fact that the migrant's departure from the village and gradual aloofness is in most cases a permanent fact.

3. The establishment and growth of the *gecekondu*

Establishment patterns

The *gecekondus* in Turkey, similar to settlements elsewhere in the world, are established not by migrants coming directly from villages or towns but by slum dwellers or low-income groups who have congregated and settled earlier in the city. The seizure of the land and the establishment of the first dwellings occur often through an act of land occupation or invasion, which creates the first enduring bond of solidarity among squatters. (The term *invasion* is used here in the sense of moving illegally onto land and not as an institutionalized form of establishing a settlement, as is often the case in some South American countries.) The organizers of the invasion are usually a small group of people, often with previous experience, who engage in the act either in response to pressure from relatives and fellow villagers or simply for profit. The participants in the invasion are usually related and known to each other; moreover, in order to strengthen their ranks new people and acquaintances, including relatives and friends from the village, may be invited to participate. The larger the number of participants and the bigger the settlement, the more difficult it becomes to demolish it, if, indeed, the authorities and the police care to do so.

The initial factors that prompted the establishment of the *gecekondus* in Nafibaba, Baltaliman, and Celâlettin Paşa, were the availability of employment and the shortage of housing and high rents in the area, notably in Rumelihisar. Employment opportunities, all within ½ to 3 miles from the settlements, became available after a series of apartment houses began to be built in the districts of Levent and Etiler, all inhabited by higher-income groups. In fact, these districts have become choice residential areas. This was followed by the establishment of two factories and the expansion of the shipyards at Istiniye on the Bosphorus. The drug and electrical appliance plants at Levent and the *sanayi çarşısı* (industrial city), consisting of car repair shops established further down the main highway, provided additional possibilities for employment. Robert College, the hosiptal of Baltaliman, and the rich families living in the fashionable district of Bebek (located south of the Nafibaba settlement),[1] provided additional employment for men and for a number of women, mostly in household jobs. Robert College (now Bogaziçi Universitesi) in Bebek, which had been a source of employment for a generation or so for some 50 people from the Black Sea area, provided additional job opportunities after it added Yüksek, or a university section, to its existing junior college section in 1955. However, the number of people employed there remained insignificant in relation to total employment.

The Nafibaba squatter settlement, as it was called then, is located on the outskirts on the hillside of the old district, or Rumelihisar (known in the old days as Boğazkesen), located on the Bosphorus. This district is contiguous to the fortress built in 1452, by Mehmed II, the Conqueror of Constantinople; and aside from a few mansions left from the time of the sultans, usually rented to American officials, it is considered a middle- to low-income area.

The land extending on the hills in the west, on which the *gecekondu* was established, belonged to the government and was transferred to the municipality. At the time of the invasion it was occupied by a retired official. Inaccessibility, because of lack of roads, and undetectability from the main thoroughfare along the Bosphorus provided the best security for the original usurper, until a group of low-paid employees at Robert College and their friends working elsewhere, pressed by the rising rents in Rumelihisar, decided to set up their own dwellings. According to the original founders interviewed, all the people in the group were from the same region and had known each other for years. Moreover, all had been living in the city for several years. The would-be invaders found out that the man who occupied this huge piece of land had no legal title to it. Subsequently, they "persuaded" him to "sell" the land at a low price (this sort of transaction is legally useful in claiming that the land was "bought") but only after ambushing and beating him soundly one night in the dark. A few days afterward the land was divided into several lots and the first 20 to 30 dwellings were erected in two days on the land thus "purchased." This occurred about 1958. Afterward the main problem was to assure the continued existence of the *gecekondu* since the land belonged to the government. The squatters knew that the survival of the settlement depended on their actual numerical strength and the resulting ability to defend it against authorities, since their action violated every building code and property law. Consequently, the *kurucular* (founders), who became eventually the peers of the squatter community, sought to attract a larger number of people to the site. The first settlers occupied larger lots that were either used as building sites for their own dwellings, reserved for their relatives, or divided and sold to other persons, usually friends or acquaintances from the same region.

The price of the lots at the time was very low. For instance, a few lots still available in the settlements surveyed in 1968 sold for 700 to 2000 liras (9 liras to the dollar; 13 liras in 1974) – that is, about 10 to 50 times less than the price of the legally acquired building lots of the same quality and size elsewhere in the city. Nafibaba was thus included in the *gecekondu* market. This market, though operating completely outside the legal real estate market, had its own structure and followed its own economic laws. There were, in fact, "*gecekondu* entrepreneurs," who sold the building materials or could be contracted in exceptional cases to build the dwelling according to specifications; one room would be erected overnight and foundations laid for other rooms. The building materials cost about 1500 liras ($165) and the total price of the dwellings, including the land, ranged between 4000 and 6000 liras in the 1966–68 period. The possibility of obtaining the deed to the land and the occupants' approximate expected length of stay in a dwelling, which varied usually in accordance with life expectancy of the settlement, as well as the chances of obtaining the title to the land, were other factors determining the market value of a *gecekondu* dwelling.

The fact that the founders of the Nafibaba *gecekondu* tried, like other people in their situation, to attract their relatives and friends to the settlements was motivated by basic social and economic considerations. The presence of relatives in the settlement was the best guarantee that one's own family will be cared for in case of sickness, unemployment, and departure for military service. This explains why families and migrants from the same village tended to cluster together in one settlement. The settlers knew that if they could obtain the title to the land, the value of their property would skyrocket, especially if the shacks were improved to become true houses. Indeed, observation has shown that after the ownership of a *gecekondu* is legalized through the acquisition of the *tapu* (land deed), the quality and the appearance of the houses improve to become indistinguishable from the lower-priced houses in the city. It is clear that the survival chances of the Nafibaba *gecekondu* depended above all on the inhabitants' solidarity, organizational skill, and concerted action. Blood relationship, village solidarity, and practical interest played important roles in achieving consensus for common action. Meanwhile, the leaders of the Nafibaba *gecekondu* expanded the boundaries of their settlement by bringing in their friends and relatives in the city as well as other acceptable migrants. In the process, some made money.

At a later state, about 1964, the settlement expanded again by invasion, this time onto privately owned land, and its population grew rapidly, chiefly with newcomers from villages. The individual who had a valid legal title agreed to sell the land to the invaders at 12 liras per square meter, which was a very low price, merely to avoid conflict with the squatters. The squatters, however, believed false rumors that the land could be obtained free and broke the agreement with the owner. Consequently, the owner went to the court and the case was eventually settled as the occupants agreed to pay a rather insignificant sum for the land. Meanwhile, the population became diversified as villagers from other provinces purchased land or dwellings from the original invaders or occupied the adjoining sites and brought in their own relatives and friends. Thus, the population of Nafibaba consisting of about 1900 people at the time of the survey – despite a strong dominant core of villagers from Kırıntı, Kayacık, and Yeniköy – became quite heterogeneous.

The settlement of Baltaliman, the second *gecekondu* studied in this work, was formed originally by workers employed by a quarry (now closed) owned by a non-Turk. Eventually, the land belonging to the government next to the quarry owner's dwelling was settled by Niyazi Altıntaş and Hasan Bahar, who had migrated from the provinces of Trabzon and Ordu on the Black Sea. Subsequently, their relatives and friends moved in and settled there. The Baltaliman settlement expanded southward up the hill and joined the Nafibaba settlement, which grew from the opposite side. The settlements eventually formed a single unit in 1971–72 (see Chapter 8).

The third *gecekondu*, known as Ahmet Celâleddin Paşa (or more commonly Celâlettin Paşa), on the outskirts of the Boyacıköy-Emirgân district, was established about 1955–58 by a few long-time residents from that district and others from adjacent areas in Istanbul. Some of these were city dwellers, whose houses had been demolished in the campaign to renovate Istanbul in the period from 1955 to 1959. Since they could not afford to buy or rent new houses, they moved and built their shacks on the present site. The second phase of development in Celâlettin Paşa began in 1962–63, when a new group of invaders occupied the land in the immediate vicinity of the first settlement. Some settlers in this second *gecekondu* claimed that they purchased the land from the rightful owners; the rest, mostly rural migrants, said that they invaded and occupied the land in the same fashion as in other squatter settlements.

Thus, the bulk of the three *gecekondus* were formed chiefly in the 1950s and have continually expanded since, despite the fact that the area occupied by the Nafibaba and part of the Baltaliman settlements was assigned to the Technical University of Istanbul as part of its new campus. Eventually the dwellers found themselves pitted against the university, which planned to turn their hillside into a zoological park. However, the Nafibaba and Baltaliman settlements, now fused, had won their case and were expecting their land deeds in 1974, as was the third settlement, because of the government decision to give deeds to all *gecekondu* dwellings built until the end of 1973.

Structure and growth

The three settlements, as expected, created an economic and commercial life of their own. At the time of the survey there were a total of 11 grocery stores, 3 coffeehouses, 2 eating places, a barber shop, a vegetable shop, and a food stand. In addition, a movie house, a soft drink stand, and a hardware store were opened in 1968. All shops were privately owned and operated by the owners themselves; eight of the owners also held jobs elsewhere in the city, either because the income from the store was insufficient or in order to increase their capital. All served the settlements almost exclusively.

Despite the owners' insistent complaint that business was slow, it was calculated that each enterprise was rather active and had an average capital of 4000 to 6000 liras and that the annual gross sale of all the shops amounted to about 1.5 million liras. Since 20 to 30 percent profit per gross sale is normal in Turkey, it was estimated that the minimum net profit of all the business places amounted to about 300,000 to 400,000 liras a year, or an average of about 20,000 liras per business place. By Turkish standards this is a rather tidy sum, which if invested properly can be very rewarding. It should be noted, however, that all the grocery stores operated by opening credit accounts to the dwellers and by selling goods at about 10 to 15 percent less than the established city enterprises. This enabled them to compete with the larger stores in the old districts. As an added attraction, the *gecekondu* stores sold fresh eggs, yogurt, and even milk produced by cows and chickens raised in the settlement as well as "home grown" potatoes and fruit. Some squatters claimed that they preferred vegetables grown in their original region because they tasted better than those grown in Istanbul area (the claim proved right after we tasted the food in their region). All this stimulated the growth of some products in the village specifically for the squatter markets in Istanbul.

The second phase in the life of a *gecekondu* is its growth. While the establishment of the *gecekondu* is essentially a physical action, its growth and development is a social phenomenon related intimately to the village and nurtured by migration. The study of migration of the residents in the three settlements may help to understand the pattern. (Another migration from *gecekondu* to western Europe and from village to abroad, which increased greatly after 1970, is outside the scope of this survey.)

The migrants did not follow a single and precise pattern of movement from village to city (Table 3.1). The interval of time from departure from village and arrival in the city varied in proportion to the force of "pull" factors in the city. The idea that migration occurs step by step from villages to larger population centers and then to cities, as put forth by Ravenstein in 1885 with regard to nineteenth-century England, is not borne out entirely in

Table 3.1. *Pattern of migration: direct or step by step (in percentages)*

	Men	Women	Unmarried
Directly from village to settlement (one step)	39	45	40
From village to a different district in Istanbul (actually to the city)	18	16	11
From village to another city or town, then to Istanbul: two steps	21	11	16
Other (includes the dwellers born in Istanbul and from towns) three or more steps migration	22	28	33
Total	100	100	100

the case of Turkish migrants. Thus, more than 50 percent of the migrants – the percentage is higher among women because they came directly from a village to join their husbands after they established themselves in the city – came directly to Istanbul without an intermediary stop in a smaller city. In general, the Turkish rural-urban migration from the early 1960s to the 1970s tended to lean toward a direct, or one-step, migration rather than multistep migration. The reasons for this tendency must be sought in the growing employment opportunities in the city as well as in the favorable political climate. The direct migration in the three Turkish *gecekondus* seems to be predominant also in some areas of Latin America. William L. Flinn indicated that in Bogotá, Colombia, "step-migration does not always occur," although "other Colombian studies, however, indicate that the migration steps take place, but that the steps are not necessarily made by the same generation and probably are not."[2] The direct versus multistep migration in the Turkish *gecekondus* studied here presents certain characteristics not very different from the Latin American settlements.

Among the married men who said that they came directly from the village, many had worked seasonally in the towns and cities in the vicinity of their native village or region. Many of these had been *gurbetçis,* who spent the winter at home and took off in search of work during the following spring. Moreover, several dozen inhabitants prior to moving to the *gecekondu* lived in various poorer sections of Istanbul, and others inhabited the old city districts adjacent to their new community (Table 3.2).

A more detailed and expanded analysis of the migration pattern confirms the findings of the general migration pattern. Thus, though the rural-urban migration to Istanbul embodies all general patterns of migration, direct migration seems to prevail. Actually, semidirect migration – from village to a city district other than the settlement – is actually a village-city migration.

Migrating to Istanbul, building a house, and finding a job in the city revolved around *akrabalık* (blood relationship) and hemşerilik (common village-town origin). The scope of and the closeness generated by *hemşerilik* grows in direct proportion to the distance from the original place. For instance, the *hemşeris* of a *gecekondu* dweller from, say, Kayacık would include those from Kırıntı and the Şiran and Alucra areas, although those from Kayacık would

Table 3.2. *Migration patterns of married men by age groups (in percentages)*

	16–25	26–35	36–45	46–
Directly from village to settlement	53	42	29	32
From village to a different district of Istanbul	19	25	14	5
From village to present district and then to the settlement	11	13	29	15
From village to another town or city and then to Istanbul	13	12	9	19
From a town (these were born in town) to Istanbul	3	3	6	10
Other	1	5	13	19
Total	100	100	100	100

Note: Some of the towns most frequently cited – number indicates frequency – as areas of residence prior to moving to Istanbul were Giresun (30), Samsun (18), Ordu (11), Izmit (11), Izmir (9), Ankara (8), and 32 other smaller towns. The first three towns cited most frequently as areas of habitation are located in close proximity to the migrants' original villages.

form the most intimate group. For Turkish villagers and their relatives and *hemşeris* in the city, blood and communal ties provide the only basis for mutual help and solidarity until these are superseded by or fused into other relations and identities of urban and national origin. Since *akrabalık* and *hemşerilik* played basic roles in the entire process of migration and the settlement in the city, it may be useful to dwell further on them.

The pioneer of rural migration into the city in the case of our three *gecekondus* was the *gurbetçi*. He had come to Istanbul for seasonal work year after year but could not bring his family either because his earnings were too low or jobs were not available on a permanent basis. Usually he lived huddled with 5 or 6 of his *hemşeris* in single rented rooms. As soon as job opportunities and wages increased and the chances of continuous employment in the city appeared reasonably secure, he began to bring his closest relatives, not at random but according to a more or less precise pattern. He brought first the ablest bodied member of the family, usually bachelor brothers and oldest son. When the job market expanded they called the other able-bodied male relatives, usually another brother or first cousin, and so on. The stiff job competition, harsh living conditions, and hard work (willingness to take the most difficult jobs and accept low wages gives the migrants, as mentioned, a competitive edge over established city workers) called for healthy, strong men – hence the predominance of the young among early migrants. The wife and the children arrived only after there was assurance of housing and continuous employment to sustain the entire family. In some cases, young boys came before their mother in order to help the father. Old parents and grandparents, and in some cases one son or daughter, were left in the village in order to provide moral and material comfort to those left behind and satisfy the natural impulse to maintain ties with *memlekıt* (homeland). The relationship with the village, moreover, provided a psychological safeguard against alienation and a practical guarantee that if economic conditions in the city deteriorated the migrant had a place to return to. Moreover, in the case of the Alevis the tradition of perpetuating the *ocak* (hearth or fraternity) – that is, their original home and tending the graves of their ancestors – played a significant part in maintaining village attachments.

Patterns of settlement in the city

Thus the villagers' migration into the city was not the consequence of a hasty decision but a gradual process conditioned by the availability of employment and housing. The newcomers formed a new community that maintained temporarily at least some of the village culture and, thus, facilitated the migrants' gradual integration into the city without a sudden break with the past. In fact, men preferred to let their wives and children live for a while with relatives in the city to become acquainted with the urban life before moving them to the *gecekondu*. Table 3.3 shows the first arrival of men, women (the women about three years after the husbands), and the unmarried in the city. They came to seek work or visit relatives and not necessarily to settle in the *gecekondu*. The percentage shifts in men's arrival dates, which are probably valid for the trend of migration in the entire country, coincide with periods of unrest or economic stagnation. Thus, those who had come 11 to 18 years ago (as of 1968) arrived during the first construction boom under the rule of Menderes' Democratic party, 1952–55. Those who had come 8 to 10 years ago arrived after Menderes was able to stabilize the economy (after receiving a $300 million loan from the West in 1958). The sudden drop in the number of those who had come 6 to 7 years ago is due to the military revolution of 1960, which unsettled the economy for about two years and threatened to control rural migration. This stagnation was followed by an economic boom from 1963 to 1967, then by massive migration, and the beginning of labor export to western Europe, often from the *gecekondus*. In some cases, as expected, the date of arrival in the *gecekondu* coincided with the first visit to the city.

Thus, 59 percent of the men, 64 percent of the women, and 69 percent of the unmarried stayed five years or less in the *gecekondu*. On the other hand, only 29 percent of the men and 47 percent of the women arrived in Istanbul during the last 1 to 5 years. Thus, at least 71 percent of the men and 53 percent of the women of the early arrivals lived in rented houses or with relatives before they moved to the *gecekondu* (Table 3.4). It is interesting to note that 72 percent of the men, 88 percent of the women, and 70 percent of the unmarried did not think to migrate anywhere else but to Istanbul. While this choice was made for cultural and historical

Table 3.3. *Squatters' date of arrival in Istanbul, as of 1968*

Years ago	Men according to age				Percentage		
	16–25	26–35	36–45	46–	Men	Women	Unmarried
1	8	3	1		3	8	10
2–3	10	9	4	3	7	17	14
4–5	13	30	15	15	19	22	31
6–7	6	21	10	6	11	16	21
8–10	10	40	17	4	18	16	13
11–18	15	42	41	8	28	16	11
18+	1	13	25	17	14	5	
Total	63	158	113	53	100	100	100

Table 3.4. *Period of stay in* gecekondu
(*in percentages*)

	Men	Women	Unmarried
Less than one year	5	8	9
1–3 years	22	27	33
4–5 years	32	29	27
6 years and more	41	36	31
Total	100	100	100

reasons as well as traditions of migration, the actual decision to migrate and the choice of the city was conditioned by immediate economic and personal reasons. (See on Table 3.5.)

Once in Istanbul the traditional system of mutual help and assistance provided the newcomers with shelter and employment, as shown in Table 3.6. It is remarkable that men found jobs within a relatively short period of time after arrival in the city (Table 3.7).

About two-thirds of those men who claimed that they found the jobs by themselves meant that they went and applied personally. In order to bolster their ego and pride they failed to mention that relatives and *hemşeris* might have informed them about the availability of jobs.[3] (See Table 3.8.)

Table 3.5. *Reasons for choosing Istanbul*
(*in percentages*)

	Men	Women	Unmarried
Better living/ employment	72	57	53
Relatives' presence	18	7	21
Husband's presence and marriage reasons		18	
Educational opportunity (children)	7	7	13
Better health care	3	6	3
Other		5	10
Total	100	100	100

The *gecekondu* has been viewed so far as a consequence of the housing shortage and high rents. For the squatters, however, another compelling personal reason to move to the *gecekondu,* a reason that emerges only after long talks with squatters, was the desire to own property. True, the memory of the material hardship in the village and the economic insecurity in the city exacerbated the squatters' desire to own property. However, if the first migrants who established the dwellings in Istanbul about 1953–58 had not been granted the title to the land by the ruling Democratic party desirous of securing votes, and if the *gecekondu* dwellers had not devised political channels for pressuring the government and municipal authorities, the urge to build the *gecekondu* might have been less. But a precedent was firmly established. Most of the *gecekondus* were not eliminated, supposedly because of laws that prohibited the summary destruction of "inhabited dwellings"; and eventually the dwellers were granted title to the land.

The new generation of squatters learned that if the *gecekondus* were preserved until election time, the chances of striking a bargain with office incumbents and candidates by offering votes in exchange for *tapus* (land deeds) would be greatly enhanced. The squatters also knew that once they acquired the *tapus,* the market value of their shacks would skyrocket, especially if the looks of the *gecekondu* improved, as invariably it did. In 1968 in the Nafibaba

Table 3.6. *Living place after arrival in Istanbul (in percentages)*

	Men	Women	Unmarried
With relatives	38	48	48
Own sources (rent)[a]	33	17	19
Working place[b]	4	13	3
With village friends	5	14	7
In own *gecekondu* dwelling[c]	20	6	23
In tents and other shelters		2	
Total	100	100	100

[a] Refers to the early period prior to the move to the *gecekondu*. Men were often without their families and stayed with friends, 5 or 6 of them in one room.

[b] Includes seasonal construction workers who slept on the construction sites in the half-built rooms and maids who stayed in their masters' homes. Some still stay with their employers despite their ownership of *gecekondu* dwellings.

[c] Those who built, bought, or rented a *gecekondu* dwelling prior to coming into the city. Often they would be without their family. Sometimes bachelors bought or built a dwelling and married afterward.

Table 3.7. *Length of job search after arrival in Istanbul (in percentages)*

	Men	Women	Unmarried
1–15 days	46	15	29
16–30 days	15	6	10
31–60 days	13	4	17
61 days to a year	24	34	40
More than a year	2	41	4
Total	100	100	100

Table 3.8. *Means used to locate job*
(*in percentages*)

	Men	Women	Unmarried
Through own efforts	40	25	26
Through friends	31	48	29
Through relatives	29	27	45
Total	100	100	100

settlement, some of the better dwellings possessing *tapus* could sell for as much as 150,000 liras; in 1974, 300,000 liras (and twice as much in Baltaliman). Thus, the squatter was aware that he had a very good chance to become a "house owner" in the city and by village standards a "rich" man. The history of friends and relatives who became urban proprietors was so tempting that additional villagers would be lured to the city. Moreover, in the status-conscious Turkish society, a house ownership propelled the squatter upward on the social ladder and into the urban middle class and facilitated his integration into the city. Governments and political parties in Turkey have encouraged house ownership as likely to increase the number of real estate proprietors and thus inhibit the spread of radicalism among the dispossessed squatters. Knowing that the chances of owning a house are relatively good, most migrants strive to build their own dwellings rather than rent houses in the city, however low the rent may be. (See Table 3.9.) Consequently, as

Table 3.9. *Ownership of houses*
(*in percentages*)

	Men	Women	Unmarried
Owns the house	84	87	70
Rents it	9	8	6
Lives with relatives but pays no rent	7	5	24
Total	100	100	100

may be expected, 84 percent of the men living in the three *gece-kondus* studied in this work owned their houses, whereas only 9 percent rented them, and 7 percent lived with relatives but did not pay rent. The rent paid by 76 percent of the men was 50 to 100 liras (or about one-sixth of their average individual earnings); 21 percent of the men paid 101 to 150 liras rent, and 3 percent paid more.

Characteristics of the dwelling

The house, usually of one room, is erected and furnished, however meagerly, overnight; thus, the inhabitants can benefit from the legal provisions that prohibit the destruction of "inhabited homes without due process." (Actually, many of the dwellings appear so well built that one can hardly believe it was achieved in a few hours.) If the house looks well settled, the squatter can claim that he has resided there for a year or more in order to benefit from the prescriptive clauses of the law.

The finishing and the expansion of the house, sometimes to 2 to 4 rooms, is done gradually by the owners themselves. The time spent on improving the houses, usually after returning home from a full day's toil, and planting trees and gardens represents a significant labor investment and results in a marked improvement of the land, much of which was unfit for regular construction anyway.[4]

The building of the house and the use of construction material show a high degree of adaptability to soil conditions and climate, which housing plans developed by the government are often not able to achieve. One moderately expensive housing development sponsored by a bank in Ankara was abandoned because of a land slide, while a *gecekondu* built on the next hill survived and thrived. The initial *gecekondu* room is often constructed of makeshift materials; however, soon afterward the shack is consolidated and expanded, often by completely replacing the original material with brick and cement. The bricks used in the *gecekondus* studied in this work were locally manufactured and used judiciously according to the soil and position of the land. If the chances of retaining the *gecekondu* appear good, the dwellers do not hesitate to use better construction materials. In a way, the *gecekondu* building has forced the local entrepreneurs to seek and make the best use of the low-cost locally available materials.

The houses in the three settlements studied used locally manufactured material, some of it purchased from dealers in the neighborhood. Some dwellings were originally built on the model of the Black Sea houses, with long triangular roofs and large attics used to store hay. These were soon replaced to conform to the prevailing style in the city – that is, less room for attic and more space for living quarters. Some of the older houses even had two stories. The whitewash seen on the Black Sea village houses was replaced with cement, which better resists the humid air of Istanbul.

In some cases the "purchase" of the land and the construction of the dwelling was financed partly by a transfer of capital from the village. Most squatters, as mentioned, owned or had shares in the houses or the land in the village, however poor those might have been. Most of these properties left in the village were used by relatives. However, a small number of squatters, a total of 34 men and 40 women, had sold their rural properties and spent the proceeds to buy or build the *gecekondu* dwelling or to meet living expenses, to pay debts, or to open small businesses in the city. The price of sold village property according to 49 percent of the men was between 2,500 and 10,000 liras and the rest below 2,500 liras.

Of the house owners in the *gecekondus*, 93, 91, and 92 percent, respectively of the men, women, and unmarried said that they built their own house; the rest said that they bought them. The price paid for the house ranged from 1,500 to 15,000 liras, the latter price was paid for established houses with two or three rooms. (If the seller had the deed, the price, as mentioned, would have been at least ten times higher.) The average price paid for a house bought in the three settlements, according to our calculations, amounted to 5,922 liras (only men's declarations), which places the *gecekondus* we studied in a slightly higher category than most. (The average *gecekondu* dwelling price was 4,000 to 5,000 liras in 1968.)

The ultimate size of the house to be achieved after acquiring the land title was determined by the number of people in the family, including relatives, financial possibilities, as well as the squatters' own image of urban life and comfort. It seems that the Turkish squatters' standards of housing and urban living followed those of the established classes rather than their own means and standards.[5] (Until about 1968, the average floor space in Turkish city apartments, notwithstanding the wasted space due to poor planning, varied between 100 and 150 square meters, which is more than the European and American average). Already the squatters' shacks were becoming real houses: only 17 percent of the dwellings had a single room; 53 percent had two rooms, and 30 percent had three or more rooms. Furthermore, 98 percent of the houses had some sort of latrine – usually outside the house enclosed within a fence. On the other hand, only 2 percent of the houses had city water, 11 percent had electricity (all these facilities were concentrated in the Baltaliman settlement), and 24 percent had baths. By 1974, water and electricity were available to all of them. For heating, 72 percent of the houses used wood and 25 percent used a combination of coal and wood. The annual average expense for heating per house was 573 liras.

Since none of the three settlements had paved streets, they became impassable at the first gust of rain. The municipality refused to bring the water because the *gecekondus'* future status was undecided; they were not classified yet as an area for *islah* (improvement) or *tasfiye* (liquidation). (By 1971 the *gecekondus* were given the classification of *islah* by the municipality and their survival was assured.) Yet, it is difficult to understand how the squattrs could have tolerated their misery when just across the street there was both water and electricity. It is even harder to understand how the "proper" residents of Rumelihisar, especially Emirgân, could have tolerated the squalor across the street.

The municipality had introduced bus service from the center of the city to the Nafibaba and Celâlettin Paşa settlements and paved the streets up to the edge of the settlements. The chief purpose of the bus service was to facilitate the squatters' transportation to employment sites withou delay or loss of time. It seems clear that the municipality, like many employers in need of cheap and readily available labor, saw the *gecekondus* only as a source of manpower and remained insensitive to their human needs; the squatters, in fact, were willing to meet the installation cost of water and electricity. (After the initial survey was conducted I wrote a series of

16 articles in the *Milliyet,* the second largest national newspaper in Turkey, analyzing the *gecekondus* and calling attention to their situation. Partly because of this publicity, the *gecekondus* were provided with water and electricity, but the street still remained largely unpaved in 1974.)

4. The social and economic structure of the *gecekondu*

Family structure

The family is the center of social life in the *gecekondu*. Consequently, the squatters married early. Of a total of 949 people interviewed, only about 126 above the age of 16 were unmarried; of these only one-fourth were women. (Two of the unmarried were rather older and their marital situation was ambiguous.) This is somewhat in line with the national female marriage age in rural areas, which was 18.86 in the 1960s. Men usually married about the age of 20, although there was among squatters a trend toward later marriages; in 1960 the average marrying age for men in Turkey was 21.82 in rural areas and 24.20 in urban areas.[1] The overwhelming majority of squatters – 90 percent – were between 16 and 45 years of age (Table 4.1). This strengthened qualitatively the labor market in the city.

Marriage and family life among most squatters, though showing definite signs of change, was still in large measure regulated by village customs. In a way this was a reflection of the fact that 92 percent of the men were born in villages, 4 percent in towns, and 4 percent in cities. The ratio for women born in villages, towns, and cities was 86, 6, and 7 percent, respectively. Most of the women – 292 of a total of 430 interviewed – were between 16 and 35. The relatively higher number of women born in the city – 58 women versus 32 men – may be explained by the fact that many women were the daughters of parents who had migrated much earlier. In a few cases men married women in the towns and cities in which they worked prior to coming to Istanbul.

An average of 61 percent of the married men and women had 1 to 3 children, and 20 percent belonging to the older age groups had 4 to 5 children. The average number of living children per family was 2.8, which corresponds more or less to the urban national average for the latest five years. The family size in the

Table 4.1. *Age of squatters*

	Men		Women		Unmarried	
	No.	%	No.	%	No.	%
16–25	63	16	125	29	121	96
26–35	158	40	167	39	3	2
36–45	119	30	91	21		
46–	53	14	47	11		
Undetermined					2	2
Total	393	100	430	100	126	100

three *gecekondus* conformed in general to the findings of other studies: average number of household members for Turkey, 5.7; for cities, 4.6; for towns, 5.2; and for villages, 6.2. Other studies give *gecekondu* household size for Istanbul as 4.7, and Ankara 5.5.[2] In view of the squatters' young age in the three settlements, the size of their families is bound to grow in the next 10 years or so. Nevertheless, the family size in the *gecekondu*, because of the various limiting factors, will remain probably below that in rural areas and may continue to diminish further in the next generation. Already there are indications that most families in the three *gecekondus* studied desired to have 2 to 4 or fewer children, thus conforming to the trend in the cities, rather than 3 to 6 children per family, as was the case in rural areas. In general, the size of the nuclear family in Turkey is diminishing, which must be attributed in some measure to the shift of the population to urban areas, to international migration, and to the changes that accompany them.

Of a total of 375 male respondents, 89 percent had been married once; 9 percent had been married twice; and 2 percent had been married more than twice. There was only one reported case of polygamy. Of 423 female respondents 92 percent had one marriage; 8 percent reported a second marriage; and none a third. Most of these second marriages occurred in the city as a consequence of individualization trends. Seventy-one percent of the men and women married from the same village, but only 31 percent of these people were related by blood to each other, usually cousins. The nuclear family in these *gecekondus* was dominant, there was a definite trend toward marriages outside the group, and closer interest in the children's education and professional training had a limiting effect on the size of the family.[3]

Literacy

The educational level of the *gecekondu* population, at least as far as the men were concerned, was definitely superior to that in the villages. Of a total of 393 male respondents, 84 percent knew how to read and write: Just about half of the literates claimed that they had learned how to read and write in village schools. Some had learned how to read and write in the military service, and others were helped by friends or attended special classes, often in order to pass a test to obtain the literacy certificate required for employment in factories. Since factory employment is steady and offers a variety of insurance benefits, it is considered better than construction or other seasonal work, despite the occasional higher wages paid by the latter. In fact, only 17 married men in the 16 to 35 age group were illiterates; the number was higher – about 45 – among those 36 years of age and over.

The literacy rate among the unmarried was very high. (See Table 4.2.) Of 126 people interviewed, 118 knew how to read and write: half of the respondents attended school in Istanbul. Only 2 unmarried men and 6 unmarried women did not know how to read and write.

Four of the married men had finished the *orta okul* (junior high) and 2 had finished *lise* (senior high); none had finished the university. The literacy rate among married women was appallingly low; of a total 430 interviewed, only 31 percent knew how to read and write. The low rate of literacy among women was the consequence of traditional discrimination and limited exposure to the outside world. The illiterate men and those who did not pursue studies beyond the first few years in elementary school cited the following as preventing their study: poverty of the family and the need to help either by working on the land or as *gurbetçis* outside the village; lack of schools in the village and inability to attend classes elsewhere; continuous migration; death of parents; failure of parents or themselves to appreciate the value of education; discrimination in favor of town boys in the case of those who sought

Table 4.2. *Literacy in* gecekondus

	Men		Women		Unmarried	
	No.	%	No.	%	No.	%
I. *Literacy*						
Literate	331	84	133	31	118	94
Illiterate	62	16	297	69	8	6
Total	393	100	430	100	126	100
II. *Schooling of literates*						
A. Elementary						
Finished	161	48	42	32	37	32
Unfinished	66	20	53	41	20	17
B. Middle (*orta okul*)						
Finished	4	1			9	7
Unfinished	8	2	2	2	13	11
Attending					9	7
C. High School (*lise*)						
Finished	2	1	2	2	3	3
Unfinished	1	1	1	1	1	1
Attending					8	7
D. Professional						
Finished	4	1	3	3	2	2
Unfinished	1	1				
Attending	2	1			2	2
E. University						
Finished						
Unfinished						
Attending	1	1			2	2
III. *Other ways of learning to read and write*						
Self	43	13	16	12	8	7
Military	28	8				
Other	10	2	14	7	4	2
Total	331	100	133	100	118	100

admittance to higher schools; and a series of other secondary personal reasons.

The women gave as reasons for illiteracy the following: the tradition that girls should be kept home to remain wholesome; parents' ignorance and conservatism in accepting a low status for daughters in the family; the need for someone to take care of orphan brothers and sisters; poverty of the family and the need to earn a living; and migration to the city.[4] The unmarried, usually of younger age, could not pursue higher studies because the village did not have the middle and higher level schools. These, however, seemed determined to acquire some education in the city if they could afford it at all. In general it seems that the failure to pursue further education was due, in addition to the economic causes, to the impractical nature of education offered in the village, hence the squatters' relative lack of interest in education while in the village. But contact with the outside world, and with the city in particular, made them appreciate better the value of education, yet, poverty prevented them from studying beyond grade school.

Economic and occupational structure

The dominant role played by economic factors in the formation, development, and eventual urban integration of the *gecekondu* has been stressed throughout this study. Occupation and occupational mobility therefore have a central place in the life and transformation of the *gecekondu*. It has been mentioned that most squatters in Turkey and elsewhere appeared to be unskilled, poverty-stricken, and unorganized laborers and hence willing to work long hours and to take jobs that the skilled and organized labor would not ordinarily accept. Consequently, as expected, employment among male squatters in the three *gecekondus* surveyed was very high; of a total of 393 male respondents, 93 percent were employed. Moreover, of the employed, 79 percent had permanent jobs and 75 percent claimed that they worked 6 or 7 days a week. Of the 27 unemployed men, 9 were sick or too old to work and 2 were retired. However, of a total of 430 women interviewed only 30 percent had outside employment. Of this total, roughly 83 percent worked as servants. Only 54 women claimed to have permanent employment requiring some skill or training. The rate of employment among the unmarried was also relatively high: Of 126 unmarrieds, 67 percent had jobs. The rest were either too young to work or were attending school. (See Table 4.3.) Among the men, 74 individuals, or a total of 20 percent of the working male population, had their own businesses, that is their own enterprises, whereas only a total of 11 women claimed to have their own businesses (tailor, beauty operator) as indicated in Table 4.3.

The high rate of employment among migrants is indicated also by some other general surveys of labor force in Istanbul. The survey results in Table 4.4 indicate that employment among newcomers from villages was high. Most of these presumably lived in the *gecekondus*.

The occupational structure in Istanbul in 1966, about the time the three *gecekondus* were surveyed, consisted largely of traditional professions such as crafts and services, which did not require a high degree of specialization, thus permitting large groups of unskilled migrants to fit relatively easily into the semitraditional urban occupational structure. (The significance of this structure has been pointed out in Chapter 1.)

Table 4.5 presents a rather accurate picture of the occupational structure of Istanbul into which presumably the squatters in the three *gecekondus* fitted. The rural migrants occupied the last four job categories. It is therefore understandable that the squatters in the three settlements surveyed in this study took every type of possible employment, usually in the low-paying job categories. The job classification in Table 4.6 was obtained by merging into 7 major categories some 50 or 60 different jobs and professions, such as builder, driver, waiter, maid, servant, dairyman, cook, mason, gas station worker, janitor, porter, coffee seller, salesman, hawker, peddler, gardener, photographer, groceryman, florist, blacksmith, watchman.

Only 42 men of a total of 393 received some training for the job they presently held; only a total of 6 women received any kind of training. The same low rate of job training prevailed among bachelors: only 5 males and 1 female received job training. This finding supports the well-known fact that Turkey's educational system emphasizes high-level technical training (unemployment is rather high among engineers, architects, and so on) while neglecting middle- and lower-level professional and vocational training. The fact that university education has a very high social value and is an important condition for professional and political mobility (members of the Senate must have a university degree) works to the detriment of vocational training. The universities are within the easy access of the established city people; and despite claims to the contrary, until

Table 4.3. *Employment situation in* Gecekondus

	Men		Women		Unmarried	
	No.	%	No.	%	No.	%
I. *Employment status*						
Employed	366	93	131	30	84	67
Unemployed	27	7	299	70	42	33
II. *Status of employed*						
A. Self-employed	74	20	11	8	18	21
Private firms	207	57	8	6	49	58
State enterprises	76	21	4	3	3	4
Undesignated	9	2	108[a]	83	14	17
B. Permanently employed	290	79	54	41	58	70
Temporarily employed	76	21	77	59	13	15
Working students					13	15
C. One job	340	98	129	98	79	94
Multiple jobs	26	2	2	2	5	6
III. *Status of unemployed*						
Free-jobless	14	52			6	26
Ill or elderly	9	33	7	2		
In the military service					3	13
Unemployed students					12	52
Retired	2	7	1			
Undesignated	2	8	291	98	2	9
IV. *Number of working days per week*						
Less than 3 days	2	1	27	21	4	5
3–5 days	77	21	50	38	14	17
6–7 days	276	75	48	37	24	29
Undetermined	11	3	6	4	42	49
V. *Hours worked per day*						
2–4 hours	3	1	11	8	3	4
5–8 hours	205	56	71	54	33	39
9–12 hours	144	39	34	26	47	56
Undetermined	14	4	15	12	1	1

[a] Servants

Table 4.4. *Household members by duration of residence in Istanbul and labor force status (12 years old and over)*

	Employed		Unemployed		Not in the labor force		Total
	Male	Female	Male	Female	Male	Female	
Duration of residence in city more than two years	340,483	68,926	23,023	9,152	104,390	428,857	974,831
Persons coming from a province or district center during past two years	16,159	5,005	1,859	858	7,150	19,162	50,193
Persons coming from villages during past two years	32,747	2,574	1,859	429	858	6,578	45,045
Total	389,389	76,505	26,741	10,439	112,398	454,597	1,070,069

Source: Labour Force Survey in Selected Main Cities (State Institute of Statistics), Ankara, 1966, p. 34.

Table 4.5. *Occupational structure of Istanbul: persons employed in normal occupations (12 years old and over)*

	Persons at work		Persons with job but not at work		
	Male	Female	Male	Female	Total
Technical, professional, and clerical workers	22,737	6,006	4,719	6,721	40,183
Managerial, administrative, and clerical workers	59,345	12,584	5,148	2,431	79,508
Salesmen and related workers	58,201	2,288	2,145	143	62,777
Farmers, lumbermen, fishermen, hunters, and related workers	3,861	143	2,002		6,006
Miners, quarrymen, and related workers					
Workers in transport, storage, and communication occupation	28,457	572	2,431	143	31,603
Craftsmen, production, process workers, and repairmen	108,966	23,881	6,578	4,719	144,144
Manual workers	35,321	3,289	1,430	429	40,469
Service workers	39,039	12,584	1,716	572	53,911
Workers in occupations not otherwise classified or not reported	5,291		2,002		7,293
Total	361,218	61,347	28,171	15,158	465,894

Source: *Labour Force Survey in Selected Main Cities* (State Institute of Statistics), Ankara, 1966, p. 32.

a few years ago at least they were instrumental in perpetuating an elitist form of social differentiation. The squatters were bound to remain a low urban class as long as their access to higher education was limited and the university remained the chief channel for the selection and the mobility of the elites. However, after the initial survey was concluded in 1968, and the *gecekondus* expanded and became urbanized, the number of students in universities increased.

The job mobility among squatters was high: of a total of 370

Table 4.6. *Occupational categories of employed migrants in the three* gecekondu *surveyed* (*in percentages*)

	Men	Women	Unmarried
Services (unskilled work, maids, servants)	39	90	25
Technical professions	17	2	25
Construction	20		20
Crafts	6	5	12
Trade	10	1	17
Agriculture	3		
Other	5	2	1
Total	100	100	100

male respondents, 55 percent had held a variety of jobs in the past that were different from the present ones. The jobs were held either in Istanbul or in other cities of Turkey. The tendency was to move from unskilled to skilled and from low technology to higher technology jobs.

It was difficult to obtain accurate information concerning the squatters' wages and annual income. There was an obstinate effort on the part of men and women to appear much poorer and more destitute than they actually were. The squatters felt that appearing relatively well to do would be held against them and possibly used as a reason for not granting them the title to the land or for forcing them to settle elsewhere. In part this reflected traditional Islamic understanding of charity and mutual help, whereby the rich have a moral duty to assist the underprivileged in whatever way possible. The poorer one is the heavier the responsibility of those capable of aiding him. The misinformation about income was corrected in part by checking the payroll of some squatters at their work place. It was even more difficult to compute the squatters' total family income, especially since some families, about 30 percent of the total, had several of their members working, and others usually young families whose children had not reached work age, had only one wage earner. Furthermore, a number of squatters received small incomes from the village in the form of money or

Table 4.7. *Living conditions compared*
with those in villages (in percentages)

	Men	Women	Unmarried
Much better	28	20	33
Good	61	64	57
Unchanged	6	10	3
Worse	5	6	7
Total	100	100	100

food, and others increased their incomes by selling vegetables, chickens, eggs, and milk produced in the settlement.

According to our calculations and estimates, the median monthly earnings of a working man (married) was 612.19 liras and of a woman (married) 459.51 liras. The unmarried earned 469.50 liras per month. The annual average earnings per family was about 8,200 liras, which compares quite favorably with the national gross per capita income of 3,143 liras (in 1967). One may assume therefore that the squatters' income, although below the average of the established city dwellers, was substantially above that of the rural inhabitants and definitely much higher than that of many of their friends and relatives left in the native villages. This important development – the increase in living standards – was technically the immediate consequence of occupational change and had profound effects on the squatters' positive attitude toward the city.

Attitudes toward the city

In view of this situation, it was natural for an overwhelming majority of squatters to believe that their living conditions in the city, compared with the standard of life in the village, had greatly improved, as shown in Table 4.7.

Better opportunities for work, the possibility for economic enterprise, and a greater choice of jobs were cited as the principal reasons for the improved living in the city. Many squatters felt that if employment in one sector of the economy decreased it was likely to rise in another newly opened field. The style of life in the city, the hope of achieving a higher standard of living and social status, the physical security (especially among those escaping vendetta), and the opportunity for specialization in a profession were among other reasons cited by squatters as making their life in the city superior to the one in the village. Those dissatisfied with city life attributed their discontent mostly to insufficient income, to the inability to adapt to urban existence, and, in the case of a few women, to their low status and heavy work, which remained, according to them, the same as in the village.

A few of those dissatisfied with the city came from richer families in the village. Their level of aspiration, expressed in terms of higher income and social status, was above that of most of the other squatters who were satisfied initially just to have a steady employment and a regular income. The migrants from richer village families discovered to their dismay that the city treated them as ordinary peasants, and, interestingly enough, some of these became aggressive entrepreneurs in order to acquire economic power and higher social status. (H. H. Hagen's theory of loss of status by samurai in Japan and their reemergence as an entrepreneurial group may have some relevance here.)

The satisfaction of the *gecekondu* residents with their present conditions is most clearly shown in their optimism concerning the children's future. In societies such as Turkey's, in which mobility was low until recently, the family plays a central role not only as a kinship group but also as a channel of value transmission and continuity; the children's achievements are the parents' yardstick for measuring their own unfulfilled potential and ability. The overwhelming majority of parents believed that their children had an excellent chance in the city to "do and achieve what we wanted to and could not" and thus lead a better life in the future (Table 4.8). A few squatters said that they had moved to the city specifically with the purpose of providing their children with better career opportunities. They regarded high education in particular, if they could afford it, as the main condition for attaining higher status and material success. Even the mere fact of growing up in a city in contact with educated people was a sufficient reason to induce some squatters to believe that their children will have a better life. "They do not know the village life," said one squatter. "Consequently they are not hindered by misgivings and inferiority com-

Table 4.8. *Outlook for children's future in city* (*in percentages*)

	Men	Women	Unmarried (when children were born)
Worse than parents	8	7	9
Better than parents	92	93	91
Total	100	100	100

plexes but can look freely forward and determinedly to a better existence in the city. . . . Already they do not hesitate to enter the best restaurants, and drink beer instead of water, and then tell me 'Father, you have led an empty life,' and feel sorry for me."

Many squatters felt that since the country was developing and living conditions were improving steadily, the chances for their children looked increasingly brighter. According to parents, their children's success in the city depended on their intellectual ability and determination to study, as well as on their own capability to support them through school. (Since school fees in Turkey are very low or nonexistent, the main problem for most *gecekondu* children is board and room while they attend classes.) Those very few who did not believe that their children had a bright future in the city attributed their pessimism to low income, the lack of an atmosphere conducive to study in the *gecekondu*, as well as to the harmful, immoral city influences.

The importance attached to education was evident also in the fact that nearly all school-age children were attending classes in the neighboring communities since none of the settlements had their own schools in 1968. Later a famous popular singer built a school in the settlement as a kind of social assistance.

The parents believed that professions, such as engineering, medicine, and law, followed by technical crafts (mechanics, machine operator) and government service, were the most desirable careers for their children. But a surprisingly high number of parents let their children choose "a career where they can utilize best their abilities."[5] Table 4.9 shows parents' career preferences for their children.

The relatively high number of *gecekondu* residents who left the choice of career to their children and the emphasis placed on ability and aptitude may well indicate a profound change in the old authoritarian concept of family where the parents' will was regarded as supreme. It may also imply that the squatters, accustomed in the village to pursue the agricultural occupations of their parents, had not given much thought to the future careers of their children. It was clear from the squatters' statements that most of them have no intention of returning to the village. This attitude, as John M. Nelson pointed out, has important consequences on the migrants' rate of money saving, investment, and attitude toward the city. These are important problems especially in relation to return migration, which apparently is more frequent in Africa than in Latin America and the Middle East, including Turkey. For instance, those who plan to stay permanently in the city may look for good houses and try to make new friends, whereas those who plan to leave may put up with all kinds of difficulties and demand fewer amenities.[6]

Impact on the national economy

The squatters' economic roles have other aspects. Squatters play a significant role in the urban development of Turkey as workers but also as consumers and indirectly provide a badly needed stimulus to agriculture. Prior to the 1950s much of the food, especially fruit and vegetables, consumed in the three major cities of Turkey – Istanbul, Ankara, and Izmir – was produced in their vicinity. The quantity and the prices of foodstuffs were determined by a more or less constant demand in the cities. However, the growth of cities after 1950, due in large part to the influx of rural migrants, increased the demand for food and caused a substantial rise in prices. Consequently, the villages in the interior of the country, which had a subsistence economy partly because of lack of demand, began to produce food for city markets. In turn, the transport of agricultural goods was greatly facilitated by the development of a good highway system and the use of motor trucks, which penetrated even the remotest villages. After 1964 this development accelerated further when some suitable agricultural areas underwent intensive mechanization and began to produce chiefly for the

Table 4.9. *Best career for children*
(*in percentages*)

	Men	Women	Unmarried
Liberal professions	30	33	32
Technical professions	29	25	24
Government service	26	29	24
Any career best suited to ability	15	13	20
Total	100	100	100

Note: Obviously bachelors did not have children but were asked the question in the belief that they were willing to have a family and had given some thought to the future of their offspring.

markets in large cities.[7] Eventually, smaller villages and remote towns were integrated in a network of roads and food producing and consuming system. Food prices, which had remained low in towns and villages, began to rise and adjusted somewhat to a national uniform price level. All this contributed greatly to increasing the income of the food producers, usually the medium and large farms. (See Chapter 7.)

The *gecekondus* played a major part in this process. The continuous rise in food prices in Turkey after 1953, especially 1968–74, was caused not only by inflation but also by the migrants' demand for food and the country's inability to produce sufficient agricultural commodities. A similar rise in demand for wearing apparel gave a great impetus to the textile industry. The spending patterns among the *gecekondu* dwellers conforms to this trend. Of a total of 372 men and 329 women who answered the questionnaire, 87 and 93 percent, respectively, said that they spent all their earnings for immediate "living expenses." Of a total of 93 unmarried people, 86 percent said the same. Though the "living expenses" as understood by squatters covered all kinds of items, including payments of debts and aid to relatives in their respective villages, still approximately 75 to 80 percent of the squatters' total earnings were spent on food. As may be expected, of a total of 376 men who answered the question, only 13 percent said that they could save money or had savings accounts; of 286 women who answered the question, only 7 percent said that they were able to save money. Only 14 percent of the unmarried said that they could save some of their earnings. The lack of saving may be attributed also to the fact that since the *gecekondus* in these areas appeared to have a good chance for survival, a considerable part of the squatters' income was spent on home improvement. This expenditure was an investment, in fact the only major one as far as the squatters were concerned; hence the importance of the dwelling as a form of financial security.

Aspirations and changing attitudes

Although most squatters were satisfied with their present life in the city, however modest that may be, nevertheless, about half of them complained that their needs were increasing and their present income did not suffice. Questioned in some detail, many answered that they ate meat once a week. However, the squatters, like those in many other Turkish households, used a great variety of rather inexpensive vegetables, oils, and fats to make relatively nutritious and tasty meals. Furthermore, men working in factories received a free lunch, as ordered by government regulations. Consequently, the squatters appeared to be in relatively satisfactory health and no cases of malnutrition have been noticed. (Nutrition habits as well as the variety of ingredients used in cooking by the *gecekondu* dwellers should be considered part of the native food culture. It would be wrong, I believe, to study nutrition in the *gecekondu* according to the food habits of the West or regard the consumption of some foods, such as huge quantities of meat, as necessary for a healthy life.) The potential for occupational mobility was high. An overwhelming majority of squatters wanted to have, if they could, better-paying jobs or at least higher wages in order to raise further their living standards. Indeed, of a total of 382 male respondents, 86 percent said that they wanted to have a better job than the one held at the present. Some 87 percent of the unmarried also wanted better jobs.

As a first choice 64 percent of the men (a total of 289 people answered the question) said that they would like to have their own private business. Some 12 percent of the men and 23 percent of the women preferred jobs in a factory, since the work in a *fabrika* – an industrial plant – represented for them a step upward in terms of personal achievement and status derived from some mastery of technical skills, higher salary, and financial security; most of those who wanted jobs in factories were presently employed in menial service jobs (Table 4.10). As second choice 72 percent of the men and 53 percent of the women (the latter had a keen desire to work outside their homes) wanted a regular job with a monthly salary. About 69 percent of the respondents wanted to earn more than 700 to 900 liras a month in order to lead a proper city life.

The squatters in general, as noted before, seem to have a special preference for private enterprise, probably because it is a form of occupation immediately available to them since some "enterprises" require limited capital. To own a small enterprise employing 4 or 5 people, preferably relatives and friends, to possess a house, and to be accepted as equal and respected by city people appear to be the average squatter's immediate economic ideal. Many of those who favor private enterprise or have already some business of their own (74 people had their own small businesses) mentioned freedom of action and decision, and especially "not being under the command of others," as the chief reasons for wanting a business of their own. A few pointed out that their own success in private enterprise would add to the country's general welfare. Many squatters who had already some business of their own wanted to enlarge it. For instance, one of them who owned a short-order stand claimed that if he had capital, he would open a restaurant "as good as the Abdullah's," which is considered to be the best in Istanbul. Another one who operated a small dairy planned to save more money, sell a cow, and buy a weaving machine with the proceeds. "I would not work for others even if they paid me 2,000 liras a month," he said, although he had planned to engage a worker to run his weaving machine if he ever purchased it. Those favoring free enterprise complained that a lack of capital was their major handicap since "there is nothing in the world you could not do with money." (The lack of capital is a major problem in Turkey. Even legitimate businesses borrow from the public at 18 percent

Table 4.10. *Job preference by sectors*
(*in percentages*)

	Men	Women	Unmarried
Private business (crafts professions)	24	14	39
Private business (trade)	40		10
Factory work	12	23	22
Government job	5	13	12
Agriculture	3		1
Other	16	50	16
Total	100	100	100

interest, and privately owned businesses borrow at interest rates as high as 50 percent). The squatters' interest in private enterprise did not stem from any philosophical commitment to the virtues of economic freedom but from practical realization that economic achievement was their only means for acquiring a higher social status and for attaining material security for themselves and their family. The incredibly high profits secured by some entrepreneurs in Turkey, some of whom were former villagers or residents of the *gecekondus,* were additional factors that inflamed the squatters' imagination about the golden rewards offered by private enterprise. It is within the framework of these conditions that the *gecekondu* seems to breed aggressive, innovative, and enterprising individuals who contribute to overall economic development but also impose on the economy as a whole their own cultural and social limitations. The enterprises of the former squatters or other migrants from the villages tend to remain closed businesses where family welfare and social status, rather than national development, seem to have priority, at least during the first generation of successful entrepreneurs.

Some other factors shape the squatter's personality in the city. The *gecekondu* represents in the squatter's own view a transitional phase. He cannot and does not want to go back to the village. He is also aware that the city regards him as an intruder undermining the urban culture and overtaxing its facilities. In these conditions the squatter finds himself both an uprooted villager and an unaccepted city dweller. Consequently, in order to move upward – that is, to be accepted – he must develop all his abilities and succeed in the only way that upward social mobility is possible – namely, through economic achievement. And when he succeeds, he is faced with the opposition and contempt of the bureaucratic and intellectual elite, who reached high position through education. It is interesting to note that while blood relatives and *hemşeris* play a vital part in the squatter's life from his departure from the village to his establishment in the city, they cannot catapult him into a social position higher than theirs. The advance in the city in terms of income and status is possible only by individual effort and achievement. However, if the squatter becomes a rich man he becomes also isolated from his villagemates, most of whom continue to remain simple workers. The parvenu squatters may possibly maintain their association with their relatives and *hemşeris,* on a more or less selective basis, though the extent of these relations and the sense of personal participation in them is severely limited. The successful squatter belongs to another social class and cannot fully identify with his villagemates still living in the *gecekondu.* In a way wealth alienates socially the successful squatter from the *gecekondu* and he moves out of it in every possible way.

The multisided challenges faced by the squatter are often reflected in his almost exaggerated sense of self-confidence and individualization, derived from conditions in the city and his relative success there. This was proven by our survey. The questionnaire had the following two questions: "Who do you rely upon and trust most in the city?" and "Who did you rely upon and trust most while you lived in the village?" These were designed to measure the squatters' reliance on relatives, elders, and friends in the village and the changes occurring in the *gecekondu.* The answers were rather unexpected. The squatters replied that they relied more on their own judgment than on the advice of the elders and relatives.[8] Expressions such as these abounded: "I trust and believe only in myself." "Outside of God, I rely on and trust nobody in Istanbul." "I have traveled enough not to trust anybody." "Who else is better to rely upon than myself." "Everybody is as poor as I am. In this place you rely only on money and God." A majority of the men said that they relied on nobody, which was a way of saying they relied only on themselves. This form of expression, boasting and speaking in the first person, is not characteristic of the Turkish culture in general; a drastic change had occurred in the personality of these former subdued and docile villagers. Or maybe the Turkish village culture stemming from the submission-commanding precepts of Islam, which were intellectualized by religious men and organized religion, and from the surviving animistic nomad culture built on personal valor and ability lost its balance in the secular materialistic culture of the city.

The squatters said that they did not rely on their relatives and elders even while in the village; however, this attitude seemed to reflect the squatters' present state of mind in the city. (Table 4.11). They believed that they survived in the city through their own resources, though they did not reject the importance of having relatives or the fact that they were instrumental in helping their migration and settlement in the city.

Table 4.11, in fact, invites long commentaries on Turkish family culture that cannot be dealt with in this study. It must be mentioned, however, that the categories appearing on the table were indicated by the respondents themselves. The apparent contradiction between relying on friends and relatives for jobs and assistance and yet not trusting them resulted from the individualization and competition experienced in the city, from the changes in the mode of life rather than from personal animosity toward relatives, as shall be analyzed further. These changes in attitude also may be explained in terms of the transformation in the traditions of egalitarianism – the idea that decisions should represent the entire group or class – inherited from the Ottoman political culture. The squatter found himself torn between the traditional communal culture and the pull of individualization and innovation in the city. Thus, the close relationship that prevailed among squatters in matters of mutual help, migration, and settlement in the city derived from the communal traditional culture, while individualized sense of self-reliance and achievement were a response to the challenge of the urban environment. The view prevailed that "relatives will help to be like them but not more." On the other hand, there was among squatters a developing tendency to accept friends on other bases than *akrabalık* or *hemşerilik,* as shall be discussed later. In sum, the trend of change among Turkish squatters seems to have

Table 4.11. *Most trustworthy and reliable people (in percentages)*

	Men		Women		Unmarried	
	In village	In city settlement	In village	In city settlement	In village	In city settlement
Nobody-oneself	46	59	59	69	40	51
Relatives	36	12	30	14	32	19
Muhtar (village head man)	4	1	3		3	
Trustworthy friends	7	16	5	9	19	20
People from the same village		5		2		3
Close neighbors	5	7	2	6	6	7
The elders	2		1			
Total	100	100	100	100	100	100

been determined by economic forces and their underlying philosophy. These may be described as a capitalist system of free enterprise supported by the government and a group of rural migrants undergoing urbanization and modernization in the framework of that economic and social system.

5. Association and leadership in three *gecekondus*

Social organization and leadership

The three *gecekondus* – the largest, Nafibaba and Baltaliman, and the smallest, Celâlettin Paşa – surveyed in this study showed remarkable similarities with regard to the squatters' origin, causes of migration, employment patterns, and family life. However, in matters of social organization, and especially adjustment to urban conditions, the three *gecekondus* differed considerably from each other. These differences will emerge more clearly after we have dealt with some general problems.

The attachments to the village culture in all three settlements is strong, as is true among nearly all rural migrants in the world. However, the village culture was not preserved intact in the squatter settlements but was constantly changing in interaction with new conditions and forces in the urban environment. The three settlements surveyed in this study appeared in general to be mobile and fluid communities oriented toward eventual integration in the city. They did not have rigid and permanent institutions but rather transitional patterns of organization and leadership established to deal with problems confronting the settlement. Yet, the *gecekondus* did have a relatively integrated and cohesive communal form of organization and several leadership sets that reflected both the migrants' village culture, and the problems confronting them in the city.

Three sets of conditions affected the organization and leadership of the *gecekondu*. (1) There was the village background, which expressed itself in adherence to prescribed values and behavior toward friends, relatives, and elders based on a strong sense of community and high regard for family. Indeed, family customs, formal respect for religion, the maintenance of a concrete identification with the village, and the priority given to the community over the individual stemmed from the village culture. Leaders in the community were expected to see to it that attachment to the village culture and values were respected and maintained. Indeed, in the *gecekondu* some leaders, usually religious men or older heads of households, were ranked in the community largely according to their roles and functions as perpetuators of the village culture. (2) There was the maintenance of order and security within the settlement and its development and physical well-being. The men who established the *gecekondu* or those who built the best house or opened a shop – that is, those who achieved a degree of success and established some prestige in the settlement, regardless of their village background – belonged to this group of leaders. (3) There were the practical considerations connected with the relations of the settlement with the outside world – the city, the political parties, and the government. Thus, the first group of factors seems to be psychologically and socially useful, whereas the second and third groups of factors aim at securing the physical well-being of the *gecekondu* and at integrating it into city and national life.

In practice, these three basic functions often overlapped as did the roles assigned to the three groups of leaders. On balance, or in case of conflict, the achievement-oriented leaders – those who had established their authority over the *gecekondu* and could best conduct its relations with the outside world – had the upper hand. In other words, the most successful leader was the one who could harmonize the old with the new.

The squatters' cultural and group activities revolved around the community, which in turn represented religious and social identities and attachments stemming from a variety of kinship associations, values, and traditional sociopolitical institutions. The identity of the Turkish villager is assumed to be formed by his family, ethnic group, religion and religious sect, *kabile* (clan), if any, and the village. The communal identity in turn was a collective expression of the same. The *kabile* ties seemed to have become either synonymous with the extended family or village or did not exist at all since there was not much evidence that the migrants preserved a sense of *kabile* affiliation or identity. (*Kabile* lacks a precise definition since Turkish villages seldom use the term. They are apt to refer, if ever, to the *aşiret* (tribe) and mostly to the extended family, which is ordinarily smaller than the *kabile*. Actually, only small parts of the country in the east or southeast may still preserve the *aşiret* organization.)

Hemşerilik (common village origin) served as a basis for establishing modern types of organizations and even for determining political choices. In the city *hemşeris* are not only individuals from the same village, but also those from the same *kaza* (district), *vilayet* (province), and even region. In fact, when asked where they came from, most squatters named first their province (Sivas or Giresun) or the district town (Şiran, Alcura, and so on) as their place of origin, and seldom the village itself; all this could be considered the beginning stage of identification with larger social and political units than the village.

The closest identification with the village and its culture prevailed in one central section of the Nafibaba settlement. The migrants from the villages of Kırıntı, Yeniköy, and Kayacık tended to congregate on one site within the settlement. The men from these villages had been instrumental in establishing the *gecekondu* and then moving their families and relatives gradually from the village into the city, almost according to a plan. Consequently, this section of the settlement was in a way a replica of the family structure prevailing in the village. The migrants coming from other regions of Turkey and living in the *gecekondu* tended to follow the same pattern of settlement. And often when referring to each other's *mahalle* – that is, to their respective quarter in the *gecekondu* – they used as reference the district or province of origin, such as *Şıranlılar mahallesi* (the quarter of those from Şiran).

The leadership both for maintenance of traditions and for solving current problems in the Nafibaba settlement as a whole belonged at the time of the survey to the migrants from the villages of Kırıntı, Kayacık, and Yeniköy. Other squatters accepted their leadership both on the basis of seniority – that is, length of stay in the city and the settlement – and because of their enterprise and knowledge of the outside world. Nearly all the people in this group were Alevis, whose own traditional concepts of egalitarian society were reflected in the *gecekondu*.[1] Yet religion was not the strongest binding tie among them; its main function seemed to be to reinforce the existing sense of village solidarity and community. Actually, the migrants from these villages belonged to at least four major families and among them there was considerable rivalry resulting partly from dissatisfaction with the Alevi religious leaders and the way they performed their duties. In fact, religion – that is, Shiism and its Turkish version, *Alevilik* – did not seem to have created but merely maintained some old forms of group and village solidarity predating the emergence of this sect in the sixteenth century. (At some point in the early days of the Republic the Alevis were described as having preserved an authentic Turkish folk culture.)

Community, tradition, and modernity

The migrants in the central group in Nafibaba were hard-working but few of them seemed to have acquired much wealth. They appeared to be disposed to help each other as well as their relatives left in the village and to be very attached to village traditions and ways of life. Their leaders rejoiced talking about their village and urged every town dweller to go and visit it. The migrants from Kırıntı, Kayacık, and Yeniköy were also the hardest working group. They made a special point of honoring excellence in every job and appeared best adapted to city life. Their women felt equal to men, talked freely with outsiders, and displayed a high level of knowledge and intellectual curiosity. They criticized the restrictions imposed on women and demanded more education and opportunity to work outside the house. They were the first to adopt modern house utensils – while insisting on preserving the village dress and wedding ceremonies and even advocating their continued use. (While interviewing and talking to members of this group, our research team felt accepted as equals. We were invited to and attended wedding ceremonies and dinners. Some of the researchers continue their friendships made with the people in this group.) Paradoxically, the people in this group appeared to be both the most traditional and the most modern; they used elements of both tradition and modernity in solving problems associated with their urbanization.

The leaders in Nafibaba were not formally elected but emerged in a natural way as the consequence of their opinions and proposals expressed in informal meetings at the coffeehouse, work place, or home. In the home meetings were attended usually by family heads of a mature age and with communal experience.

There was not in the whole group one man who was regarded as a permanent or supreme leader. This was close to a form of traditional communal leadership brought over from the village. Probably the main reason for the survival of the village culture among this group was the fact that migrants from the same village settled together in large groups and perpetuated their traditional culture. The rest of the squatters in Nafibaba, about two-thirds of the population, were predominantly Sunni (orthodox Muslim). They had come in smaller numbers from other towns and regions in Turkey. (See Chapter 2.) This was a heterogeneous group occupationally speaking, consisting of factory workers, small businessmen, drivers, and so on. Some were very poor; others were relatively well to do. Their attitudes alternated between a high degree of optimism to neutralism toward the city and attachment to their original village, depending largely on the degree of success achieved in the city and the size of the village or family group in the city. Some of the people in this group had come from well-to-do families in villages or even towns and used the *gecekondu* as a transitional stage on the way to better jobs and possibly better houses in the established sections of Istanbul. These formed their own regional enclaves, especially those from the province of Sivas, who were also Alevis but were less cohesive than the first group. The squatters in these latter groups appeared to be slightly more insecure but were also more individualistic, aggressive, and competitive, truly eager to try new occupations. Their family attachments were strong, whereas their sense of communal responsibility was less pronounced. They were numerous but, deprived of regional solidarity among themselves and without a strong village nucleus, they followed the leadership of those from Kırıntı and Yeniköy. These latter leaders, however, aware of the numerical strength of squatters from other regions, were anxious to involve them in the *gecekondu* affairs as much as possible. All regional groups in Nafibaba cooperated well because of common interest in the survival of the *gecekondu* and because the similarities among them derived from the village background were still greater than the differences that separated them from the old city dwellers. Leaders here operated on the basis of consensus, and decisions were reached after substantive deliberation in groups.

The situation in the Baltaliman settlement, which was a few

hundred yards down the hill from Nafibaba and about one-sixth its size, was quite different. This settlement, as mentioned previously, grew first around a quarry. The first two houses seem to have been established with the consensus of the quarry owner, a woman of Greek origin who still lived in the area. However, the expansion of the Baltaliman settlement and its stratification took place under the leadership of three families (Altıntaş and Bahar in particular) from Trabzon, Ordu, and one from Istanbul that had migrated earlier from a Black Sea town. In other words, all the three leading families in the Baltaliman settlement had come from the Black Sea coast. In fact, this settlement was called Karadenizliler (from the Black Sea) among squatters. The three leading families owned the shops in the settlement and also served other areas outside the *gecekondu*. One family had an oil delivery truck, which by Turkish standards constituted an excellent asset, and another family operated a firewood depot. The houses of these families were of excellent quality, comparable to the dwellings in the better sections of the city. It was quite apparent that these families had accumulated wealth after establishing themselves in the settlement. The three leading families were better educated, enterprising, hard-working, and energetic than the average *gecekondu* resident – hardly distinguishable from established city people. They controlled the Baltaliman settlement in every respect and also exerted some influence in the Nafibaba area. The other residents of the Baltaliman settlement were predominantly villagers who settled there, in part at least, with the approval of the leaders, since most residents in Baltaliman were their relatives and friends from villages along the Black Sea coast. The leaders in Baltaliman succeeded in creating a tight and cohesive community, which was relatively urbanized and somewhat less attached to the village, chiefly because of the higher level of income, the resulting friendship with city people, and the higher proportion of those coming from towns. Internal cohesion, near unanimity of consensus in decisions, and control of votes permitted the leaders to deal effectively with the political parties and the municipality. Here the central uniting link was prosperity and authority. Consequently, Baltaliman, the only one among the three settlements, had water and electricity in 1968 and was certain to acquire the title to the land on which the houses were built. The leadership here was definitely of the authoritarian "peer" type, but their decisions were voluntarily accepted by the rank-and-file squatters because the leaders were relatively rich, had power, and exerted influence outside the *gecekondu,* which benefited the community as a whole.

The Celâlettin Paşa *gecekondu* had some striking characteristics of its own. The first settlers, as mentioned, consisted of residents from the same or neighboring areas. They moved to the settlement individually without group affiliation in the 1950s, apparently with the approval of the authorities and party leaders, after their houses had been demolished in a campaign to renovate Istanbul. Some of these squatters had come from villages some 20 years before. Now they provided services in Emirgan, a favorite tea-drinking spot on the Bosphorus, and apparently assumed the role of "strong boys" in local party politics. This group of early squatters in Celâlettin Paşa was small, had lost much of its village roots, and considered itself part of the city, although the established residents did not yet accept them as such.

The second and larger group of squatters came to the area after 1965, from scores of different villages and regions; villagers from the Suşehri district in Sivas province tried to cluster together but without being able to create a true community. The people in this group seemed to have lost somewhat the sense of community and tradition and appeared unable to devise a common line of action, except occasionally in some extreme cases where the survival of the *gecekondu* was threatened. Moreover, this group was looked down on and treated as ignorant villagers by the first group and by the established families living across the street.

The relative disintegration of the Celâlettin Paşa settlement resulted largely from the diversity of settlers (semirural, semiurban, slum who had lost their communal ties, new arrivals totally alien to the city), the lack of accepted leaders, and the failure to reorganize a community and provide for cultural continuity. It is interesting to note that this settlement was able to elect neither the communal type of leaders prevailing in the Nafibaba nor the authoritarian but capable family "peer" leadership of Baltaliman. Consequently, *de facto* leadership here was assumed by the chairman of the formally established *Gecekonduyu Güzelleştirme Derneği* (Association for Settlement Improvement), a squatter who considered himself a city dweller. The sense of disintegration, insecurity, and division prevailing in Celâlettin Paşa in a way decided the choice of the leader. He was an autocrat, a bully in fact, who did not know how to read and write and relied on sheer force and intimidation to rule the settlement. Without internal solidarity and consensus, he had no alternative but to use force if order was to be secured, the functions and obligations of the *gecekondu* toward the outside world properly discharged, and ultimately the survival of the *gecekondu* assured.[2] But this very situation – the lack of a strong communal spirit and community life – forced many squatters to look on their family as the only source of social and psychological support. All this seemed to have strengthened the nuclear family and weakened somewhat the attachments to relatives, and even to native villages. A few squatters here felt a degree of alienation and isolation that they tried to overcome by joining trade unions and other organizations. Interestingly enough, the growing pressure on the nuclear family for all kinds of psychological, moral, and social support increased family conflicts. The squatters in this group seemed to yearn for enlightened leadership and were ready to undergo any sacrifice if they could achieve some group identity and speed up integration and even assimilation into the city. The acute anomie prevailing in this group prepared it for rapid urbanization, but this was an act of desperation, a forced solution rather than a goal decided freely, as was the case with squatters in the Nafibaba and Baltaliman settlements. Moreover, these two settlements, which had established internal order and security, had achieved a degree of cohesiveness based in good part on traditional factors of solidarity, such as the village community and family leadership; whereas the Celâlettin Paşa settlement faced acute disintegration because it lost most of these bonds.

The crime record in all three communities proved that the above considerations were indeed correct. The police officials interviewed in Rumelihisar and Emirgân and the study of the daily criminal files in these precincts for a period of eight months (January–August, 1968) indicated that the Celâlettin Paşa settlement faced acute problems of internal disorder. It was true that the total overall crime rate in all three settlements was about half below the national rate and about two-thirds below the rate in Istanbul. Moreover, the total number of 28 "crimes" committed in eight months in all three settlements included no homicide, but a series of offenses deriving from the violation of building codes, conflicts caused by the undefined boundaries of house lots, possession of weapons, *hakaret* (insults; the high importance attached to honor in Turkey swells the volume of such "crimes"), petty thefts, a few minor offenses, and family conflicts. Actually, few of these unlawful acts reached the court, since they were occasionally settled locally by the leaders of the community, and even fewer of them drew court sentences. Often a complaint to the police, which dutifully registered it as *suç* (crime), sufficed to calm the parties.

The most significant aspect of this "criminal" record was the fact that 12 of the so-called crimes, of a total of 28, were committed in the Celâlettin Paşa *gecekondu,* although its population was less than one-fourth of the total number of squatters interviewed – thus placing its "crime" rate above the national average. Moreover, 5 of the crimes in Celâlettin Paşa consisted of possession of weapons, which may be considered a symptom of the physical insecurity prevailing in that settlement and of the lack of communal agencies, traditional or otherwise, to prevent and solve small personal conflicts. The rest of the "crimes" in Celâlettin Paşa stemmed from family conflicts – assaults, in fact – caused largely by the developing psychological disintegration of family life, inability to adjust fully to the psychological requirements of a nuclear family, and lack of family agents, as in the extended family, to mediate and resolve conflicts.

Table 5.1 gives a detailed picture of the "crimes" in the three *gecekondus.* The frequency and types of crimes – if considered in the light of their structure, leadership, internal cohesiveness, and the lack of what may be called the continuity of the communal and traditional organizations – are so eloquent in their implications as to make further elaboration unnecessary.

Religion and community

Aside from frequent visits to and from the village, the factors responsible for perpetuating the village culture in the *gecekondu* were the presence of large groups of migrants from the same village, the maintenance of some kinship attachments, and the presence of individuals who occupied leadership positions in the village as heads of kinship or religious groups or as representatives of an

Table 5.1. *Crimes in* Gecekondus, *January–August, 1968*

Nafibaba and Baltaliman		Celâlettin Paşa	
Type	Number	Type	Number
Thefts (culprit not apprehended)	6	Gambling	1
Theft (alleged culprits tried)	2	Possession of dangerous weapons; guns and knives, firing of guns	3
Thefts (culprit condemned)	1	Wounds inflicted by guns and knives because of border conflict	2
Assault (culprit tried)	1	Insult deriving from attempted assault on women	1
Assault and insult (caused by quarrels because of children; being tried)	2	Adultery (a man living with another woman complained that his wife went to live with another man)	1
Insult (caused by property boundaries; parties reconciled in court	1	Assault and beating (by men who had severe family conflicts; one threw his wife out on the street)	2
Conflict over boundaries (settled in court)	1	Assault (because of border conflicts)	1
Igfal (deceit, or sexual intercourse with promise to marry; case involved a woman living in other settlement)	1	Insult (because of border conflicts)	1
Other	1		
Total number of incidents	16	Total number of incidents	12

official body. Thus, the Coşkunlar (Sofular), known as honest, virtuous, hard-working, enterprising, ambitious, ready to take advantage of economic opportunities, including trade – but not as ostentatious, proud, or aggressive people – were well respected in the village and in the *gecekondu* where their word carried weight.[3]

Interestingly enough, the Coşkuns built their position through achievements and honesty, but also through observance of Alevi traditions based on conviction rather than office obligations. Members of this family had visited Karbala (the Shiite shrine in Iraq) and brought back religious souvenirs, including pictures of the

Prophet sitting with Ali and his sons. The *imams* (leaders of Alevis) Hasan and Huseyin were flanked by two angels, something hardly conceivable among the iconoclast Sunnis. The pictures were distributed freely to friends and relatives.

Formally, however, the religious-communal leadership – *şıhlık* (sheikh) – of the Alevis belonged to the Günel family. The leader at the time of the research, Ibrahim Günel, called *baba dede* (grand-grandfather), or simply *dede* (grandfather), lived in the village but visited Istanbul once a year and was honored by the Alevis in the city. He claimed that his position, which was hereditary, demanded impartiality, hard work, and continuous education, as demonstrated by his daily reading. The other group of Alevis – those from Sivas province – belonged to a different sect and had their own customs and leaders but were less conscious of their identity and less interested in their specific religious traditions than those from the Kırıntı. In fact, even among those from Kırıntı the emphasis on Alevi traditions came from the Günel family, which wanted to maintain its former high status in the village by stressing the importance of religious identity and affiliations. The religious leadership among the Sunni was represented by the *imam*. (For Alevis, *imam* usually means the head of the sect; for Sunnis a prayer leader.)

Religion in the *gecekondu* must be seen as only part of a broader village-communal culture. While an overwhelming majority of squatters claim to be good Muslims, many confessed that they do not perform the rituals of Islam, except perhaps fasting.[4] A few men and women in the *gecekondu* seem to interpret all events in accordance with religious precepts and, yet, they live harmoniously with their relatives and friends, who occasionally deride their beliefs as being "superstitious." Only one or two men among those interviewed claimed that their greatest ambition in life is to become a *mufti* (religious chief). Some religious men offer free religious education to *gecekondu* children but defend workers' rights and advocate the full adoption of technology, modern education, and science. Even in the squatters' villages some religious leaders – *hocas* or *imams,* as they are called locally – turned into fierce advocates of democracy and urged their villagemates to participate in elections, claiming that the Marxist Labor party active during that period promoted laudable social programs. They also urged village children to attend the Imam-Hatip (clergy) schools. Other *hocas* believed that democracy began with Omar (the second Caliph, 634–644), since he instituted welfare measures that are considered an inherent part of a democratic order. The reconciliation of these diverse attitudes may be explained partly by the fact that to be a Muslim for the villager and the *gecekondu* dwellers means first of all to be part of a community. In other words, religious affiliation is part of a broader social identification with a community, with the acceptance of communal ethics and behavioral norms. Religion for the squatters is a concrete set of rules and regulations connected with the realities of life rather than an abstract system of ethics. The concrete expression of all these is the community.

In the eyes of villager and squatter alike, any individual who accepts the supremacy of the community, as they understand it, is a member of the group. The fact that the community explains and justifies its existence by religious, scientific, or political principles has little importance as long as that justification and explanation do not have a disintegrating effect on their communal life. Scholars have defined the Muslims' sense of communal attachment as deriving from the *umma,* the ideal Islamic community that includes all believers. The communal life provides the squatter with a sense of psychological security and belongingness, as well as group identity, which is his rationale for accepting the supremacy of the community. It must be stressed however, that the concept of community in the *gecekondu* has been undergoing subtle changes under the impact of industrial and urban conditions, as shall be discussed later. I believe that the idea of community, which is so much a part of modern Turkish society[5] and responsible for its cohesion, will continue in some form despite these changes.

G. H. Sewell has cited religion, notably that of the Alevi-Shiites, as a primary identity group variable, which determined the place and role of ethnic and village identities.[6] There is no question that the Alevis are conscious of their religious identity and prone to defend their doctrine. Some claim better knowledge and observance of Islamic rules than the Sunni and delight in telling stories of how they defeated the orthodox Sunni in religious discussions. Sewell mentions that the orthodox *imam* in his area of study acknowledged that the Alevis sought him out and argued with him over points of doctrine.[7] The Alevis living in the three *gecekondus* in Istanbul organized special gatherings in honor of *dedebaba,* or simply *dede,* their sheikh, during his annual visits to Istanbul and offered him gifts and dues. They also participated with other Alevis in the religious ceremonies held in Kuruçeşme and Beşiktaş. In fact, the migration to and the contact with the city seemed to have sharpened the Alevis' sense of identity. For instance, the Alevi squatters in Istanbul became identified with the Bektashi groups in the city and began practicing their rituals. Consequently, they organized commemorative meetings honoring Hacı Bektaş Veli, who founded the order, possibly in the twelfth century, and even strove to attend festivities in the founder's town of Hacı Bektaş in the province of Nevşehir in central Anatolia. Actually, the Kızılbaş Alevis used the association with the Bektashis as a means of gaining solidarity and integrating themselves into a larger urban religious order. Moreover, the squatter Alevis began reading books on Bektaşi doctrine, revived customs, and adapted symbols likely to strengthen their newly emerging religious identity in the city.[8] Furthermore, ingroup marriages among the Alevis were more frequent than among Sunnis. If taken at face value, this seems to indicate a deepening of religious consciousness; actually, as shall be explained later, this was a vehicle for identification and integration into the city and the nation.

Indeed, the developments leading to the acceptance of secular urban values and to integration into a national political culture were far stronger than the efforts to strengthen the Alevi culture and traditions. For instance, the Alevi youth showed open animosity toward the *şıh* (sheikh) and did not approve of their parents' paying him dues merely because he was a religious leader; soon the sheikh stopped coming to Istanbul, and apparently dues are no longer paid to him or his successors. In the village itself the Alevi were openly critical of their religious leaders and accused them of having abused their position and distorted the meaning of religion. In many other cases, the Alevis, similar to the Sunnis, claimed that religion was strong in the village because villagers did not have an alternative but city dwellers realized that "there are many other things in life besides religion."

The weakening impact of religion is evident in the fact that as late as 1968 these settlements did not have a mosque (since then two mosques have been built largely as a consequence of outside political factors) and the historical Alevi-Sunni rivalries seem to have disappeared or lost their virulence, at least in the three *gece-kondus* studied. Many Sunnis in the settlement referred to the Alevis as "children of God like us" and did not seem to discriminate against them except in a few isolated cases. (The strong orthodoxy displayed by migrants from the Black Sea littoral may be in part due to the fierce Muslim-Christian rivalries that prevailed in the area in the nineteenth century.) One could hear among Sunnis statements such as, "You can see that they are Alevis because they support the Republican party"; or "These Alevis are strange people, you can never guess what they are up to"; or "We could not build a mosque here because of the Alevis"; but occasional conflicts among Alevis and Sunnis were rapidly resolved thanks to the authority of settlement leaders.[9] In fact, many squatters confessed confidentially that Alevi leaders were rapidly losing their influence in the settlement, as proven by subsequent events (chapter 8).

The status of women

The surviving effects of the village culture are evident in the status of women. The inferior position of women in the village resulting from division of labor and a hierarchy of values, although showing signs of change, seems to have been preserved in the *gecekondu*.[10] Women formed a society of their own, subordinate to but harmonious with that of men. There were behavioral differences among women from various provinces. Those coming from Sivas and Gümüşhane wanted to acquire jobs outside the home and showed interest in urban cultural activities and in the education of women; those coming from the Black Sea littoral – notably from the provinces of Rize and Trabzon, and Kastamonu in the interior – appeared rather conservative and accepted their husbands' decisions without question. In a few rare cases husbands coming from these areas did not agree to their wives' being interviewed because "they did not know these things," although, when interviewed, these women seemed quite aware of developments affecting their lives. But inside families women assumed more authority than men and appeared in general pleased to settle in the city and take advantage of urban educational and cultural facilities. (See chapter 6.)

The sense of outrage and revolt among women in general, because of their low status, seemed to be acute and violent, indeed. This may become more evident if the level of their social and political consciousness reaches an advanced stage. When questioned in depth, women in the *gecekondus* showed resentment against the low status assigned to them. In fact, many women welcomed the interviews as an opportunity to air their discontent and lodge complaints in the hope of obtaining some help. Some women enjoyed the interview so much that they suggested additional questions related to their family life, especially to their relations with the in-laws. (The desire to avoid the in-laws' interference in family life was one of the reasons cited by women for migration from the village.) The differences of outlook, style of living, and level of aspiration showed much sharper variation among the *gecekondu* women than men. A few portraits of women, although representing exceptions, may better illustrate this point.

H. A. lives in a three-room house. The dwelling is well kept. She dresses well and considers herself and her family well above the others. The husband has a job of his own and earns up to 2,000 liras a month. The family possesses a refrigerator, and a clothes washing machine. Similar to the middle-class families she has instituted a reception day attended by her friends, mostly from the city. Her two daughters attend school, are well-dressed and can afford the luxury of going swimming (with the mother) three times a week.

S. G. lives with her niece since her own son and daughter, who live in the next house, have abandoned her. Her other daughter, living elsewhere in Istanbul, occasionally comes to wash her clothes and feed her. But many days S. G. is hungry. Often she talks meaninglessly, sings in despair and complains of pains. She cannot send her niece to school. Trying to escape the village poverty, she has found worse misery in the city and in the process she has lost all hope.

S. B. lives with her six children. Her husband went with another woman. Her family history is frightening indeed. She married at the age of 14. Her sister was married to a rich man in the village, who already had two wives, and eventually she committed suicide. S. B. has succeeded in training two of her daughters as hairdressers, while two others are attending school, the rest are too young. Her house is well kept and seems to have all the comforts. The children are healthy and sociable, hardly distinguishable from those in the city. S. B. works as a maid in a rich man's house. It is only when discussing her work that her discontent, which seems to dominate her entire personality, bursts into the open. "I married young and had lots of children and worked to raise them. I never knew what youth was. My husband went to a young woman because I was worn out and useless. Now, I clean the dirt of this rich couple while the lady is relaxing on the beach or is entertaining her friends at home. My children take me occasionally with them to a picnic and ask me whether I have fun. I do not know what they mean. What is fun?" Her daughters, who are quite compassionate, try to comfort her.

L. U. lives in a rather good house. Her husband works in a factory. She seems responsible for starting a small successful dairy business. Though grass and water is scarce, she still manages to feed her cow. She does not belittle housework but feels that she deserves, primarily because she comes from a good family, a higher social status and important responsibility. Her grandfather had reached the rank of captain in the Ottoman army, which later proved useful in securing him a high rank in the village. She believes firmly in the industrialization of Turkey and in equal job opportunities for everybody, including women. Her highest ideal aspiration is to become an industrialist in order to open factories that would benefit everyone. She feels capable of undertaking all the responsibilities assumed by men. L. U. believes firmly that the two sexes are absolutely equal. If opportunities were available, L. U. would like to train as an astronaut and fly into space. Her political views are firm and determined in favor of democracy, which she defines as a "system in which the people cannot live without government and the government cannot function without people and their consent and participation." Her daughter, on the other hand, is very shy and retiring.

If literacy, employment, and freedom among women reach a higher level of development, then, one may expect them to participate in the *gecekondu* affairs. But for the time being the women's participation in the conduct of the settlement affairs is nearly nonexistent and this constitutes one of the most unfortunate aspects of the social order prevailing in the *gecekondus*. Yet, new conditions of life, occupational changes, life in the city, and exposure to urban influences are affecting women and will definitely pave the way to meaningful changes in their status in the near future.

(Ethnic and linguistic differences in the three *gecekondus* studied did not seem to have affected the social organization of the *gecekondu* or the selection of leaders, largely because an overwhelming majority of squatters were of Turkish stock.)[11]

Formal institutions and public opinion

The *kahvehane,* or coffeehouse, may be regarded as a social club where problems are discussed and debated and informal decisions are reached. (This is a misnomer because the beverage most frequently consumed is tea since coffee is expensive.) Actually, the coffeehouse should be regarded more as a communication center rather than a social institution. Though known for centuries in Turkish towns, it spread into Turkish villages rather recently as an answer to the increased need for a place for communication, gathering, and business transaction.[12] Every major *mahalle* in a *gecekondu* has its own coffeehouse frequented usually by men from one region. There is also a major coffeehouse that functions as a central gathering place. Leaders and *gecekondu* dwellers meet in the coffeehouse usually in the evening to exchange views, settle problems, and make decisions. Outsiders coming into the *gecekondu* visited the coffeehouses to get information or make political propaganda statements.[13] (Incidentally, the coffeehouse is operated as a business venture and not as a community or public service.)

The preceding section dealt with elements of the traditional village culture that conditioned the social organization and the selection of leaders in the *gecekondu,* whose main function was to maintain a village type of community in the settlement. Superimposed on these informal and traditional organizations and leaders were formal organizations and elected leaders who, though fulfilling occasionally traditional village functions, dealt mostly with current problems related to the survival, administration, order, and security of the settlement and its relations with the city and the government. The *muhtarlık* (head man office), the *Gecekonduyu Güzelleştirme Derneği,* the trade unions, and the political parties – the last will be discussed at length in Chapter 8 – appeared as the main formal organizations.

The *muhtarlık* is an official institution established in Turkey for the first time about 1864, as a consequence of the administrative reforms. The subsequent village law of 1924 further defined the functions of this office. In essence the *muhtar* represents the official recognition extended by the central authorities to the traditional community leaders, known under various names in the past. In villages the *muhtar* is the representative of the community and has considerable authority as the representative of the central government administration.[14] In towns the *muhtar,* although less important than in the villages, performs such basic functions as issuing identity and domicile certificates and preparing factual reports on local problems on which higher authorities base their decisions.[15] Thus, the *muhtar* occupied a key position in *gecekondu* life, and squatters tried to gain influence and control over the position, as shall be shown in detail in Chapter 8.

The *Gecekonduyu Güzelleştirme Derneği* is found in nearly every major squatter settlement in Turkey. The Dernek is located in a specially constructed building in the Nafibaba settlement that serves at times as a meeting place and classroom, as a hall for festivities, ceremonies, cultural activities, and other social functions and especially as a channel of formal communications with the city authorities and the government.

The Dernek, established in accordance with the provisions of the Association Law, formalizes the informal decisions made in the coffeehouses and other informal meeting places. It also plays a major role as a more dignified point of contact between the outside parties and the squatters, especially for the representatives of the government and high party leaders. The Dernek theoretically represents the entire community since membership is open to everyone including outsiders. In reality is it a "peer association"; decisions concerning the community as a whole are not taken by the entire membership but only by a handful of leaders. The rank-and-file squatters accept the "peer" decisions as best suited to the interests of the entire settlement. The idea that the leader personifies the settlement is an obvious by-product of the communal solidarity prevailing in the *gecekondu*. The Dernek is actually a rational – that is, interest-oriented – organization. It bridges the natural and traditional forms of association rooted in the family, kinship, and village, and those based on interest, class, or occupation in the city. All decisions concerning the community as a whole are formalized in the Dernek and enforced through it in the entire settlement, regardless of the settlers' origin and religious affiliation. In sum, the Derneks create a degree of formal integration in the settlement, establish working relations with the city and the government as a whole, and defend the interests of the squatters before official organizations in a manner similar to Latin American organizations.[16]

Trade unionism does not seem to play much of a role in the *gecekondu*. A total of 99 men, but only 6 women and 8 unmarried, were trade union members. Another 45 men, 8 women, and 8 unmarrieds belonged to the *Society of Mutual Help* (which is synonymous with the *Gecekonduyu Güzelleştirme Derneği*); and 69 men, 13 women, and 8 bachelors belonged to a series of other associations. A large number of squatters also belonged to special associations established with the purpose of developing their native villages (see Chapter 6). There was no evidence that the trade union members have yet had an ideological impact on the settlement. The prestige of factory workers as masters of a technology was high in the settlement but their trade union position did not seem to bear much weight on the internal affairs of the *gecekondu*. Apparently, industrial workers considered their membership in the *gecekondu* as superseding their loyalty to the trade union. In some instances male squatters praised the trade unions for securing them higher wages but still seemed to regard their membership in them as a practical necessity rather than a basic political or ideological commitment. On balance, the communal membership in the *gecekondu* carried more weight than professional or class affiliation. This was natural since most of the squatters had been industrial workers for only short periods of time and had not had the opportunity to become politically conscious and place class affiliations above traditional attachments.

The leaders involved in the struggle to control the *muhtarlık* or the Dernek are engaged in establishing order in the *gecekondus* or in conducting relations with the outside world. They were formally elected on the basis of their achievements inside and outside the *gecekondu*, either in dealings with the government or in some private business. The founders of the *gecekondu*, who belong usually to this group, enjoy a certain prestige and often become the spokesmen for the settlement. These founder-leaders possess firsthand knowledge of all matters concerning the *gecekondu*, including the ability to communicate and plan common action with leaders of other squatter settlements. At times they engage in city-wide political activities among squatters. They strive to preserve peace and order, to prevent crime, prostitution, and other undesired acts in the *gecekondu*, which could undermine internal solidarity and might prompt the intervention of municipal and government authorities. These leaders bargain with the political parties, the police, and other outside agencies on behalf of the *gecekondu*, which effectively help integrate the community. These leaders seldom come from established village families; they are, in other words, "self-made men," who often have a vested interest in the *gecekondu;* some own small businesses, such as a grocery store or coffeehouse, or land still available for construction there. Actually, few people in the *gecekondu* can afford, under normal conditions, to "own" extensive tracts of land since these are likely to be usurped forcibly by "have nots" or other rival groups backed by their own relatives or friends.

The occupations of the squatters play an important role in determining their ranking in the settlement. The most prestigious group consists of private successful entrepreneurs. The second group is made up of industrial workers because their steady jobs, insurance benefits, and mechanical and technical skills are considered a special mark of achievement and ability. The third group consists of craftsmen and artisans, such as masons and carpenters. The fourth group is made up of service workers, although those working for the municipality or other respectable establishments rank somewhere between the industrial workers and the craftsmen.[17]

The *gecekondu* leaders enjoy considerable prestige among squatters and relatives coming from the same village since their achievements symbolize the potential achievements of all people from the same village.[18] Often a newcomer is likely to give as reference the name of a *gecekondu* leader from his own village or men with well-established occupations, although he does not know them personally. He is sure, however, that they know each other's families. In many cases the successful entrepreneur and professional becomes a model and adviser as well as the yardstick for measuring the success of the newcomers from the same village.

6. The urbanization of the *gecekondu*

Phases of urbanization

Squatters' urbanization is envisaged in this chapter within the framework of economic development, population growth, and migration, as mentioned (Chapter 1), and specific processes of individual and collective sociopolitical and psychological acculturation.[1] Moreover, villages and cities are regarded here as part of larger social and economic systems; each affects the other socially, politically, and culturally, in accordance with changes in the broader systems. The communal organization in the squatter settlement is a mediating, practical organization that maintains solidarity among migrants and facilitates their integration into the city. Elements of the village culture and of the sense of identification with the land and the community may be permanently incorporated into the city in the emerging new political and national culture in the third world countries. As mentioned before, the city in the third world is undergoing a profound transformation through the incorporation of technology, science, and differentiated administrative and professional services into its structure and functions. Today, much of what is new for the villager in the city is also new for the urban dweller.

The current urbanization in Turkey as elsewhere in the third world has been regarded in this study chiefly as a consequence of rural migration. In turn, migration and urbanization have been considered as reflecting both general historical experiences common to all or most third world nations and specific developments involving only a region or a culture.

In common with other third world countries, Turkey was affected in the nineteenth century by the development of a global market economy and demand for agricultural commodities, which created a corresponding urban growth and profoundly altered the traditional social structure.[2] The specific factors affecting current

137

urbanization in Turkey involved, first, a historical and cultural view of the city as the highest and potentially the most "virtuous" and comfortable form of life,[3] and, second, the equation of modernization with urbanization. The reforms after 1923, which emphasized the development of cities and turned them into symbols of modernity and aspiration, strengthened further in the public mind the correlation between modernization and urbanization.[4] The fact that Turkish villagers already had positive views toward the city certainly was a factor in their migration and willingness to integrate themselves into the city. And if conditions permitted, probably most Turkish villagers would come and settle in the city, as indicated by a study of rural attitudes.[5]

In this study the model for analyzing the Turkish squatter's urbanization was not based on preconceived patterns but was developed through empirical observation and familiarity with the way the migrant regarded his own urbanization and how he carried it out. Consequently, while this study accepts the survival of the village culture and modes of organization in the city, it also takes the view that the migrant adapts himself to urban conditions and gradually changes his physical living and cultural outlook. He does so, as Ned Levine put it, by striking a "positive relationship between old culture contacts" and "new culture contacts" and seeking familiar people whose contacts "will help him to acculturate and, at the same time, maintenance of contacts with the village should give a reference point from which he can compare himself."[6] This study therefore looks on the migrant's contacts with the village as a psychological necessity and as a yardstick to measure his own achievement and transformation in the city.

Finally, the migrant's relation to the city has been regarded essentially as marginal and determined to a large extent by economic factors. The availability of steady employment, increasing income, opportunities to affect the government, and occupational mobility appear as the key factors in facilitating the migrant's integration into the city, thus ending his marginality. Consequently, the term *urbanization* encompasses both the migrant's "integration" through occupational change and gradual adoption of physical and cultural aspects of urban life and the city's adoption of some elements of folk culture.

Though urbanization begins in a way with the villager's decision

to leave his community, the actual process enters its truly transforming phase only after he establishes himself in the *gecekondu*.
Field observation suggests that the urbanization of Turkey's
migrant-squatters occurs in four phases. The first phase is marked
by the adoption of urban dress and some urban habits as preparatory steps toward assuming city views and attitudes. Though
a superficial change, city dress symbolizes for the squatter his
transition to a higher form of societal existence. He may retain
much of his village personality under his often awkwardly fitted
city (Western) clothes, but in his mind a change of dress represents a proof of his desire and readiness to conform to the material,
and eventually to the cultural, aspects of city life. Women, on the
other hand, who remain somewhat more attached to their village
culture, partly because of limited contact with the city, retain their
rural dress longer than men. The general modernization of Turkey
has assigned to the dress change a rather symbolic function in the
process of social transformation. This does not imply a loss of
former cultural identity but a redefinition of that identity within
the framework of new social and political conditions.[7]

The second phase of urbanization consists of the migrant's adoption and sharing, if available, of such city facilities as water, electricity, and transportation, and also of regularly buying his food
and clothing in shops. This is also the time for building a dwelling
and developing closer identification with the settlement. This phase
represents the physical aspect of city integration, and its successful
completion depends on the squatter's ability to secure steady employment and adequate earnings, as well as on the willingness of
municipal authorities to provide him with urban utilities. The relatively successful completion of the two phases usually produces
satisfaction with life in the city.

The third phase of urbanization, which often parallels the first
two, consists of the squatter's willingness to establish relations with
other city people. The squatter creates for himself a new self-image
modeled on urban forms that he considers superior or ideal. This
appears to be a rather critical stage in the sense that the squatter
may decide that some of his values, notably those related to the
family and to community relations, are better than those prevailing
in the city; he may thus develop resistance to change. Such a development is conditioned in part by the squatter's age, level of

attachment to the village, length of stay in the city, level of communication with the city residents, and participation in urban economic, social, and political activities.

The fourth and concluding phase of urbanization consists of the squatter's full identification with the city – that is, his personal conviction that he does not belong to the village but to the city. The best measure of this transformation should be sought not so much in the squatter's attachment to the city as in his feeling of alienation from the village. One may be inclined to think that the squatter's surviving attachments to the village and interest in his relatives living there may prevent or delay his full integration into the city. Our observations tend to support the opposite viewpoint. The idea of having "roots" and a place to return to, however destitute that may be, in case of extreme difficulty in the city is reassuring to the squatter. Many squatters said that they returned occasionally to the village during their first difficult years in the city to rest and to gain self-confidence. Others said that the grim poverty of the village rekindled their determination to stay and succeed in the city; still others said that the village visit enabled them to measure the level of their own progress and change in the city.

Squatters' life in the city

These views concerning the migrants' urbanization derive from the squatters' answers to a questionnaire. Since many of the questions asked in this section related to the squatters' actual life in the city, the answers were more precise than those given to other general questions. In general, 90 percent of the men, 92 percent of the women, and 87 percent of the unmarried said that they were very or reasonably satisfied with having established themselves in Istanbul, as shown in Table 6.1.

The essential factor in determining the degree of satisfaction was the difference between the low standard of life in the village and the relatively satisfactory one in the settlement. The city is a better place to live because all living facilities devised by modern technology are concentrated there. The expectation of a better life in the future adds to the satisfaction. Many squatters are aware that their life in the city, handicapped by lack of education and social status, started at a very low level; but they believe that they have

Table 6.1 *Degree of satisfaction in living in the city (in percentages)*

	Men	Women	Unmarried
Very satisfied	43	68	61
Reasonably satisfied	47	24	23
Very little satisfied	5	5	3
Unsatisfied	5	2	10
Other		1	3
Total	100	100	100

come a long way. One could still discern occasionally in the squatters' comments some traces of the old idea of social immutability and class differences. Expressions such as "A poor person in the village is a poor person in the city" and "We could aspire only to a third-class existence" indicated that the squatters' satisfaction derived from the belief that one who started at a very low level could rise only gradually.[8]

Men in general derived their satisfaction from having steady employment and better earnings, a house, however modest, or a profession or business of their own, better food and clothing, regular work hours, schools for children, possibilities for amusement, medical facilities, personal security, and civilized relations.

A minority of the men who were dissatisfied with their life in the city came from richer village families. They had moved into the city in order to achieve greater success but found themselves stranded in the *gecekondu*. Others were dissatisfied because they came to the city with a hope of studying but could not. A few were dissatisfied with the city because of unfulfilled romantic visions of luxury and amusement.

The majority of women said they were very satisfied with being in the city because they had an easier life and found there great choice of food and clothing, "if one had the money to buy them." They also found in the city security and some freedom from interference by relatives and elders.[9] Moreover, many women wanted refrigerators and washing machines and more opportunities to enjoy the city life. Some compared their present situation with the dismal life in the village. One said, "We were like blind people in the village; we got our eyesight in the city." Some women did not hesitate to refer sarcastically to their own embarrassment and awkwardness in their initial dealings with city people. Others regretted the fact that they had borne more children than it was necessary or desirable; still others were happy to have a chance to work outside their homes. The satisfaction of women with life in the city was also evident not only in their readiness to answer the questions about the city, but also in their lengthy comments about the good aspects of urban life.

The unmarried were satisfied with the city chiefly because of the educational facilities and social activities (amusement) available and the possibilities for contracting a suitable marriage. Some of the young men and women had either formed an exaggerated view of Istanbul as children or had come to the city at a very young age and took city facilities for granted. Consequently, they judged the city facilities available to them not in contrast to the privations endured in the village, as did their elders, but in relation to their own expectations of city life. They felt that they were deprived of many facilities available to the established residents of the city, hence the relatively high percentage of dissatisfaction.

The reasons for the satisfaction derived from life in Istanbul came in the form of lengthy comments during interviews with the respondents. Table 6.2 gives an approximate classification of these answers and comments according to the importance attached to them by respondents. The adoption of city dress was complete among bachelors and among men, while a few of the older women and some of the recently arrived women maintained some of the native costumes. There was not a single veiled woman, though in a few cases women showed reluctance to speak with strangers. In general, the squatters were pleased with the abundance and quality of city clothing and did not hesitate to wear fashionable dress provided their income allowed it.

The majority of all respondents (64 percent of the males, 56 percent of the females, and 67 percent of the unmarried) did not yet consider themselves city dwellers (Table 6.3). The squatters' personal views about their own urbanization were based first on a series of tangible criteria. Almost half of the men and women explained that they could not call themselves *şehirli,* or city folk, because they did not live like the established residents. Others ex-

Table 6.2 *Reasons for deriving satisfaction from being in the city*

	Men (371 Respondents)		Women (403 Respondents)		Unmarried (119 Respondents)	
	No.	%	No.	%	No.	%
Opportunity for employment and better living	228	44	171	30	50	38
Predominance of civilization and good manners	42	8	17	3	15	11
Availability of educational opportunities	36	7	33	6	16	12
Higher quality of life (in relation to village)	35	7	108	19	8	6
Availability of health facilities	34	6	20	4	2	2
Fulfilled part of expectations	29	6	28	5	3	2
Wider choice of food, clothing, and cleanliness	29	6	68	12	14	11
Possibility of owning a house	28	5	49	9	4	3
Reunion with the family	26	5	38	7	2	2
Availability of entertainment	22	4	7	1	12	9
Discovered the city to be better than expected	13	2	4		4	3
Developed attachment to the city	1		16	3	1	1
Other	1		8	1		
Total	524	100	567	100	131	100

Note: The number of answers to this question is larger than that of the respondents because some of them cited two or more factors as reasons for their satisfaction with the city.

Table 6.3. *Identification with the city (in percentages)*

	Men	Women	Unmarried
Consider themselves city dwellers	36	44	33
Do not consider themselves city dwellers	64	56	67
Total	100	100	100

plained that the unsatisfactory living conditions in the *gecekondus* and failure to acquire the legal titles to the houses prevented their integration into the city. The surviving attachment to the village (notably among the unmarried, most of whom were 16 to 20 years of age and had parents and close relatives in the village) and the failure to adopt urban manners, modes of thought, and the city dialect were cited as other impediments to integration into the city. On the other hand, those (36 percent of the men and 44 percent of the women) who said that they considered themselves city dwellers attributed this mostly to the fact that they were actually living in Istanbul and had spent a good part of their lives in urban areas (Table 6.4). This latter view was expressed mostly by men who had been engaged in seasonal work and had been separated from the village for a long time. A few men and women, but many more unmarried, who claimed that they were integrated into the city attributed it chiefly to the fact that they worked regular hours like the established city residents.

The high rate of nonidentification with the city among the unmarried derived from their higher expectations and a more critical appraisal of their own position in relation to the established city residents. The identification with the city increased proportionately to the length of residence in urban areas and the age at the time of arrival; Table 6.5 lists the chief reasons for nonidentification with the city.

The importance attached to the availability of urban facilities as one of the major conditions for identification with and integration into the city was underscored by the recent establishment of a municipal bus line running from the *gecekondus* to the central areas of Istanbul in order to facilitate the squatters' transportation to various work places and shopping areas. An overwhelming

Table 6.4. *Reasons for identifying with the city*

	Men		Women		Unmarried	
	No.	%	No.	%	No.	%
Resided in Istanbul	26	27	75	62	4	14
Lived in cities since an early age (seasonal worker)	22	23				
Led an urban dweller's life	7	7	15	12	12	43
Adopted urban thought and manner	8	9	11	9	7	25
Separated entirely from village	10	11				
Became-accustomed to city	12	13				
Other	9	10	21	17	5	18
Total	94	100	122	100	28	100

Table 6.5. *Reasons for not identifying with the city*

	Men		Women		Unmarried	
	No.	%	No.	%	No.	%
Unable to live like other urban dwellers	117	48	92	48	20	35
Living in *gecekondu* insecure	54	22	20	10	7	13
Attachment to village	46	19	53	27	18	32
Difference in thought, manner, dialect	22	9	20	10	7	13
Other	6	2	10	5	4	7
Total	245	100	195	100	56	100

majority of men, women, and unmarried – 91, 97, and 96 percent, respectively – believed that the bus service helped them both to adapt to city life and to bring them closer to the city people, despite the latters' occasional contemptuous treatment. The squatters derived a feeling of equality from the fact that they traveled in common with other city residents. "Before the bus came," explained a squatter, "we were a village near Istanbul. Now we have become a *semt,* a district on the outskirts of the city." Others said that traveling on the bus forced them to learn polite manners and helped them save the time lost walking to work places. While expressing gratitude for bus service, the squatters – except for those at Baltaliman, who had city water and electricity – still felt that the municipality discriminated against them by not providing city amenities and schools. (These were provided later.) Nevertheless, the municipal and government officials kept tight control over sanitation by inoculating the squatters against epidemic diseases and by disinfecting toilets and swamp areas against malaria. Many squatters, aware that the introduction of public amenities depended first on securing a decision to retain and improve the settlement, as promised by politicians at election time, appeared more interested in obtaining the land deeds than the amenities. Many were grateful that the muncipality did not liquidate their settlement altogether, as entitled by law. This "humanitarian" attitude on the part of authorities often stemmed from the bribes paid by squatters to the municipal building agents and police officials, one of whom owned a house in the *gecekondu.* Moreover, relatively few squatters regarded municipal services as their due, as they did their political freedom. This reluctance might have stemmed from awareness that the municipal services were financed by taxes paid mostly by established city businesses and residents. Although the municipality collected building taxes from each *gecekondu* dwelling the revenue was rather inadequate to compensate for all city services needed by the squatters.

The adoption of urban habits

The squatters' urbanization can be measured also according to their adoption of habits associated with city life style; reading newspapers regularly, listening to the radio, seeing movies, and adopting some form of organized recreation (in Turkish this is often expressed as *dinlenme* or *eğlence* – amusement or entertainment) associated with urbanization and modernization were well established in the *gecekondu.* Radio and newspapers have penetrated even the most remote villages because of the availability of inexpensive radio sets and an efficient national newspaper distribution system. During the time the survey was conducted, television was available only in Ankara and Istanbul, but it now reaches almost the entire country. Radio and newspapers, therefore, are not an exclusive feature of city life, although the lack of electricity and the illiteracy in villages are likely to make their usage less frequent there.

The high rate of literacy (see Table 4.2) among the men and the unmarried (that is, those mostly between 16 and 20 years of age) accounted for the high percentage of newspaper and book reading, as shown in Table 6.6.

About half of the newspaper-reading squatters bought the popular daily *Hurriyet* (Freedom), which had a national circulation of close to 1 million; this was followed at some respectable distance by *Milliyet* (Nationality), *Cumhuriyet* (Republic), and *Tercüman* (Interpreter), which had social-democratic, social-national, and popular democratic slants, respectively. Party newspapers such as *Son Havadis* (Last News; siding with the ruling Justice party), *Ulus* (Nation; People's Republican party), and the sensational *Bugün* (Today) found only a total of 26 readers among the men. Some 63 percent of the men and the unmarried said that newspaper reading had become a daily routine; 31 percent said they read the paper once every few days; and the rest read the

Table 6.6. *Squatters' reading habits*

	Men		Women		Unmarried	
	No.	%	No.	%	No.	%
Newspapers						
Yes	303	80	89	23	108	89
No	76	20	297	77	13	11
Magazines						
Yes	71	19	32	8	51	41
No	312	81	347	92	70	59
Books						
Yes	145	38	36	9	81	67
No	238	62	345	91	40	33

Note: (Questions were asked separately for each category.)

paper only occasionally. Only 34 women said that they read the newspaper daily, and 38 women read it once every few days – all this being a by-product of low literacy among women (see Chapter 4). On the other hand, younger men showed interest in cultivating their intellect and in specializing in professions by reading books on a wide variety of subjects.[10]

More than two-thirds of all the squatters interviewed possessed radios and tuned in daily to various programs.[11] The most popular programs, which account for about 35 and 42 percent of the listening time of men and women, respectively, consisted of *milli* (national folk) music and news broadcasts followed by discussions and interviews, which filled about 13 percent of the squatters' listening time. Barely 11 percent of the men and women combined listened to light (popular) and Western music. It rose to 18 percent with the unmarried, who seemed to be interested also in plays and educational programs. Only 17 men, 23 women, and one unmarried – a young girl – said that they listened to the Koran reading on the radio. (See Table 6.7.)

The younger people tended to go to the movies more frequently; women in general claimed that movie going was not included in their upbringing. In the past the lack of transportation facilities to the city might have prevented many people from going to the movies. However, many squatters may have been reluctant to admit seeing movies, lest it seem a waste of money incompatible with their poverty. On the other hand, an open-air movie opened in Nafibaba settlement during the summer of 1968 and showed a series of native films. It organized also popular music concerts, which were well attended and thus provided convincing proof of the squatters' interest in movies and entertainment. Incidentally, interest in entertainment was quite high among all squatters, especially the unmarried.

About 50 percent of all the squatters interviewed stated that their major form of recreation (entertainment) consisted of gatherings with relatives and *hemşeris*, visits to their homes, picnics, and swimming. The rest pointed to reading, soccer, theater, embroidery, folk dancing, and card playing as the main form of recreation. Only 8 percent of the men, 13 percent of the women, and 3 percent of the unmarried said that they did not engage in any form of recreational activity.

Table 6.7. *Communication and recreation*

	Men		Women		Unmarried	
	No.	%	No.	%	No.	%
Read newspapers						
Yes	303	80	89	23	108	89
No	76	20	297	77	13	11
Read magazines						
Yes	71	19	32	8	51	41
No	312	81	347	92	70	59
Read books						
Yes	145	38	36	9	81	67
No	238	62	345	91	40	33
Own a radio						
Yes	277	71	291	69	89	78
No	112	29	131	31	35	22
Listen to[a]						
National songs	261	35	265	42	88	30
Light music	25	3	16	3	24	8
Western music	15	2	19	3	31	10
News	260	35	172	28	66	22
Discussions	98	13	74	12	41	14
Plays	20	3	41	6	15	5
Quizzes, educational	23	3	1		12	4
Advertisements	15	2	4	1	7	2
Sports	14	2	5	1	12	4
Koran	17	2	23	4	1	1
Go to the cinema						
Yes	248	64	162	38	87	70
No	141	36	261	62	38	30
Frequency of movie attendance						
1–2 times per month	94	38	63	39	31	27
3–4 times per month	58	23	38	24	31	27
5–8 times per month	15	6	11	7	23	20
Over 8 times per month	18	7	3	2	24	21
1–3 times per year	53	21	38	24	6	5
4–8 times per year	7	3	4	3		
Over 8 times per year	3	2	2	1		

[a] In number of answers given.

In general, recreation in the *gecekondu* was not well organized, but depended on each individual's initiative and imagination and on the available opportunities. The legal weekend holiday in Turkey, which begins Saturday at one o'clock and lasts until Monday morning (at the time of the survey), provided the squatters with a welcome period of free time that had been conspicuously absent in their village life. Many devoted their free time to improving their dwellings; others used it to visit the city, see relatives, and watch soccer games; the latter was a passionate partisan affair. The plans made for the weekend, the special clothes worn at this time, and the clusters of relaxed men in the coffeehouses on Sunday showed that regular recreation had begun to become part of *gecekondu* life. While in the village they either toiled continuously in the summer, sat idle through the winter, or wandered around the country in search for work. Making a distinction between work and rest, with special time allotted to each one, was on its way to becoming another city habit.

Relations with city dwellers

The squatters' integration into the city may be measured also according to their contact with the people and businesses in the older established sections of Istanbul. This contact and the resulting exposure to different ways of thought, manners, and speech had profound educational impact on the newcomers. The villagers' impressions of the city during their sporadic visits before migration are formed, if they do not have friends and relatives, by the cold, impersonal, and often contemptuous treatment on the part of city folks. These impressions are reinforced further by the villagers' belief that some townsmen may deceive and exploit them.[12] The migrants therefore, have to cope occasionally with these preconceived ideas while gradually discovering the "inner core" – that is, the true personality, motivations, and goals – of the city people and thus develop an empathy toward them.

The squatters' contact with the city and desire to know its inhabitants therefore plays a significant part in their urbanization. If the rural migrants were exclusively "an extension of the village into the city" or "urban villages," as many have described them, then the squatters would keep their relations with the city at a minimum and remain a closed community. The attitudes of *gece-kondu* residents concerning contact with the city do not support the view that the settlement is a closed community. An overwhelming majority of the men and the unmarried, 85 and 86 percent, respectively, claimed that they visited the central city 2 to 7 times a week; 64 percent of the women, most of whom were working as servants, visited the city at least once a week. The rest paid rare visits to the city. The frequency of the visits becomes even more striking if one considers the fact that most of the men were employed in the vicinity of the squatter settlement and not in the city proper; the central areas of Istanbul are located 3 to 5 miles from the settlement. The reasons for visits were – in order of priority – shopping, work, entertainment and recreation, and fulfillment of various official formalities. A large number of the women, 71 percent, went into the city mainly in order to shop; 43 percent of the men went there for the same purpose. Some 18 percent of the unmarried men and 13 percent of unmarried women went into the city chiefly for entertainment and recreation.

The nature and scope of the squatters' relations with the city people may be a better indication of their desire to integrate and identify themselves with the city. A relatively high percentage of squatters had personal relations with new city acquaintances, although the percentage of those who had relations with relatives and old friends from the village was higher (Table 6.8). Women preferred to deal less with friends from the village, possibly because of personal rivalries and fear of gossip. More than half of the people with whom the squatters had some relations lived either in the neighboring districts or other areas of Istanbul (Table 6.9). It must be stressed, however, that the urbanizing contact with city people is effective only if the squatters' economic and educational situation improves further.[13]

The squatters of an older age and who stayed long in the city seemed less attached to their relatives and showed increasing interest in new friends. When interviewed more closely, it became quite evident that older squatters were becoming dissatisfied because of a series of obligations and responsibilities stemming from blood relations. It seemed that kinship relations played a dominant and useful part during the initial phase of migration and settlement in the city, but afterward the value of rational, interest-oriented

Table 6.8. *Personal relations in the city (in percentages)*

	Men	Women
With relatives	32	39
New friends	39	37
Old village friends	26	19
Nobody	3	5
Total	100	100

Table 6.9. *Location of friends (in percentages)*

	Men	Women
Same settlement	46	48
Neighboring districts	22	20
Other areas of Istanbul	32	32
Total	100	100

relations with outsiders prevailed. This interest went hand in hand with the broadening scope of squatters professional, political, and civic activities and with their tendency to judge other men on the basis of achievement rather than kinship ties. In fact, kinship obligations and attachments diminished somewhat as health and welfare services in the city became available. (Most work places employing more than five people are subject to insurance. The scope of insurance was broadened recently.) In summary, the *gecekondu* showed a definite tendency toward attaching less importance to distant relatives, instead of treating all of them more or less as equals, as was often the case in the extended household in the village.

Changes in the concept of family

The impact of urbanization on the concept of family can be seen best in the bachelors' attitudes toward marriage and the qualifications they sought in their future consort. (See also Chapter 4.) The overwhelming majority of male parents, as mentioned before, married village girls. Probably their main criteria for choosing a wife in the village was *namus,* honor – that is, whether or not the marriage candidate had prior relations with other men and could be considered *aile kadını* (family woman), capable of fulfilling preestablished expectations of marital life: womanhood, motherhood, and so on. (in towns *aile kızı* means a girl from a respectable family.)

The unmarried men and women in the *gecekondus* seemed to have developed definite opinions about marriage. Forty-five percent of the bachelor men wanted to marry women from the villages; 76 percent of the women preferred to marry city men. The rest wanted the future consort to be from the village but to have city experience, a few had no opinion at all (Table 6.10).

Just about half of the bachelors wanted to choose their bride or groom independently; the remaining were evenly divided among those who wanted to leave the choice to their families or wanted to act in accord with them. Women in particular showed an unusual sense of independence in wanting to have a say in the choice of their future husbands. Of 36 women only 5 agreed to let their parents choose the husband (Table 6.11).

The unmarried men and women desiring to marry in the city were against the *başlık* (the amount of money given by the men to the bride's father and often used to purchase household items for the couple) primarily because it created material hardship for both sides and appeared as the bride's sale price. Women in particular opposed vehemently the idea of *başlık* as a degrading treatment.[14] But a minority of men seemed inclined to accept the *başlık* simply because it was part of family traditions. Men in general appeared less liberal in their family views, partly because it downgraded their established superiority and partly because it created difficult adjustment problems. Both bachelor men and women desiring to find a bride or groom in the city felt that their level of life, concepts, and aspirations were so urbanized as to make incompatible marriage with a village person. Young squatter girls, in particular, preferred to marry men from the city because of their urban upbringing, which made them well mannered and respectful of women. Men, on the other hand, appeared inclined to marry village women because of common family traditions, their thrift (a common complaint was that city women tend to be big spenders),

Table 6.10. *Where wife-husband
should come from (in percentages)*

	Men	Women
From the city	38	76
From the village	45	24
From the village with residence in the city	7	
Anyplace	10	
Total	100	100

Table 6.11. *Who should choose wife-husband*

	Men		Women	
	No.	%	No.	%
Only himself-herself	40	46	17	47
Only parents	24	28	5	14
Himself-herself and parents	22	26	14	39
Total	86	100	36	100

and their better adjustment to the poor conditions prevailing in the *gecekondus.* (Some men felt that by marrying a village woman they would give her a better life and higher status, and she would be grateful.)

The qualifications sought by bachelor men and women in their future wives or husbands ranked as follows: honesty-morality (23 percent), a good mother-father (17 percent), education (15 percent), a good friend (14 percent), beauty (11 percent), a good profession (11 percent), money (7 percent). The first two qualifications reflected some of the traditional Turkish family values prevailing in both towns and villages. The rest, however, were to a very large extent borrowed from the urban culture, either through contact with city people or frequent reading of newspapers and books, and watching movies. In fact, even the first two qualifications reflected more the urban dweller's idealized image of parenthood and family virtues than the villager's natural attitude toward them. (In philosophical terms this overlapping of various family concepts may be explained as a result of the transition from a more or less natural state of freedom to a freedom defined and regulated rationally according to the predominant urban culture. Other extensive studies of *gecekondu* families have brought forth the change in the family structure.)[15]

The squatters developed rather extensive relations with the city people. A total of 47 percent of the men and 46 percent of the unmarried said that they had established friendships with people in the city outside of their settlement (Table 6.12). Specifically, 68 percent of the new friends consisted of people on the work site, 21 percent were new acquaintances made on various occasions, and only 11 percent were people from their native region. However, only 17 percent of the women respondents had made new friends among the city people. When asked directly whether they wanted to establish closer relations with the city people 81, 73, and 90 percent of the men, women, and unmarried, respectively, said yes.

The squatters wanted to know the city people better for the following reasons: to acquire knowledge, manners, and ideas of the urbanites; to promote their own professional and practical interests; to satisfy the yearning to become *medeni* (civilized or emancipated); to become fully assimilated into the city; and to satisfy the need for friendship. Incidentally, more than 52 percent of the women and bachelors cited the desire to acquire city manners and ideas and to become *medeni* as the chief reason for seeking closer relations with city people. The squatters who did not want to establish closer relations said that the differences between the city people and the *gecekondu* residents were too deep and that they did not trust the urban dwellers or were too shy to contact them.

The established city population, however, showed no apparent desire to know and integrate with the squatters. Even the better educated, while acknowledging the existence of objective factors behind rural migration, blamed the squatters for undermining the established urban ways of life and manners and for spoiling the physical appearance of the city. The migrants were accused for crowding in buses and trains and amusement parks, for the heavy

Table 6.12. *Actual and desired relationships with city people*
(*in percentages*)

	Men	Women	Unmarried
Having relations	47	17	46
Not having relations	53	83	54
Desiring closer relations	81	73	90
Not desiring closer relations	19	27	10

traffic caused by the *dolmuş* (taxis) often operated by *gecekondu* residents, and for a variety of other urban difficulties. The *gece-kondus* in their eyes were sources of crime, prostitution, and drug addiction, although, as indicated earlier, this was not true. Often on holidays, city people and their children would visit the *gece-kondu* areas as a curiosity. Few seemed to care that the *gecekondus* provided the city with cheap services and abundant manpower for its industrial and commercial activities. Few city residents could see that the squatters were a part of a process of change and in-dustrialization that was transforming not only the rural people into city dwellers but also the city itself into something new. For the time being it was not expected that the city, the government, or some other agency would provide any service specifically desig-nated to quicken the squatters' urban integration. In fact, many city residents advocated the use of strong means to stop the rural migration and even to send the squatters back to their villages. However, the processes operating through the political parties and election mechanism integrated the squatters and the city people, regardless of their wishes.[16]

Squatters' self-image and aspirations

The squatter's own view of his *gecekondu* and his residence there was quite firm and positive. An average of 75 percent of all *gece-kondu* residents stated that they were not embarrassed because of their residence in the *gecekondu*. A sense of pride and truthfulness mixed with determination, which may be considered some of the characteristics of the Turkish village culture, seemed to be the source of this attitude. The most frequently cited reasons by *gece-kondu* dwellers for their attitude were the following: This was their life and they were not ashamed of it, the *gecekondu* represented an improvement in their existence, they desired to be accepted as they were, and they had become used to this situation. Only 10 women and 11 men, all of older age, seemed resigned to accept their current situation as permanent. Those who were embarrassed to say that they resided in the *gecekondu* attributed it to the fact that the city dwellers still considered them inferior. Others attributed their embarrassment to their own personal failures, to the unwillingness of the old urbanites to consider them true *şehirli* (city people), to poverty, ignorance, and lack of city manners. On the other hand, 66 percent of the men, 57 percent of the women, and 77 percent of the unmarried wanted to live, if they could afford it, in other districts of Istanbul, usually in the better areas. The reasons given for the desire to live in a better district included the availability of water and electricity there, the proximity of the area to their work place, its good reputation, and the high level of education prevailing there. This desire to live elsewhere did not necessarily express a dissatisfaction with the *gecekondu* (in fact, many squatters preferred to stay in their present houses rather than move into apartment buildings) but rather a high level of expectation and optimism in the future. The squatters' potential for integration into the city was expressed best probably by the rising level of aspiration and confidence in their own ability to define and reach goals based on achievement. These goals could be achieved mostly in an urban environment with a mobile social structure and an expanding economy, all of which the squatters considered to be already part of their own world.

The answers to a series of questions involving the migrants' views on their children's future and their aspirations and ability to achieve them may best illustrate the point. The squatters believed generally that the city offered their children the best opportunities for advancement and possibilities for reaching the highest positions in society if they had the ability. In other words, the squatters felt that a rural or *gecekondu* background was not an inhibiting factor in the advancement of their children since they or their children would inevitably become part of the city. (A variety of political and historical reasons specific to Turkey, including the idea of nation-community, tend to create an egalitarian state of mind in society at large. The lack of a landed aristocracy and of sharply differentiated social classes in the past strengthened this state of mind.) Indeed, 69 percent of the men, 83 percent of the women, and 72 percent of the unmarried believed that their children already born or to be born could reach the highest position available if they had the ability. The factors deemed likely to enhance the children's attainment of higher social positions are shown in Table 6.13.

Those who believed that their children could not reach the highest position commensurate with their ability attributed it to economic causes, such as poverty, and to lack of backing, which was understood as a form of nepotism. Asked to name the most effective means for *anyone* to reach the highest position in Turkey, squatters named education (usually expressed as *bilgi,* which means knowledge acquired in schools), followed by money, ability, and proper backing (*himaye,* nepotism or protection). (See Table 6.14.)

It should be mentioned, however, that the squatters qualified their statement about money by saying that one needed money in order to study and to make the best use of his ability. Many, in fact, said that money can buy only things, whereas ability and a suitable environment to develop it can lead one to wealth as well as to high position, as indicated by excerpts from interviews.[17]

The squatters were asked to name a specific position, occupation, or profession to which they personally aspired ideally at the moment and would dedicate their lives to it if they had the qualifications necessary to practice it.[18] (See Table 6.15.)

On the other hand, an overwhelming majority of *gecekondu* residents believed that they could have reached far higher positions in life than the present one if they had had the means. The question was posed conditionally as "If you had the possibilities, what is the highest position your ability would have allowed you to reach?" There were no categories indicated by the questionnaire. Consequently, the answers must be interpreted not as what the squatters wanted to be but what they thought they could be if all opportunities were available, including education, money, and proper friends. While the answers in Table 6.15 reflected interest in earn-

Table 6.13. *Factors enhancing the migrant children's upward mobility (in percentages)*

	Men	Women	Unmarried
Education	46	59	42
Self-confidence and ability	30	22	32
Democracy-freedom	11	4	6
Honesty and perseverance	3	6	7
Money and backing by the powerful[a]	3	2	9
Other	7	7	4
Total	100	100	100

[a] Backing, or nepotism, was expressed in a slang expression, *torpil* (torpedo) – that is, the influence of a third person powerful enough to ram through all bureaucratic and social obstacles.

Table 6.14. *Means of reaching high position in Turkey (in percentages)*

	Men	Women	Unmarried
Knowledge (education)	27	26	24
Money	26	24	23
Ability	22	24	24
Backing by the powerful	14	14	16
Faith and determination	11	12	13
Total	100	100	100

ing and income, the answers in Table 6.16 stemmed chiefly from status considerations, often in line with the idea of social ranking and prestige in the village; for instance, government position carries more prestige in rural areas than in the city.

The migrants' answers lend themselves to a variety of interpretations related to the social change in Turkey as a whole. For instance, the high government offices, for centuries considered the highest position in society, are considered desirable by many more people in the *gecekondus* than among the intelligentsia at large. Women also showed an astonishing degree of self-confidence,

Table 6.15. *The most desirable occupations* (*in percentages*)

	Men	Women	Unmarried
Liberal professions (doctor, engineer, lawyer)	24	22	37
Government service (officials, judges)	17	13	13
Business	12	1	10
Army career (officer)	9		9
Teaching	7	20	13
Politics	6	1	2
Crafts	3	6	5
Nursing		5	2
Anything educational (to become learned)		8	2
Housewife		4	
Secretary			1
Never thought of it – doesn't care	9	6	
Other	13	14	6
Total	100	100	100

Table 6.16. *The highest reachable position* (*in percentages*)

	Men	Women	Unmarried
High government official	20	30	25
Big businessman	24	20	20
Deputy in the parliament	8	12	12
Prime minister	5	6	9
President	13	4	9
High army officer	7		2
Physician	6	7	6
Teacher	4	7	4
Engineer	5		5
Factory worker	2		
Other	6	14	8
Total	100	100	100

which contrasts sharply with their apathy toward some political matters. From the viewpoint of this study the most important aspect of these answers was the squatters' self-esteem and confidence. These are some of the characteristics of a modern open society with high mobility. The squatters undoubtedly were not only becoming members but were actually shaping such a society.

Underneath the migrants' conflicting attitudes and views toward the city and aspirations, the process of integration into the urban life continued its course. As time passed, the squatters, often without realizing it, became more and more estranged from the village and from their relatives living there, not by design but by the force of circumstances. Though closely related to each other on one level by blood relations and village background, three generations – the parents in the village, the migrating squatters, and their children born and raised in the city – were gradually separated from each other by different occupations, modes of life, and experience. The personal narration of A. S., who had come to the city 15 years earlier, is the best proof of the differences among the three generations.

Now and then my father comes from the village to visit us. During his first visit he wore a heavy woolen shirt. He was sweating heavily by the time he had climbed the hill. At the top of the hill I looked at my perspiring father and I felt embarrassed. I, his son, wore a light, cool nylon shirt while he, my father, was suffocating in a homemade coarse cloth. He wore rubber shoes which froze his feet in the winter and cooked them in the summer, while I wore comfortable leather shoes. A man in the city must wear clean clothes, otherwise the city gentlemen do not hesitate to show their disgust and contempt. I am paying special attention to clean clothes. My father's clothes were old and dirty and I was apprehensive to walk around with him. I was in fact afraid that someone might ask who he was. The differences between us were so great that I could not say that he was my father. . . . In the summer I sent the children to the village to vacation and go swimming. Last year, I went along with them. One day my daughter who has just entered the fourth grade showed me the wheat field and asked, "Father, what is this?" I was shocked and stunned for quite some time. Can you imagine? I toiled over the land and fought bitterly to make a living, and finally gave up and migrated to Istanbul just because the land did not produce enough. All I knew was the land and what it produced, and, now, my own children did not know what wheat looked like.

After the interview was concluded, we saw some boys, including A. S.'s son, playing in the street. Their game was *tayyarecilik*

(aviation). Two acted as pilots while two others with cardboard
pieces attached to their belts as parachutes jumped from the
"plane," which consisted of two clumsy boxes to which two pieces
of timber were attached as wings. All were born in Istanbul and
none had seen a plane except in the sky and perhaps in films, but
already they dreamt of flying, of being something that their parents
and grandparents could not imagine, even in their wildest dreams.

Istanbul was for centuries the city of government elites and their
supporting socioeconomic groups. It exerted considerable cultural
influence on the countryside without being subjected much to the
counterimpact of the folk culture or to the views and problems of
the Anatolian towns and villages. The city, instead of being the
living product of economic and social forces, was a mythical goal
one aspired to reach by living in it, often at the expense of the
countryside folks. Culturally, Istanbul was the repository of three
conflicting traditions that survived and thrived in their own social
environment, which often corresponded to a class division. The
European culture in its many forms belonged to the rich upper
classes of professionals, industrialists, and bankers living in the
fashionable districts (Şişli, Maçka, and so on) and the islands. The
so-called classical Turkish culture – that is, a surviving residue of
the combination of upper-class Ottoman culture and Islamic traditions – belonged to the craftsmen, religious men, and a variety of
middle-income groups. The popular culture, a rather odd combination of urban Islamic culture, Ottoman arts and music, and
folklore – in fact, this can be called the folklore of Istanbul – belonged to the lower classes, to that amalgam of ethnic, linguistic,
and racial groups that filled Istanbul in the nineteenth century.
Actually, these three cultures and the social groups and their sub-
groups formed three, or even more, adjacent or concentric cities
under one name. There was a common economy and a city administration but not much else to integrate them and develop in
all of them a sense of urban community and a common political
personality.

   The rural migration after 1950, aided by economic development,
industrialization, intensive communication, and the resulting occupational and social mobility, was the key factor that established
the foundations for an urban cultural change. A new urban culture

based partly on the countryside folklore, on which elements from the three existing cultures are being grafted, is emerging now in Istanbul. Culture is understood here not only as a system of values and normative rules, but also as a philosophy of life, as a means for defining social goals and the ways to accomplish them. The migrants' culture, notwithstanding its simple forms, is the culture of an overwhelming majority who lived in the countryside and were deprived of direct access to political power and to the comforts associated usually with city life. That culture expressed the suffering as well as the aspirations and goals of the countryside people – their creative spirit and dynamism. The migrants brought that culture into the city. Perhaps it is symbolic that Aziz Nesin, one of Turkey's greatest social satirists and novelists, with influence among the Turkish youth, came from the village of Gölve (district of Şebinkarahisar) – that is, from a migrant-sending village (see Chapter 7). It is no exaggeration to say that today Turkish cities are undergoing a process of nationalization – of cultural and linguistic Turkification – by rapidly shattering the sterile forms inherited from the Ottomans while giving new meaning and direction to those borrowed from the West. And to the extent the city culture becomes representative of the entire population, it assumes the character of a national culture.

The effects of this cultural transformation can be seen, for instance, in the radio and TV programs, a substantial part of which are dedicated now to folklore – to the countryside culture in its many forms. In a number of cases, groups from the *gecekondus* sing and dance for national audiences. A case may be worth citing. On the national radio, on July 10, 1974, at 9:30 P.M., Ahmet Ulus played on his *saz* (string instrument) a piece from Karacaoğlan, a seventeenth-century folk singer in the style of *saz şairleri,* or folk minstrels. It turned out that the player, a young boy of about 11 years of age, was the son of a *gecekondu* inhabitant. The father took his son, whenever possible, to the village to study and learn the style of folk minstrels and singers, which the son helped popularize in the *gecekondu* and then on the radio. Folklore dances from all regions of Turkey are today an accepted form of entertainment in all cities, something unheard of 20 years ago. In fact, wedding ceremonies and other forms of collective amusement that lacked spirit and spontaniety, especially while trying to imitate the

European styles of entertainment, have begun to adopt folk songs and dances in which men and women participate. For the first time, efforts are being made to introduce in schools courses in music, dance, home economics, and so on, that would give children of squatters and nonsquatters a new understanding of their own country and culture.

The migrants' role in changing the city and its culture is certainly worthy of further and deeper investigation.

7. *Gecekondu*-village relations and rural changes

This chapter deals with two interrelated problems: the migrants' continued relations with the village as part of their city adjustment and their urban impact on the economy and the social conditions in their native village. The preceding chapter defended the view that the squatters were urbanizing by integrating themselves into the city and rejected the notion that the squatter settlement constituted a permanent extension of the village into the city. Rural attachments may appear to some observers to delay or even undermine the squatters' integration into the city. However, the problem must be posed differently. As mentioned, urbanization in the third world today does not require or depend on the migrants' total and sudden alienation from the village and its culture. The village, in fact, plays a vital psychological role in facilitating the migrants' adjustment to and integration into the city. On the other hand, the migrants' visit to the village and their attachment to relatives living there must be seen as the consequence of natural and cultural factors that may well survive in a variety of forms even in the most advanced phase of urbanization. There are long-time residents in Turkish cities who maintain relations with their village relatives despite their wealth and sophistication.

The emerging new city in Turkey as elsewhere in the third world is undergoing, as mentioned before, a profound economic and sociocultural transformation, in part caused by the incoming rural migrants, who infuse it with the natural and dynamic spirit of the folk culture. A key problem is to determine whether or not the squatter's attachment to and relations with his native village remain the same as they were in the past. The manner in which these attachments are interpreted and justified rather than the mere fact that they exist at all constitutes the best yardstick for measuring the squatters' deruralization – and implicitly their urbanization. The chief indicators of this change may be found in the critical views that the migrant-squatter develops toward his village and the relatives there, and the comparisons he makes between rural life and city life.

Field observations show that the squatter-migrant changes his attitude and adopts a new outlook toward the village while living in the city and that he becomes a channel for transmitting new ideas and even for initiating changes in the rural areas through relations with his native village. In other words, he assumes the role of an agent of change, not only in transmitting to the village outside ideas that have become his own but also by initiating in the village – for a variety of personal and kinship reasons – economic, social, and cultural changes. The fact that the squatter-migrant is close to his relatives and friends living in the village increases his potential for influence among them, since he can interpret events and ideas and transmit information and opinion through customary forms accepted by the village culture. Moreover, he is trusted as a relative and as a member of the community, and consequently his personal impact may be greater than many elaborate "development" programs imposed by impersonal and often mistrusted bureaucrats.

Village development is a key preoccupation among villagers as well as the migrants in the city. In their eyes rural development or modernization can be achieved by raising living standards, by securing higher levels of literacy and better communication with the urban centers, by improving agriculture, and, finally, by integrating the village into broader economic and social units with the purpose of making life more comfortable – or by bringing *medeniyet* (civilization) there.[1]

Rural development in Turkey as elsewhere depends on outside stimuli. The squatters visiting the village inadvertently assume the role of informal modernizing agents, as already mentioned, and become part of the stimuli. It is evident that these innovating agents, whatever their origin and qualifications, cannot achieve wide and lasting changes in the village without the support of national programs for economic and social development and without a suitable political atmosphere. It should be mentioned, therefore, that the squatters' modernizing role was facilitated by a variety of general development plans adopted by the government, as well as by a favorable political atmosphere stemming from a liberal multiparty democracy that secured massive rural participation in politics. All this general influence helped open the village to the outside world and increased its receptivity to innovation and change, mediated often by migrants in the city. Finally, the squatters' modernizing role must be related not only to national programs but also to the development philosophies of the local agents, including the village *muhtar* (head man), who assumes vital intermediary functions in establishing village contacts with the migrants in the city, in securing financial assistance from them, and in initiating a variety of projects in the village.

Relations with the village

The overwhelming majority of the *gecekondu* residents had relatives in the village: 95, 91, and 93 percent, respectively, for the men, women, and unmarried. Of 897 respondents included in all three categories in all three settlements, only 66 people said that they did not have any relatives left in the village. These were undoubtedly people who were born and raised in towns and cities and settled in the *gecekondu* in order to avoid paying rent. The recent arrivals who could not bring their families into the city or had a job that did not permit them to take proper care of their wives or children left them in the village. Almost half of the men and women respondents had mothers and fathers or brothers living in the village, while the rest had only uncles, aunts, and cousins or both.[2] The number and the kinds of relatives left in the village are shown on Table 7.1. (The relatively high percentage of fathers and mothers left in the village is a further proof of the fact that the migrants belong to the younger age groups, as mentioned before.) An overwhelming majority of squatters said that they received visitors from the village. More than half of those who received visitors were hosts to one to five people each year and the rest to six or more. Most village visitors were relatives who came just to visit their kin; the rest came to explore employment possibilities or to seek medical care. The distribution of the village visitors is shown in Table 7.2. *Gecekondu* residents, in turn, visited the village rather frequently though somewhat less than their relatives visited the city. See Table 7.3.

Table 7.1. *Squatters' relatives residing in the village* (*in percentages*)

	Men	Women	Unmarried
Own family (wife, husband, children)	3	5	
Mother, father, brother	44	44	24
Uncles, aunts	39	23	52
Other (cousins)	14	28	24
Total	100	100	100

Table 7.2. *Squatters' visitors from the village*

	Men		Women		Unmarried	
	No.	%	No.	%	No.	%
Frequency of village guests:						
Received guests	312	81	320	77	89	75
Did not receive guests	73	19	96	23	30	25
Number of guests received year before:						
1–5	164	58	232	79	63	78
6–10	65	23	31	10	8	10
More than 10	53	19	32	11	10	12
Relationship to guests:						
Relatives	250	73	282	81	80	73
Close friends	91	27	65	19	29	27
Reason for visits:						
Customary visits	201	50	225	57	69	64
Seeking work	110	28	83	21	24	22
Medical care	87	22	57	15	13	12
Other			28	7	2	2

The reasons that squatters visited the village are as follows: to see the relatives (48 percent), to maintain family traditions (to attend wedding ceremonies and funerals), to circumcise their children, to get married, and to help their relatives with field work,

Table 7.3. *Squatters' visits to the village*

	Men		Women		Unmarried	
	No.	%	No.	%	No.	%
Visited	272	72	237	57	61	54
Did not visit	107	28	177	43	53	46
Total	379	100	414	100	114	100

usually at harvest time. (The total number of people who mentioned field work was 33 – 17 men, 12 women, and 4 unmarried.) A number of squatters mentioned specifically that they went to visit the village for *moral düzeltmek* (uplift of morale). Only a few cited permanent attachment to the village or the desire to maintain connections there as key reasons for village visits. Those who did not visit the village at all cited as chief reasons poverty and the absence of relatives there. Interesting enough, however, was the fact that 21 percent of the men and 50 percent of the unmarried who grew up mostly in the city and did not visit the village cited specifically their feeling of strangeness to the village as the chief reason for not visiting.

The extent of the relations between the squatter settlements and the village was dramatized by the existence of two independent bus lines. Twice a week a bus left the squatter settlement for Şiran and served on the way Suşehri and Alucra, the migrants' *kazas,* or district towns. From there onward, they reached the village by jeep, truck, or on foot. In a way it was the symbol of the ability of the poor peasants living in these districts to reach the city of their highest aspirations; as one put it, "We made it from Şiran all the way to Istanbul." The village and the city had come closer in more than one way, thanks to the squatters. The bus line was, indeed, one of the chief channels of communication, which facilitated the flow of people, newspapers, books, and a variety of goods from the city to the village and vice versa. The incessant trips to and from the city, the buses loaded with peasants, chickens, bags of potatoes, onions, beans, and so on, might cause the uninitiated observer to think that the city was being rapidly ruralized while the village remained immersed in its backwardness. Nothing can be farther from the truth. The intensive communication between the city and the village was actually a two-way street. The village sent people to the city and received through them money and ideas.

The squatters' interest in their native village was in many cases maintained and stimulated by the people in the village or the town itself. For instance, the mayor of Koyulhisar, an exceptionally enterprising leader, described his efforts in this respect as follows: "We are urging the people who migrated from this area to send money, or to come and stay, to vacation a few months and spend their money here. They do send money and come and stay. But the main goal is to be here together with them all and strive in common to develop the country." (Very proud of his region, the mayor claimed that people from his area were already very civilized and Istanbul did not change them drastically, except for their eating and dressing habits.)

The squatters' interest in their village was prompted by practical as well as family and kinship reasons. Indeed, 59, 55, and 52 percent of the men, women, and unmarried, respectively, said that their interest in their native village stemmed from practical reasons. Only 30 percent of the men and 18 percent of the women cited a concern for their relatives' welfare or blood relations as the main reason for their interest in the village. The squatters cited as the chief reasons for their interest in the village the presence of personal property, usually land, in the village; the possibility of starting some business there after accumulating money in the city; the security gained by the knowledge of having a place to take refuge in case of economic crisis in the city; an interest in a place for retirement; the need for a place to visit; as well as desire for human communication. It is interesting to note that a number of squatters maintained some relations with the village so that if forced to leave the city for lack of a dwelling, adverse economic conditions, or government pressure, they would have a place to go.

About 22 percent of the men and 38 percent of the women who maintained relations with the village had regular correspondence with the people living there. As may be expected, a sizable number of squatters helped their relatives in the village by sending them money, food, old clothes, or by allowing them to cultivate their land and use their rural houses. Thus, 31 percent of 386 male respondents said that they provided some help to their relatives in the village. The opposite was also true. A number of squatters, usually the younger ones and those who had rural properties, received some assistance from the village, mostly in the form of small amounts of food sent by parents or relatives as the migrants' share in their village property.[3] There were also frequent cases in which squatters sent money and received in exchange locally produced food. The assistance sent from the city to the village, however, was much greater on balance, and, most importantly, it consisted of cash. It appeared that 64 percent of the total assistance sent from the city was in cash; only 27 percent of the total assistance received from the village was in cash. The increased cash flow into the village, it must be stressed, had profound effect on the local economy and the surrounding rural areas since it induced changes in the village as a whole. Indeed, the squatters' help was prompted by a feeling of personal obligation toward their relatives, but also toward the village itself. Indeed, the help to the relatives was sent from individuals, whereas the help to the village was sent from the entire community residing in the city. Consequently, it is necessary to deal briefly with this second important form of assistance.

"Gecekondu" role in village development

An important aspect of the migrant's interest in his native village and in its modernization is his ability as city resident to envisage the dire rural conditions and subsequently to develop a sense of social responsibility toward his village as a whole. This empathy had its roots in kinship relations but was formulated in a practical manner in accordance with the social and political ideology prevailing in the city.[4] For instance, some young squatters who attended school expressed a desire to return as teachers to their villages and help them develop or at least to bring their poverty to public attention. (This idea belonged to a young bachelor attending a school of journalism. The young men in the *gecekondus* had subjective ideological views about village problems and considered themselves responsible for finding a solution to rural underdevelopment.)

The most outstanding example of squatters' interest in village development was a series of associations established by squatters from a specific village with the purpose of developing it. These associations, found in all of the three settlements, bore the name of a village and its purpose – for example, Düzyaylayı Kalkındırma Derneği (Association for the Development of Düzyayla). At the time of the survey in 1968, there were at least seven such associations. Later the number increased to about 20. The district of Şebinkarahisar, with some 50 migrant-sending villages, had a nearly equal number of development associations throughout Istanbul. For instance, the Association for the Development of Kırıntı had 40 members among the squatters and about 60 in the village itself. The individual city member paid a monthly fee of 10 liras; the annual village fee was 10 liras per family. The purpose of the association was to help the village raise its economic and educational standards. It sent to Kırıntı a number of books, including texts dealing with agriculture, as well as a variety of tools and even simple machinery. The association also provided funds to villagers from Kırıntı who came to Istanbul seeking medical care. Another similar organization, the Association for Assistance to Yeniyöl (Anna), established by squatters from that village, contributed 7,000 liras to a program designated to bring water to the village and eventually use it for irrigation. Another organization of the same kind was established by squatters from the village of Düzyayla; it had 80 members in the village and 100 in Istanbul. This association organized a festival in Istanbul and used the proceeds to build the road leading from the village to the town of Hafik. Another organization paid 45,000 liras to have a telephone line established between the village and the district town and even initiated a plan to relocate the village at a better site.

This empathy among the squatters toward their native village was in a way the measure of their own identification with the city. This may be evaluated best by taking account of their reaction toward rural life. More than a majority of all squatters visiting the village said that they felt ill at ease there. Indeed, 59, 38, and 47 percent of the men, women, and unmarried, respectively, claimed that they became *tedirgin* (a mixture of nervousness and uneasiness) while in the village.[5] Many said that they found themselves changed and unable to get along with village people or accept their traditions or live amid the difficult conditions prevailing in rural areas. (See Table 7.4.)

Table 7.4. *Reasons for uneasiness while visiting the village*
(*in percentages*)

	Men	Women	Unmarried
Not used to village life	34	37	50
Alienation (used to city life)	14	20	36
Inability to get along with villagers	11	10	
Living difficulties	14	31	8
Other	27	2	6
Total	100	100	100

The minority who felt comfortable while in the village cited the presence of relatives and familiarity with rural surroundings (usually those who had stayed a short period in the city) as chief reasons for their contentment. Interestingly enough, about 17 percent of the men included in the satisfied category said that they felt comfortable in the village because of the rest it afforded them, since the purpose of the visit was vacation, a luxury totally unknown in the past. Consequently, even this last group can be considered "attached" to the village only because they were there for a short time and took advantage of whatever opportunity for rest and enjoyment it offered.

In comparing themselves with the villagers, an overwhelming majority – 80 percent of all squatters – believed that their life in the city was definitely superior to that of the villagers in every respect; 8 percent thought that it was the same, and only 7 percent claimed outright that their life standard was below the villagers'. This correlates well with the villagers' own views that those who migrated to the city lived well there.[6] Those who considered rural life better than city life felt that villagers had more freedom and independence and better chances to acquire wealth than city dwellers, provided that they gained the skill and knowledge of the latter. This information came in answer to a question that was the preparatory step to another question – namely, whether the squatter considered himself more advanced than the village people. This question was designated to elicit a subjective evaluative answer. The Turkish words used in the questionnaire were *ileri* and *geri* (advanced and backward), which are part of the colloquial Turkish expressing both the quantitative and qualitative aspects of progress. They are used also as political-ideological epithets. The result is shown in Table 7.5.

When asked to cite the reason for their "advanced" situation in comparison with that of the villagers, the squatters gave one or several explanations, which are ranked according to frequency (see Table 7.6).

The results, if compared with the answers concerning the preference for living in the city (see Chapters 2 and 3), show a remarkable degree of consistency, including the women's interest in the city because of its material facilities rather than its cultural opportunities. Possibly the most convincing proof for squatters' growing identification with the city was their firm determination not to return permanently to the village. Indeed, 73, 65, and 81 percent of the men, women, and unmarried, respectively, indicated that they did not envisage returning to the village even when old and retired, despite the possible lower cost of living and the presence of relatives there. And yet the squatters continued to maintain relations with the village and affect its development, as discussed below.

The second aspect of squatter-city-village relations concerns the impact on the village of migration as a whole and of the migrants as individuals – a vital aspect that has not been sufficiently explored. The information below concerning the effect of migration was gathered from rather extensive field observations in some of the squatters' original villages.

Effects of migration on the village

The effects of rural migration in each village varied according to the type of soil and vegetation, availability of water, population density, marketing facilities for locally produced foods, and other factors. In order to facilitate the study of the effects of migration on rural areas the villages that sent migrants to the three *gece-kondus* studied in this work have been divided into three categories largely on the basis of location, which had a determining effect on their economy and demography. These categories are mountain, semimountainous, and valley villages.

Table 7.5. *How squatters compared themselves with villagers* (*in percentages*)

	Men	Women	Unmarried
Squatters are more advanced	81	78	90
Squatters are more backward	5	9	3
Squatters are the same	14	13	7
Total	100	100	100

Mountain villages

The mountain villages in the area south of the Black Sea littoral are located at a high altitude averaging 3000 to 5000 feet. Their summers are short; the crop-growing season is about four months long; rainfall is relatively good in the fall and winter. Heavy snow falls from early December to March, which makes communication extremely difficult. The soil is adequate only for grass and for some tree varieties such as a local wild pear, known locally as *ahlat,* which can be grafted to produce bigger pears with excellent taste. Special varieties of apple and plum trees can also be successfully raised. The mountain slopes are steep. The soil is rather porous and cannot retain humidity. The deep, v-shaped valleys contain fast-running streams that cannot be crossed easily in the winter but are dry in the summer. A few impressionistic lines I jotted after a trip to the village of Gölve may give an idea about the land.

I am sitting next to Arslan the jeepdriver. We are climbing a mountain about 25 degrees steep. The dirt road is about four yards wide. My right foot is stretched rigidly against the jeep's floor. I hold tight to the door bar with my right hand and Arslan's seat with my left hand so I won't be thrown out of the jeep. The front wheels are in a ditch cut in the road by water from a recent downpour while the rear wheels are wiggling left and right to get out from another ditch. I look over Arslan's shoulders down into a ravine about 500 feet deep to see if there is a tree or any obstacle to hold the jeep if it slides over. There is nothing; only dry grass and occasional small amounts of soil washed down by rain. An accident here would be fatal. In the back seat Unal Nalbantoğlu from Hacettepe University, who is assisting me in the research, has difficulty keeping steady. But Arslan, the driver, is unperturbed.

Table 7.6. *Measurement criteria of advancement-progress*
(*in percentages*)

	Men	Women	Unmarried
Better dress	19	21	20
Better food	18	21	17
Better living-housing conditions	19	27	17
Better language (use of Istanbul dialect)	13	8	14
Different (superior) ideas	17	9	19
Superior manners – knowledge	8	5	8
Better work conditions	5	6	3
Use of recreation		1	2
Other	1	2	
Total	100	100	100

"The grader was here a few days ago," he says. "This is O.K. I got so used to these roads that I cannot drive on asphalt – paved roads – anymore." On the way back Arslan drove the jeep toward the village of Konak. The road, four yards wide, occupied the hill crest perched on steep slopes ravished by rains. The jeep stopped abruptly, for the road ended. The view is extraordinarily panoramic and beautiful if one can admire it by forgetting that one sits on a promontory surrounded on three sides by frightening precipices. The only safe way is to back the jeep, which Arslan does easily as though all his life he lived on the brink of death. The village of Konak down half way from the mountain was able to dam several small streams into a simple reservoir. It used the water for irrigation purposes. Konak, which is considered a rich village by local standards, has few migrants and is the envy of the poorer villages around it. But a trip from any of these villages to Konak or to the district city of Şebinkarahisar is a real adventure. It takes two hours by tractor, which is the most frequently used means of transportation, or about eight hours on foot from Gölve to Şebinkarahisar. Yet Gölve has a national distinction; this is the village of Aziz Nesin, the outstanding Turkish novelist and satirist about whom several doctoral dissertations are being written in the United States and Europe.

The main occupation in these mountain villages some 70 or 80 years ago was cattle and sheep raising. At that time the mountains were covered by forests. Eventually trees were cut in order to raise crops to feed the population on a land that was good only for grazing. A large number of these villages were apparently at one time summer settlements of sheep- and cattle-raising mountaineers – a good number of them were nomads – who eventually settled here when the economy of the area was altered drastically by changes in world economy and in the local demography. (See chapters 2 and 3.) The villages of Gölve and Anna (Yeniyöl) can be taken as prototypes of mountain villages and of migration therefrom. The total population of Gölve 20 years ago consisted of 150 families, or about 900 to 1000 people; Anna (Yeniyöl) had about 2000 people. None of these villages, like all in their category, are concentrated in one place either because the land does not permit the building of very many houses together or because people wanted to be closer to their fields.

Gölve today (1974) has five *mahalles,* or quarters, located one to four miles from each other – Ardıçırası, Ayan, Eksiköy, Atölen, and Gere. Anna in turn has three major *mahalles* – Pınarönü, Kavaklı, and Ortamahalle – subdivided into about 20 *mahalles,* each one consisting of a cluster of houses, usually one extended family, as their name often indicated.[7] Communication between these *mahalles* was difficult, especially in winter. Consequently, it was necessary to build schools in each major *mahalle,* in a way a waste of national funds since these schools would be attended by only a few pupils. (I calculated that a proper school system and teachers for Anna would have cost three to five times the total annual production of the village.) Nevertheless, Anna had in 1974 two schoolhouses located at a central point and three teachers, all financed from the national budget. The total livestock in Anna in the summer of 1974 consisted of about 350 sheep, 350 goats, and 500 cattle. However, the total land belonging to Gölve and Anna was enormous, extending approximately 6 to 8 miles east to west and 4 to 5 miles south to north. But it was poor. The richest man in Anna, Zihni Yılmaz (the *muhtar,* who died recently), owned 500 *dönüms,* or about 100 acres, of relatively good land that became partly productive thanks to the availability of chemical fertilizer. But this land was just barely enough to meet the subsistence needs of his son and nephew, who subsequently abandoned it. There was only one tractor in Anna and two in Gölve. The survival and development of mountain villages depended, it seems, on cattle raising and dairy farming rather than the cultivation of wheat. A sound dairy industry can be established in the area only through massive capital investment to change the entire local economy and reassemble villages in a central place. (A plan proposed to centralize Gölve was turned down by villagers who were willing to migrate to the city but not to new housing projects to be developed in their immediate surroundings.)

The creation of marketing facilities for the local products was another condition for developing these villages. Since this could not be done, the villagers took the next alternative: They migrated to cities when the opportunity presented itself. As a consequence of migration, the mountain villages in the Black Sea area (Mindaval region of Alucra district is another migrant-sending area and is in the same situation as the villages described here) lost most of their population through migration to the city. In the summer of 1974 the total population of Gölve's five *mahalles* had dropped to about 36 families, or 200 people, and that of Anna to about 450 people – that is, to about one-fourth of their original population. Thus, both Gölve and Anna had three or four times more people living in various towns and cities (not all the migrants from these villages lived in the settlements surveyed in this study). Most of the villages in the *kaza* of Şebinkarahisar had long established traditions of *gurbetçilik*. Consequently, the *gurbetçi* villages were the first to send permanent migrants to the city. These were followed by inhabitants from other villages that were in a relatively better economic condition. In other words, migration from this area began as a consequence of objective factors but later gained a momentum of its own as the lure of cities attracted others not so hard-pressed as the *gurbetçi*. Paradoxical as it may sound, despite the rapid growth of population, the lack of densely populated settlements was one of the major handicaps preventing concerted community action and development in mountain villages, if one could speak of development at all. (In fact, a few villagers complained that on those rare occasions when they needed help they could not find workers to hire even though wages were up to 100 liras a day, almost twice the average wage earned in the city.)

In the past the *gurbetçis* provided a major part of the income of these mountain villages. Today a part of their income is still provided by squatters in the city. In fact, the villages of Gölve and Anna derive about 50 to 60 percent of their income from remittances from people outside the village. However, emigration from these villages has taken away a large part of the surplus population and has relieved the pressure on the land, enabling those remaining to live better, in part by cultivating larger tracts of land per capita and by receiving help from relatives in the city and abroad.

Yet, the future of these mountain villages remains uncertain in view of the enormous investment in roads, agriculture, and so on, necessary to make them self-sufficient. It is quite possible that some migrants may return to their native villages and, with the money earned in the city and western Europe (this new dimension of migration will be discussed briefly later), organize cooperatives and initiate enterprises suitable to the climate and soil of the area. But the total dispersal and disintegration of these villages seems to be a stronger possibility, especially after the old people in the village die, the migrants in the city become fully urbanized, their ties to the village weaken, and their assistance to the village ceases. In some cases it is the squatters' nostalgia, sense of attachment to the land, the memory (and graves) of parents, and other non-economic reasons that make them keep the mountain villages alive. Even now there are very few young men in these villages since they leave for the city as soon as they are able to work. The village population consists of old men and women and the children of parents working in the city.

Semimountainous villages

The second category of migrant-sending villages are the semimountainous ones, which probably underwent the most significant changes as a consequence of migration. These villages appear at times divided into several *mahalles* or are assembled in a single large unit. For instance, Ovacık had four sections: the central section, which is the seat of the *muhtarlık,* Yukarı Armutlu, Aşagı Armutlu, and Etir. On the other hand, Sarıyer had one satellite village – Kayadibi – whereas Suboyu (Bige), Kırıntı, and Düzyayla (the latter in the Sivas province) formed a single unit. The semimountainous villages are located at lower elevation, closer to the district capital, with better access to the main highways and to the town; their climate is somewhat warmer; water is available, though not sufficient; and they are in general better protected against winds. But most important, these villages often possess relatively large tracts of flat, fertile land that can be made highly productive through the adoption of modern methods of agriculture and even machinery. For instance, Ovacık, Kırıntı, and Suboyu have small tracts of very good land. Houses in these villages are built close to each other and are larger, sturdier, and more comfortable.

Migration from the semimountainous villages varies, largely depending on economic factors – that is, the ability of the land to adequately feed the population. The four units of Ovacık have sent out only about 30 percent of their population, compared with 70 to 90 percent of mountain villages. Interestingly enough, the *mahalle* – actually a village on its own called Etir – of Ovacık sent out relatively few migrants, despite the fact that its location resembles the mountain villages. This was due to the fact that Etir – a cattle-raising settlement – organized its dairy production and found a market for its products. Emigration was 55 percent in Suboyu and about 45 percent in Sarıyer proper. Kırıntı, on the other hand, the best-organized and most prosperous of villages in this category, consisted in 1974 of about 110 families, or 780 people. There were, according to the natives, 2200 people from this village living in Istanbul, Samsun, and Giresun and 60 people working in West Germany. These semimountainous villages also received money from their relatives. Kırıntı, for instance, received annually some 500,000 liras from outside. At least a part of this money was invested in agriculture and crafts, rather than being spent solely on food. (A few of these villages such as Kayadibi and central Ovacık had been originally inhabited by Greeks. Their place was taken by Turkish migrants from Greece exchanged for Greek residents according to an agreement in 1924. Some of these Balkan migrants stayed for a few years and then went to settle in the western part of Turkey. Subsequently, their place was taken by people from other villages, usually from those located in mountainous areas. Some Balkan migrants are still there, as was the case with Trup-çular village.)

A serious problem in these semimountainous villages was caused by economic stagnation and regression after 1913–18, which among other things prevented the villagers possessing some skill from finding employment. For instance, some villagers in this area were excellent carpenters, stone cutters, and had worked in the past on construction jobs in the villages and towns in their neighborhood. When such jobs became scarce many migrated to the city and found employment in the construction industry and showed their skill in building their own squatter houses. A second economic problem after World War I stemmed from the fact that available land was no longer sufficient to feed the growing population. Thus, migration from these villages had a salutary effect in providing those remaining at home with relief from excessive population pressure and with new sources of revenue from outside, which was partly invested locally and stimulated economic activity. Moreover, while the migrants from mountain villages went mostly to large cities, those from the semimountainous villages went also to the closest town or city. For instance, some of the few migrants from Etir went to Şebinkarahisar. One of them, a carpenter, Recep Ekmekçiler, had worked in various villages in the past, and then opened a rather successful carpentry shop (they sold the land in the village and invested the money in their town enterprise) in Şebinkarahisar and on the side engaged in transportation and building businesses.

In general, migration in mountain and semimountainous villages had a definite impact on population growth and economic development. It has lowered the rate of population increase in these areas by shifting the surplus population to cities where it engaged in truly productive occupations. The provisional results of the national census for 1970 indicated that the annual population growth in Turkey as a whole dropped to about 2.6 percent from 1965 to 1970. However, the annual population growth in the provinces of Giresun, Gümüşhane, and Sivas was less than the national average, as shown in Table 7.7. The *kazas* actually lost population. (See Tables 7.7, 7.8, and 7.9.)

The decrease in population pressures in these villages had lessened the demand for food since the same land had to feed fewer mouths. In other words, the departure of a number of men and their families had helped increase the remaining villagers' living standard simply by leaving more food for them. Indeed, about 60 percent of *gecekondu* residents who had property in the village said that their houses and lands were being used by their parents and brothers. Some migrants who possessed better-quality land, usually in semimountainous villages, rented it to other villagers who now, in view of the changes in the village economy, often used it to raise cash crops. For instance, one *dönüm* of land in Ovacık was rented in 1974 for 300 to 1500 liras per year depending on the land quality. It appeared that now only relatively good land

Table 7.7. Population shifts in migrants' districts, 1965–70

	the districts (in 1000s) Total population of			Population of rural areas, bucaks and villages (in 1000s)		
	1965	1970	Annual increase (%)	1965	1970	Annual increase (%)
Turkey	31,391	35,667	2.6	20,544	21,849	1.3
Giresun Province: Alucra	36	36		34	33	— 0.6
Şebinkarahisar	30	30		21	20	— 1.0
Giresun City and other towns	362	381	1.0	296	304	0.4
Gümüşhane Province: Bayburt	104	110	1.2	89	90	0.2
Şiran	30	29	0.7	28	26	— 1.4
Gümüşhane City and other towns	129	143	2.0	114	121	1.2
Sivas Province: Hafik	56	53	— 1.1	53	53	
Koyulhisar	28	29	0.7	26	26	
Suşehri (the town expanded after 1970)	58	61	1.1	50	51	0.4
Sivas City and others	563	586	0.8	406	389	— 0.8
Total of Giresun Gümüşhane, and Sivas	1,396	1,458	0.8	1,117	1,113	— 0.07
Trabzon Province: Araklı	49	52	1.2	45	47	0.9
Sürmene	47	49	0.8	42	43	0.5
Trabzon City and other towns	500	561	2.4	400	433	1.6
Total of Giresun, Gümüşhane, Sivas, and Trabzon	1,992	2,120	1.6	1,604	1,636	0.4

Source: 25 Ekim 1970 Genel Nüfus Sayımı, Telgrafla Alınan Geçiçi Sonuçlar, Ankara, 1970. Figures rounded. A comparison of population shifts in the provinces that receive immigrants and those that send emigrants based on a longer period of time still shows that the increase rates in the latter were much below rates in the former, notably from 1960 to 1965. (See Table 7.8)

was being cultivated, which, economically speaking, brought a
satisfactory return for the capital and labor invested in it. The
food produced in the semimountainous villages after the departure
of the emigrants provided the village population with a rather adequate diet and a small portion of it was sold for cash. Thus, the
living standard in some villages improved to the point where peasants could work longer hours, produce more, save some money,
and finally invest it in agriculture. Investment in agriculture was
something the villagers living in the destitute northeastern region
had not been accustomed to before.

In the past, land had been used to produce food, mostly corn
and beans, nearly all of which was used to quell the villagers' hun-
ger. The desperate peasants cut whole forests in one night and
used the land haphazardly to plant corn or other crops, only to
see the soil washed into the sea in a matter of years. Now, however, in semimountainous villages land was beginning to be used
properly, and some crops were chosen because of their suitability
to the soil and their cash value. For instance, in some villages, such
as Kayacık, the poplar tree was being cultivated systematically for
sale to furniture makers. (One full-grown tree sold for 500 to
2000 liras in 1974.) A *dönüm* (about one-fifth of an acre) may
be planted with up to 200 poplar trees, depending on the quality
of the land and the availability of water. But it takes about 20
years for the poplar tree to reach the cutting size. Some villagers
grafted the wild pear tree, which grew abundantly in the region,
and obtained fruit of excellent quality, which was sold to fruit dealers in Istanbul. Cherry, apricot, and other cold-resistant trees were
also being successfully introduced. Some villagers raised livestock
with the specific purpose of selling it to meat-consuming centers
such as Istanbul and Ankara. Others were engaged in a lucrative
business as livestock collectors and transporters. One such businessman – a villager with many relatives in the squatter settlements
– said that he planned to buy a jeep to tour the neighboring villages to buy additional livestock and to sell them goods purchased
in the city. He was already exporting the locally produced beans
and potatoes to the *gecekondu* residents who preferred homegrown
vegetables. Another villager, a former squatter, bought a taxi with
the money earned in Istanbul and was engaged in the transportation business.

Table 7.8. *Population increase in migrant-receiving provinces*

	1950	1955	% increase	1960	% increase	1965	% increase
Istanbul	1,166,477	1,533,822	31.5	1,188,092	22.7	2,293,823	21.9
Ankara	819,693	1,120,864	36.7	1,321,380	17.9	1,644,302	24.4
Izmir[a]	768,411	910,496	18.5	1,063,490	16.8	1,234,667	16.1
Adana[a]	508,518	628,505	23.6	760,803	21.0	902,712	18.7

Source: Population statistics of the *Turkish Statistical Institute.*
[a] Adana and Izmir receive the migrants from the central and southeastern parts of the country.

Table 7.9. *Population increase in migrant's provinces[a]*

	1950	1955	% increase	1960	% increase	1965	% increase
Sivas	542,004	590,869	9.0	669,922	13.4	704,613	5.3
Trabzon	420,279	462,249	10.0	532,999	15.3	595,782	11.8
Giresun	299,555	334,297	11.6	381,453	14.1	428,015	12.2
Gümüşhane	203,994	211,563	3.7	243,115	14.9	262,731	8.1

Source: Population statistics of the *Turkish Statistical Institute.*
[a] According to a study, the provinces in Turkey that receive the most migrants are Adana, Amasya, Ankara, Hatay, Istanbul, Izmir, Mersin (İçel), Samsun, and Zonguldak. The provinces that send the most migrants are Bilecik, Çankırı, Erzincan, Gümüşhane, Tekirdağ, and Rize. These are exact figures but were rounded in Table 7.7 to obtain a simpler figure for comparative purposes. Erol Tümertekin, *Türkiye' de İç Göçler*, pp. 103–4.

In Koyulhisar the cultivation of fruit and vegetables, notably tomatoes, was very advanced. Lately beehives were being successfully introduced. It was also estimated that the village of Kırıntı could double its annual income if it switched from wheat and oat growing to bee raising since its cultivable land, about 2000 dönüms, or 400 acres, was not sufficient to adequately feed its 780 people. Moreover, there was interest in opening a canning plant as well as in prospecting for minerals in the Koyulhisar and Suşehri districts. Some villagers asked the government specifically for carpet-weaving teachers so as to enable the girls and women to earn money by working in the village, at least during winter months. Already in 1974 some weaving machines were being tested in Şebinkarahisar. Some villagers, because of the increased income, began to use coal to heat their homes instead of *tezek* (dried dung), which had been for generations the chief source of heat for the Anatolian peasant. The manure was now used as organic fertilizer in the fields, which, along with chemical fertilizer, helped increase the quality and quantity of vegetables.

A rather striking development occurred in the villages of Kahrasan, Koyuncular, and Yağmurlu in the province of Trabzon. In the past the men in these villages had been seasonal workers while their wives raised corn and hazelnuts at home in rather negligible quantities; apparently hazelnuts produced satisfactory crops only once in four years. An experiment with raising tea shrubs began in 1953, and it proved to be very successful; consequently, a tea factory was established in the town of Sürmene. Employment provided by the tea-processing plants visibly ameliorated the economic situation in these villages. Consequently, migration from these villages not only came to an end but made employers apprehensive that the growing need for manpower would force them to hire people outside of the province. Nearly all the men above the age of 25 in these villages had been seasonal migrant workers at one time or other in the past and had acquired more pragmatic and flexible attitudes that proved instrumental in rapidly replacing their traditional crops with tea when the latter proved to be financially more rewarding.

The inhabitants in semimountainous villages acknowledge the positive impact of migration in general, and of the migrants in particular, in providing economic help to the village and in generalizing interest in schools, in better living and dressing. Thus, economic development in migrant villages, especially in the semi-mountainous ones, was facilitated by the lessening of demand for subsistence purposes and by monetary assistance and ideas from outside. All this helped not only to moderately increase the general welfare in the village but to restore the ecological processes to their natural course. The cash crops enabled many villagers to buy wheat and eat bread and use the corn that had been their major food staple in the past to feed the horses and cows. Consequently, the farm animals – horses instead of oxen – still used in agriculture became stronger and could now pull the heavy steel plough that tilled the soil inches deeper than the wooden plough, which could only scratch the top. Actually, many semimountainous villages bought tractors, usually seven to eight tractors per village against one or two for the mountain villages. Some villages had raised goats for generations since they were the only animals that could climb rocks to nibble the shrubs and roam over wide areas in search of food. But goats also ate the tree buds and the leaves, preventing the growth of the trees; this became a major cause in the deforestation of Turkey. Now villages that had some other means of survival learned not to raise goats. Some villages began to raise a special variety of sheep chiefly for its wool, which had a good market value. Areas with a relatively abundant rainfall and without goats turned green, as small trees began to grow and nature was allowed once more to follow its ecological course.

The situation described above is a trend of development rather than an accomplished fact. Some mountain villagers still depend on the help of their relatives; some of the villages have been destroyed and depopulated by poverty, land slide, and migration. These are truly ghost villages where the few remaining old people stay as guards and depend entirely "on the salary paid by the *gurbetçi*" (the villages still refer to migrants in the city as such), as one of them put it. Yet, on balance, the economic impact of migration and the help received from outside have been beneficial in stimulating long-range developments. About 40 percent of the men and women and 70 percent of the unmarried felt that after their departure there was sufficient land in the village to assure adequate living for their relatives still residing there.

Valley villages

The indirect impact of migration in villages may be noticed also in the changes occurring in land ownership and land cultivation patterns. However, before dealing with this problem it is necessary to discuss briefly the effect of migration on valley villages – the third category – since land ownership and other more complex problems of agricultural economics concern them more than mountain and semimountainous villages. Most of these villages are located on bottom lands along rivers and highways. Their soil, especially in the Suşehri (Water City) district, is excellent. One of these villages is Güneyli, located on the main road between Suşehri and Şebinkarahisar, and is a prototype. It has a population of about 800 people. Similar to villages of its kind, Güneyli may be considered a rich village. It had in 1974 some 25 tractors and derived excellent income, about 25,000 liras per family, from a variety of crops, especially sugar beets sold to the refinery in Erzincan. (Actually, the Suşehri valley had an economic boom in 1974. The total number of tractors in the district amounted to about 3,000 machines, and 3,500 people were on the waiting list. This compares favorably with the total number of tractors in Turkey in 1946, which was about 2,500.)

Güneyli had sent some 20 families as migrants to cities. Those who left were the landless or insufficiently landed peasants. In other words, these were truly marginal villagers. Some worked as wageearners in the summer on the land of the rich; others were sharecroppers. They left the village in order to seek better wages and a higher status as factory workers, house owners, craftsmen, and businessmen in the cities. Their departure deprived the richer villagers of cheap manpower, indirectly forced them to adopt machinery, and made them cost-conscious about their agricultural operations – that is, it compelled them to modernize their farms.

In a number of other cases, the land that belonged to the migrants was sold or rented to the richer men in the village or town. Consequently, the land that had been parceled into small lots or was unsuitable for large-scale agriculture was now being assembled, however politically undesirable, into fewer hands. Some of these farmers formed or joined agricultural cooperatives and began to introduce modern machinery, as mentioned. They tried to raise the best cash crops by improving the land and its production, but they were faced with a series of problems.[8] Soil analysis (to determine its suitability for specific crops), the use of fertilizers, crop rotation, and especially problems connected with irrigation became major topics of discussion among the villagers. The agricultural program on the national radio, which included discussions on new methods of land cultivation and similar problems, was the most popular broadcast in these areas. Furthermore, the interest in schools, and notably in technical matters related to irrigation and fertilizers, increased rapidly both in the valley and semimountainous villages. Some villagers demanded trained technicians and agricultural specialists to teach them how to increase crop yields. Because of this chain of events related directly to rural conditions, the Turkish peasant, unjustly considered conservative for long, came to appreciate the practical value of science and technology.

However, the economic development in valley villages and their constantly increasing need for water created a series of new conflicts with the mountain and semimountainous villages located on the upper part of the streams. These less-privileged villages wanted to share the increasing wealth in the valley villages either by taking over some of their land or by using the water for their own purposes. For instance, the village of Güneyli was engaged in a bitter conflict with the village located on the slopes of the mountain rising behind it, a conflict that had already caused the death of one person and many court suits. In a number of cases villagers already without much hope for a better life became frustrated by these conflicts, which have often degenerated into village vendettas, and decided to migrate to the cities. In fact, a substantial part of the population growth in Suşehri – its population grew from 3,000 to 12,000 in a few years – was due to migration from poor mountain villages, although only a few of these migrated because of local conflicts.

The economic and behavioral impact of the "gecekondu"

Migration had an important cultural and educational effect in valley villages. Because of their better economic situation and independence, paradoxically enough, these villages were relatively closed to the outside world. Their relatives, friends, and even former servants (many were relatives anyway) in the city provided them with channels of communication as well as with information on machinery, food, and other problems. The same migration to the city psychologically rehabilitated the former landless and poor villagers by giving them a higher status because of their urban life, and many did not hesitate to refer to their former masters as "rich but still peasants."

A powerful economic stimulant to the economy of the region studied in this work, and to the national economy of Turkey in general, was provided by remittances sent by Turkish workers employed in western Europe, mostly in Germany. This international migration (temporary), begun in 1970, brought the total number of Turkish workers in western Europe to about 1.1 million at the end of 1974. Their total remittances in 1974 amounted roughly to $1.2 billion. A good many of these workers went to Europe directly from the region as well as the *gecekondus* studied in this work. According to official sources, the district of Şiran received annually 10 to 20 million liras from workers in Europe. This was an enormous amount of money by local standards; it created inflation and raised the food and land prices, as many workers from the area employed in Europe tried to buy real estate not in their villages but in the district town. The effect of international migration was more evident in towns than in villages. But squatters living in Turkish cities remained far more influential in effecting changes in the village than those living abroad. (International migration is a new topic that falls beyond the scope of this study and will not be dealt with further.) [9]

The sociocultural and educational impact of migrants was evident in all three categories of villages. The effects of communication – that is, ideas and information conveyed from urban centers – and of new leadership were manifest in village politics as well as in the change of attitudes, manners, and living styles. The election of village leaders – *muhtars* – and of the members of the village councils is influenced to a large extent by migrants. The *muhtar* is the most important village administrator both for the local and the central governments. The office is elective and has a degree of autonomy. Since the migrants in the city are a major source of financial assistance, the village in general and the *muhtar* in particular try to be agreeable to them not only in providing them with various documents needed in the city (*nufus cüzdanı,* or citizenship papers, domicile certificates, marriage papers, and, most important, draft notices for the army service), but also in adopting attitudes and policies suitable to their views. The Derneks (Association) for developing the village is one of the squatters' formal channels for affecting village politics. Some of the *muhtars* said that the *gurbetçis* were respected and were offered special treatment while in the village, lest an unfriendly attitude drive them away and quicken their estrangement from the village.

In some cases, as happened in Gölve, squatters from the city came to cast their votes in the election of the village *muhtar;* apparently there was some duplication here in the case of those who had established a domicile in the city. Consequently, the *muhtars* often visited the squatters in the city and paid special attention to their views and suggestions. For instance, the assistance from city migrants to the village of Anna in 1974 showed a sharp decline largely because of a conflict about opening a *Kuran kursu* (Koran reading) course, which the migrants established in Istanbul opposed. This conflict had also undermined the very existence of the Dernek established in the city to develop the village. In some cases the *gecekondu* residents were directly instrumental in influencing the election of the village *muhtar.* In other cases, the new *muhtar* had lived in the city prior to his return to the village, possibly to assume the responsibility for family affairs or engage in business. The villagers considered that the knowledge acquired by such a *muhtar* about the outside world, notably about bureaucratic procedures, and his city experience were qualifications entitling him to leadership. The perennial *muhtar* of Suboyu village, for instance, owed his position to the fact that he had worked in Istanbul before his military service some 20 years earlier. "Had I known that the situation in the city would be so good I would have stayed there," he says in jest. He is a rich man, who has a house in the city that he rented to others. In another village a *muhtar* who had the special qualification of having lived in the city had been elected consecutively for four terms. Although the villagers complained that he was a sharp and biting critic of their shortcomings, nevertheless they were sure to vote for him again, if he decided to run, because he provided them with creative and enlightened leadership. In many other cases the *muhtar* and his family had the multiple role of village leader, innovator, and entrepreneur.

The portrait of the *muhtar* and his brothers in the village of Düzyayla may provide the best illustration for these views. The *muhtar* was a former *gecekondu* resident of Istanbul, where he had lived for several years before returning to his village. This *muhtar* was elected without opposition because the villagers wanted to prove their absolute confidence in him, since as a member of the village council he had displayed outstanding qualities as leader and innovator. Much of the progress in the village, such as roads, water, and public toilets, was attributed to his initiative and know-how. The *muhtar* (about 32 years old at the time of the interview) was a rather taciturn man, but his ideas were clear and his decisions very firm. His leadership abilities had secured him also the confidence of the government officials in the *kaza*.

The *muhtar*'s older brother established himself in Istanbul and seemed to be the leader of the squatters from Düzyayla, living in the Nafibaba settlement. He visited the village in the summer in order to help his brothers, and occasionally brought along his 12-year-old son to "see the difficult conditions of life in the village so as to strive to work harder in the city." Apparently he shared some of the money he earned in Istanbul with his brother, possibly by investing it in agriculture. The *muhtar*'s younger brother (23 years old) had worked in Istanbul in an automobile repair shop. Unable to advance as fast as he desired, he returned to the village. He became the operator of a tractor, which belonged to the entire family (a newly purchased item), but hoped eventually to return to Istanbul to improve his mechanical skills. He was an avid soccer player and, consequently, teamed up a number of village youngsters and played the game with them. The older village residents were at first shocked by the fact that a "grown-up man" (at 23 years of age he should have settled down) taught the village children bizarre city games, such as soccer, and amused himself playing it. Eventually they became reconciled to this mode of recreation.

The *muhtar*'s youngest brother (18 year old) had a stomach ailment and could not work in the field. He dreamed about living in the city. He made efforts to portray his family as well to do and saw the general village situation in a rather positive light. He claimed that everyone in the village had a radio and visited cities.

Moreover, he was very interested in soccer, which he discussed at length.

The *bekçi* (village guard) in Düzyayla was the *muhtar's* most trusted and respected assistant. He enforced the work rules by contacting and reminding the villagers of their responsibilities. His persuasive ability was outstanding. He and the *muhtar* made an excellent team. In a number of other villages, young men, most of whom had worked or visited their relatives in the city, assumed the leadership in the village by ousting the old conservative *muhtars* and councilmen. They instituted sanitation programs, expanded the existing schools, and secured regular class attendance by village children. Moreover, they introduced a series of agricultural innovations. Even in a few villages in which the established rich families continued to elect their henchmen as *muhtars,* there was a definite tendency to bow to the migrants' pressure and bring new men to power. In fact, the social supremacy of these families was challenged because villagers who received help from their relatives in the city became less dependent on the rich and often defied them by voting for their own office candidates. Actually, some of the successful migrants still living in the *gecekondus* were envied by the established village families, who often uttered remarks such as "He [the squatter] worked for us for years, then he went to the city and became rich and now does not even greet us."

The changes in the attitudes, dress, and customs due to the influence of the migrants are an accepted fact in the villages. The inhabitants of mountain and semimountainous villages were rather emphatic in singling out the old *gurbetçis* and the *gecekondu* residents as the chief agents of change. A comparison of the *gurbetçi* villages with a few rare, non-*gurbetçi* villages reveals that the latter have remained relatively more conservative, particularly in family relations, and shown some resistance to innovation, education, and even contact with the outside world. The inhabitants of the *gurbetçi* villages show eagerness to talk to outsiders, are curious about events beyond the village. In fact, the squatters in the city and the inhabitants of *gurbetçi* villages describe these conservative villagers as *geri* (backward), although economically these are relatively more advanced. Despite their poverty the inhabitants of mountain villages give the impression of having no difficulty in establishing communication with city people since their knowledge of Istanbul and intensive communication with it is so intimate. Paradoxical as it may appear, the people from the poorer villages appear the most "modernized," thanks to communication with the city where they have so many relatives.

The relative disappearance of *taassup* (bigotry) in all its forms, notably in religious and family affairs, is another change noticed in the migrant villages. Although parents preserve considerable authority over their children, including their marriage decisions, this is exercised not as the parents' exclusive right but rather as a kind of family affair in which the consensus of the children is sought. This change is due obviously to the influence of the city relatives, who are openly credited with more wisdom and experience in these matters. The idea of adopting city attitudes in family matters has become important, since some mothers hope to marry their daughters to city men, preferably those who have migrated from their own village. The pragmatic attitude of the Turkish peasant with regard to squatters is evident in the proverb often cited by villagers: "Go and seek advice not from the one who claims to know much but from the one who had traveled and seen much" or "A wandering fox is smarter than a sleeping lion."

In the squatters' villages the youth have all adopted city dress to the extent that it is difficult to distinguish them from their relatives in the city. In a few places, women in particular insist on wearing their exceptionally beautiful *üç etek,* the traditional local dress. Men oppose this because such a dress, involving complex embroidery, costs about four times more than the normal city dress for women. Some of the village houses have been built according to city models, by using better construction material and partitioning the house into bedroom, living room, kitchen, and so on. Even the toilet, which was built apart from the house in the past, is now incorporated into the dwelling.

Several squatters have built retirement houses in the village but, except for very few, they have not returned to live there. Another city influence is evident in the food used for breakfast. In the past Turkish peasants in central and northeastern Anatolia usually ate *tarhana* (a tasty and nutritious soup made with wheat flour, dry vegetables, fat, and so on) for breakfast. Now villagers tend to eat cheese and olives and drink tea for breakfast, as do city people. Tea, in fact, is found in every village, however humble. But this modern kind of breakfast has increased the villagers' food expenditure, especially for sugar, and has made them even more dependent on city goods, although the locally produced soup for breakfast had an excellent nutritional value and taste.

A few villagers are rather apprehensive about the influence of the city dwellers on village morality; many others openly admit that the village morality has greatly improved in the last five or six years because of better living conditions. Thus, *kız kaçırma* (abduction, sometimes in order to avoid wedding expenses), though still practiced, is on the decrease. Village customs, such as firing guns at wedding ceremonies or stealing objects well guarded or difficult to carry in order to prove bravery and intelligence, are being rapidly abandoned. Moreover, the *gurbetçi* – that is, the villagers' kinsman in the city – has a basic role in suppressing village quarrels, reconciling the feuding families, and in instilling in all of them a sense of village identity and pride. The parties listen to him not only because of his experience and knowledge gained in the city and the higher status he derives from it, but also because he is above petty quarrels. Some attribute the revival of *imece* (communal work for improving public services) in some villages to the suggestions and pressures of the *gurbetçi*. In Kırıntı in particular *imece* is widely practiced. Consequently, roads, bridges, and schools have been built and repaired and sanitary public toilets established in many villages where there is a sufficient number of people – in semimountainous and valley villages.

The radio, the record player, and lately the tape recorder reached the village first via the migrants. The transistor radio in particular has become a common commodity. Some village homes possess two or three sets; at times, even the village shepherd carries one in the hills while grazing his herd.

The village has come close to the city and to the world at large. One has a feeling that because the city, and especially the modernity it represents, has come so close to the village some villagers have begun to show some reluctance to move to the city. In fact, some seem to have begun to think about bringing to the village the knowledge and the means that created the urban welfare. The migrant in the city has been, in good measure, responsible for having created a new state of mind and new conditions in the village. And maybe all that he has helped bring to the villager carries with it a promise, possibly a solution, to the problems that had forced him move to the city. He might have found the remedy to the very problems that had forced him to migrate.

8. Politics and party affiliation in the *gecekondu*

The stages of integration

Politics and sociopolitical processes covering all aspects of individual and collective life have profound transforming and integrative functions in the *gecekondu*. Probably no other activity is as instrumental as political action in achieving the squatters' urban and national integration.[1] This study has adopted the view that the squatter's position with regard to the village and the city is marginal and that the degree of marginality with regard to either changes according to the squatter's urban occupation, level of income, and length of stay in the city. Integration into the city, or urbanization, which puts an end to marginality, has been regarded as a part of a broader process of political acculturation and internalization of urban and national values, which transforms the squatter's personality and even the culture of the city in which he lives. The process of integration-urbanization politicizes many values and concepts in the migrant-squatter's traditional culture by relating them in an active situational manner to his status and needs in the city. This chain of migration-squatterization-urbanization, or integration-politicization, among migrants occurs in several stages in the form of interrelated and overlapping socioeconomic processes built around marginality.

Marginality

Marginality begins with the decision to leave the village and is based on a subjective evaluation of objective conditions in the village (the place of origin) and in the place of destination (the town or city). At the beginning marginality to the village is minimal and to the city maximal. It alters subsequently in accordance with the migrant's occupation, income, and so on, in the city. The change in the degree of city marginality occurs through actions induced or created mostly by the migrant and his relatives and friends and conditioned by the urban and economic environment, and by government decisions. Thus, from the start, the migrant-squatter sees his marginal relation to the city and the village, as well as the potential remedy. In other words, the drastic change in the migrant's social position mobilizes him psychologically for political action. If the sociopolitical conditions in a locality or the political regime in the country allows for self-initiated individual or group actions designated to satisfy some needs and demands, the squatter's psychological mobilization leads to concrete action.

Integration into a squatter community

Integration into a squatter community is the second major step preparatory to urban integration. A powerful sense of community and solidarity at the local level is essential for successful political action and integration into the city, provided that the implicit or explicit purpose of that community is related to such an integration. The squatters' defense of their dwellings and land and the perceived economic security to be gained from the ownership of urban property have powerful integrative effects on the squatter community. This is not, it should be stressed, a village community, despite strong elements of rural culture in it, but a transitional one created in answer to specific urban conditions. The need to defend the squatter community increases the sense of interdependence and assures participation in political action inside and outside the settlement.

Awareness of needs

Individual and group awareness of needs in the settlement has profound political effects on the squatters.[2] These needs may be divided into three categories: (1) the immediate objective needs, stemming from the actual living conditions prevailing in the settlement, such as food, clothing, and water; (2) the perceived needs related to squatters' occupation, professional training, children's education, and so on; (3) the aspired, or long-range, needs, such as moving up the social ladder, occupying a position, operating an enterprise, which are part of what the squatter considers to be the real life of a successful city dweller. The idea of ameliorative action, and the level of it that is political action, as Cornelius saw it, depends on the level of consciousness concerning those needs.

Satisfaction of needs through demand making

Formulating demands and entrusting them to an individual deemed capable of satisfying those demands has the side effect of transforming elements of the traditional culture into current political symbols and values that have practical relevance. In the case of the Turkish squatters, the demand making transformed the traditional and mythical *devlet baba* (father state), an aloof, authoritarian semideity, into a living government – into human organization that could be manipulated to do or undo certain acts, especially with regard to the *gecekondus*. In other words, demands formulated on the basis of objective needs led inevitably to the rational, interest-oriented search for individuals capable of taking concrete action to satisfy those needs. This, to put it simply, was the conversion of traditional elements of political culture into dynamic factors of current political action, whereby the government was expected to satisfy individual needs rather than merely discharge cultural, religious, or communal integrative functions as in the past. Moreover, the formulation of demands, and especially addressing them to higher forums in the city and the government, compelled the squatter to realize that he and his settlement were part of a bigger entity – the city and the nation – which also possessed the power to drastically alter his life.

The legitimization of demands

Legitimization of demands is of major importance in the squatters' internalization of the urban and national political culture. The squatter must provide a rationale for himself and for others to justify his demands addressed to the city and the national government. He may claim that he is entitled to some recognition and satisfaction of demands because he is part of what may be called the national community or the country. The squatters in Turkey, for instance, claim loudly that they are also *vatan evladı* (a son of the fatherland), that they have the same language and customs and are as patriotic, if not more, than the rest of the city and the country. They may claim that the satisfaction of their demands is part of national goals that they would share even more fully if they were integrated into the system. Moreover, they do not hesitate to associate themselves with modernity, secularism, and reforms often by using the language of the power elites. In doing so, the squatter identifies himself with and gradually internalizes the political symbols and values of the dominant ruling political groups, which often are the spokesmen and promoters of the national political culture. Thus, the squatter identifies himself with the urban-national political culture to a degree far more pronounced than the older city residents or villagers simply because he does it consciously and self-interestedly. Some of the marginal ethnic and linguistic groups may be assimilated culturally into the larger group during this phase of squatters' urban integration.

The values and symbols, the rights and obligations associated with egalitarian participatory political democracy work to a large extent to the migrant-squatter's benefit. Indeed, today's understanding of democracy stressing the individual rights and freedoms without regard to ethnic or social origin provides the squatter with a strong political ideological platform for formulating and insisting on his demands. Yet, all these developments inevitably associate the squatter with the system and hasten his integration into the city and the national political culture, a process that began in the village very slowly and accelerated in the city.[3]

Political action

The culminating phase in this process of political mobilization and acculturation, and urban integration,[4] fed by powerful forces stemming from the squatter's marginality, is concrete political action. Such action provides satisfaction for the migrant's demands and needs. The organization of political activity within the settlement and the contact and bargaining with holders of or candidates for political offices and with political parties are part of the politics of demand satisfaction. It is quite understandable therefore that politics in the squatter settlement is not inspired by radical ideologies. However, such ideologies can find acceptance in the settlement if the normal channels for demand satisfaction and political participation are closed to squatters.

Politics in the settlements of Nafibaba, Baltaliman, and Celâlettin Paşa in Istanbul was studied at both local and national levels by analyzing the election of the *muhtar* and the squatters' behavior in national elections. The squatters' answers to political questions posed during interviews expressed a high level of political consciousness, which might have been absent in the village.

The principal goal pursued by the *gecekondu* dwellers in local and national politics was to assure the survival of the settlement, to secure its incorporation into the city, and to obtain the benefits that this incorporation entailed. In this respect *gecekondu* politics is transitional – that is to say, it follows an expedient course until the settlement is fully incorporated into the city. Afterward, the *gecekondu* politics may conform more closely to the national trends. In the current phase of the migrants' transition from a rural to an urban existence, politics intensifies communication and social mobilization and facilitates the Turkish *gecekondu* dwellers' participation in city affairs, and thus speeds up their integration into an urban environment.

The formal associations established by the *gecekondu* dwellers, such as *Gecekonduyu Güzelleştirme Derneği* or the Derneks, whose outward purpose is to improve the settlement's appearance, function also as liaison office between dwellers and political parties and conduct political bargains with city and even national politicians. The Derneks are also the focal point of group activity where a new type of leadership emerges, based not on the previous religious, tribal, or communal authority held in the village of origin, but chiefly on organizational skill and ability to represent and defend the interests of the settlement in political and administrative circles. (See Chapter 5.) Belonging to political parties and campaigning and voting in elections provide the *gecekondu* dwellers with additional opportunities to establish communication and to relate, on an equal footing, to the other members of the national political community.

The traditional background of squatters' political culture

The squatters' political culture has its traditional roots in both the communal and the Ottoman political culture. The two seem to have converged to shape the squatters' basic political attitudes in their villages of origin. The political culture disseminated by the Ottoman central authority in the past took account of the communal, religious, and ethnic loyalties of the subjects. It subsumed their loyalties within a hierarchical bureaucratic structure whose function was to preserve and perpetuate the communal, religious, and ethnic groups, whatever their specific denomination. This political culture was eminently suited to the communal type of relations that prevailed in the villages; it maintained the equality among community members and promoted obedience toward the higher authorities at all levels. Thus, this approach established a congruence of authority between the lowest social unit and the highest forums of power. It is probably this feature that distinguished the Ottoman political system from those of the other Islamic empires where local and central authorities were not always congruent.

The Ottoman system aimed at maintaining the social and political status quo, and the ruling bureaucratic group achieved it through group balance. Notwithstanding abuses and pressure by the bureaucratic-dynastic order, the government portrayed itself as created to seek the good of the community through justice. Society itself was considered a consequence of man's search for mutual help. The principal goals of the political order were conceived within the framework of a philosophy that called for providing order, security, and the observance of the law so that both the society and the government could fulfill their missions. Traces of this powerful Ottoman culture, which filtered to villages throughout centuries, were evident in the squatters' political behavior. Egalitarianism and the belief that the wish of the humblest peasant and the will of the government were somehow congruent – or should be made so – appeared to be among the outstanding features of the migrants' political culture. Incidentally, these traditional political beliefs were partly responsible for facilitating the acceptance of democracy and the modern election system among villagers.

Certain surviving effects of the Ottoman political culture can be seen in the squatter's concepts about *devlet* (state) and *hükümet* (authority, also government). The squatters view the state as an indispensable political organization that cannot be forsaken in any way. Its role is perceived to be similar to that of a father. The idea that man must live in some form of organized political society is the squatters' cardinal political belief. The state is regarded as established for the people's common good and protection, and as a sort of moral being that can not do wrong. If it fails in its protective mission the fault is attributed to the men who act on behalf of the state. The *gecekondu* dwellers seldom criticize the state or the municipality directly as being inherently bad or useless. They have, in fact, a rather optimistic belief that the state is benevolent and ultimately will protect them and, incidentally, issue the legal titles to their houses. This magnanimous state is regarded as a protector, a provider, a mystical father, and consequently there is nothing immoral in establishing a house on its property. "We have built our dwelling," explained a squatter, "on the land of our father, the state. We took it and built on it. We came and settled on this empty land which belonged to the father state. Is this a crime? Do you think that it would have been better to steal or beg instead of taking refuge on its land? The state land was empty. We decided to earn a living by using it and pay our taxes and thus make it productive." (According to the traditional Ottoman-Islamic law, *ihya* – that is, making land productive or useful – in some ways creates a bond of ownership between that land and the person who rehabilitates it.) Other squatters repeated the maxim *"Allah devlete zeval vermesin"* (May God preserve the state), which is still one of the most often heard expressions in Turkey.

Authority is regarded as a necessary instrument for the state to fulfill its mission. It is, in fact, the essence of state. However, the squatters no longer regard, as might have been the case in the village, divine will as the source of state authority. Neither do they accept the upholding of some sacred precept as a sufficient argument to legitimize the use of that authority. They see the essential justification for the existence of the state in its continuous endeavor to materialize the protective and providing missions regarded to be the very essence of the state in a manner useful to the individuals, including the squatters themselves.

Leaders play an important part in relating the community to the state. In accordance with communal traditions, the leader provides a two-way channel: first, in transmitting the authority of the state to the community, and, second, in conveying the community's demands upward to the state's *vekil* (representative). The best leader is the one who can interpret and convey most effectively and accurately the sentiments and aspirations of the community to the highest forums and who can also find means to fulfill them. The community and its welfare appear as the chief goals that ultimately justify many of the demands and the steps taken to realize them.

This mixture of mysticism and pragmatism may explain both the squatters' respect for the community and the state and the petty political deals they make to obtain material benefits for the *gecekondu*. The squatters' idea of community and state derives from the traditional village culture, whereas the demands related to the welfare of the *gecekondu* represent a new dimension of the political culture evolving in the *gecekondu*. Most of the demands voiced by the *gecekondu* dwellers have their basis not in the traditional culture but in concrete needs and in the modern ideas of social rights that are barely taking root – hence a high degree of idealization on a theoretical level and an equally high degree of materialism on the practical level.

The impact of modern political ideas on the changing traditional political culture is evident. Some modern elements in the political culture of the squatter community derive from the national experience of the 1920s. Turkey became a Republic in 1923. A series of new institutions such as a unicameral assembly, a centralized bureaucracy, modern fiscal and educational organizations, and a variety of cultural reforms gave the political system an outwardly modern outlook. These changes were imposed by the Republican People's party (RPP), which ruled Turkey until 1945–50. After that period a parliamentary system with universal suffrage, direct elections, opposition parties, and a relatively free press were introduced gradually or were allowed to emerge by themselves. Eventually the Democratic party (DP) won the elections in 1950, largely through the peasant vote, and again in 1954 and 1957, but in 1960 the government of premier Adnan Menderes was toppled by a military coup.

The electoral success of the DP leaders was due to their prag-

matic and realistic understanding of the Turkish communal philosophy and of the fundamentals of the leadership tradition in
villages and towns. They supplemented this understanding with a
policy of economic incentives, bringing some relief and satisfaction
to a considerable number of villagers. Menderes not only relied on
the communal traditions prevailing in the Turkish villages but he
also revitalized them through the use of modern concepts and
practices, such as political equality, suffrage, and national elections.
He eventually taught the populace to equate equality, rights, and
freedoms with demands for welfare and material progress. He then
exploited the demands thus formulated for his own political ends;
however, by doing so Menderes moved Turkish politics to a new
stage for demand-making and demand-satisfying action.

Civilian rule in Turkey was reestablished in 1961, following the
adoption of a new constitution based on a rather sophisticated
model of liberal parliamentary democracy. A two-house legislature,
a constitutional court, and checks on the executive guaranteed all
freedoms and rights including elections. Thus, for half a century
since 1923, Turkey has been governed as a republic. A quarter of
a century of this time was spent under democratic rule. The most
dramatic impact of the democratic political experience was felt by
the lower classes. The direct vote, regular elections, personal relations with legislators, and relatively easy access to government offices, as well as a number of material benefits derived from party
politics, gave the lower classes, especially the peasants, a sense of
importance and of equality with the upper classes; this subsequently
enhanced their attachment to democracy as the origin of all these
rights and benefits. Moreover, a quarter of a century of democratic
experience intensified social mobility and exposed all Turks, but
especially the peasants and lower urban classes long ignored by the
elites, to intensive political education. The effects of this education
may be seen in the squatters' opinions concerning some key concepts and institutions of modern politics. Interest in and knowledge
of politics are in themselves evidence of political mobilization.

Party politics

Participation in party politics as measured by reported turnout
levels at elections was very high among *gecekondu* dwellers. Participation rates were notably high among men above age 35, pos-

sibly indicating better appreciation of the advantages of general suffrage among those who could remember the pressures of the one-party rule. An average of 81 percent of the men and 63 percent of the women said that they voted regularly in all elections. In the senatorial and local elections of 1968, 89 percent of 388 male respondents and 71 percent of 430 female respondents said that they participated in the elections, which compares favorably with the 71.2 percent national participation in the general elections of 1965, 64.3 percent in 1969, and 66.8 in 1973. True, the election of the *muhtars* in 1968 might have generated special interest because of its immediate relevance to the *gecekondu* interests. Still, even in the 1965 elections the rate of participation among squatters was higher than the national one; it was 78 percent among the men and 72 percent among the women.

The squatters seemed to consider voting a manifestation of communal opinion. According to the squatters' own interpretation, the opinions of various communities converged to form the national consensus, which has mandatory power. Voting, therefore, is a way of transforming the communal opinion into a political will and into a political vehicle for obtaining material benefits. Many squatters also held the view that one had a duty to vote for his chosen party, as shall be seen later. Consequently, a very high percentage of the squatters believed in the importance of voting, as shown in Table 8.1.

The particular reasons given for the belief in the importance of voting showed great variation; 31 percent of the men and 42 percent of the women believed that voting is important because it lends support to and secures the victory of one's chosen party. Preference for a particular party carried in the squatters' view the obligation to assure its success. In other words, option makes loyalty mandatory. Twenty-four percent of the men and only 10 percent of the women believed that voting is effective in electing the national leaders – that is, "the men who shall guide us." On the other hand, 17 percent of the men and only 3 percent of the women considered voting a citizenship duty in the modern sense. Seven percent of the men and 19 percent of the women thought that voting in general is a means to secure material gains. The rest believed that voting provides the means to avoid dictatorship, to subject the administration to public control, to assure the progress of the country, to raise the quality of government, and to express

Table 8.1. *Belief in the importance of voting*
(*in percentages*)

	Men	Women	Unmarried
Important	85	66	79
Not important	9	9	5
Does not know	6	25	16
Total	100	100	100

a consensus.[5] Those who did not have faith in voting – 31 men and 30 women only – attributed their skepticism chiefly to the facts that voting does not secure them any visible benefits, that their vote cannot affect the country's administration in the least, that politicians do not keep their word, and that voting stimulates intra-party struggle and rivalry in the country.

Parliamentary democracy, as mentioned before, was introduced in Turkey after World War II through the acceptance of a multi-party system and of direct elections. It had not been preceded by a long period of preparation and indoctrination. Consequently, squatters were rather confused about the meaning of democracy. Nevertheless, 59 percent of the men and an insignificant 7 percent of the women replied that they knew and understood the meaning of democracy. (See Table 8.2.) An additional 12 percent of the men said either that there was not any democracy in Turkey or that it was not properly implemented. These latter belonged mostly to the socialist Labor party (TLP).

The respondents seemed to regard equality as the chief characteristic of democracy. Emphasis on freedom, self-government, economic opportunity, and proper service by government officials implied a perception of democracy as a means to end the inequality between the elites and the masses, and, much less, as an avenue leading to the establishment of social equality between the rich and the poor. The same view of equality as the principal characteristic of democracy prevailed among peasants, although their opinions on economic and social equality were rather vague. However, the squatters, as well as the villagers, whose political opinion I tested on other occasions, were not predisposed toward abstract conceptualization.

Table 8.2. *The meaning of democracy*
(*in percentages*)

	Men	Unmarried
Freedom to act as one wishes	26	15
A regime of freedom for all	15	10
A lack of repression	10	13
Functional government (a government to satisfy human needs)	8	14
Economic opportunity	7	13
Equality of rights	6	8
Proper service by officials	5	7
Self-government	4	10
The defense of individual rights	4	1
The state of law	4	2
The right to complain	1	
Other	10	7
Total	100	100

Note: Women were not included because a very small number answered this question.

The squatters had a much clearer comprehension of the role of political parties, with which they were acquainted closely through practical experience (Table 8.3). In fact, the meaning and functions attributed to political parties often coincided with what an individual raised in an established parliamentary system may regard as being the definition of democracy. The majority of the men and the unmarried believed that political parties in a multiparty system were useful instruments of government, whereas almost half of the women pleaded ignorance on the matter.

The essential functions of political parties, according to the respondents, were the following: to control the government, to enable a competitive selection of best policies, to adopt development plans, to provide political education, and the like, as shown in Table 8.4.

Respondents, notably the men, made rather subtle comments on the advantages and disadvantages of the two-party and multiparty systems.[6] National unity and economic development with political

Table 8.3. *Opinion on political parties* (*in percentages*)

	Men	Women	Unmarried
Parties are useful	72	37	66
Parties are not useful			
– one party is sufficient	22	19	24
No opinion	6	44	10
Total	100	100	100

Table 8.4. *Reasons for the existence of political parties* (*in percentages*)

	Men	Women	Unmarried
Control of government	32	5	10
Mutual criticism and selection of best policies	16	21	11
Competition and the achievement of progress	13	15	13
Prevention of dictatorship	12	10	16
Providing forums to discuss economic development	13	16	19
Focusing attention on the individual citizen	8	13	15
Providing political education	2		10
Constituting a bulwark against the return of the sultanate	4	1	6
Other or do not know		19	
Total	100	100	100

stability were the chief reasons given by those who favored the two-party system; individual freedom, private enterprise, and control over the government were emphasized by those who supported the multiparty arrangement. A minority who had an unfavorable opinion about the usefulness of political parties actually preferred a one-party over a multiparty system. Over 50 percent of those who did not believe in the usefulness of political parties thought that parties disrupted national unity and created disorder. (See Table 8.5.)

Table 8.5. *Reasons for opposition to political parties* (*in percentages*)

	Men	Women	Unmarried
Disorder and division	53	56	50
Internecine fights	16	11	10
Very limited usefulness	12	11	20
Preference for strong government (one-party system)	14	19	15
Other	5	3	5
Total	100	100	100

Those who rejected political parties seem to have been guided essentially by a sense of group solidarity rooted in communal unity and by fear that political activities would disrupt it. Thus, once more communal background seemed to carry considerable weight over individual opinions about political parties and politics. It must be stressed, however, that this was true for only a small minority.

The *gecekondu* settlers were firmly convinced that their association with the political parties was motivated by a moral obligation toward the country and the government rather than by personal gain. Indeed, notwithstanding contradictions in actual practice, only 5 percent of the men and 3 percent of the women believed that voting for a *specific* party provided personal benefits to the voter. The Turkish political culture developed by the elites in the past, and still surviving in the era of multiparty politics, remains encumbered with rigid stereotyped ideals of perfection, morality, abnegation, and sacrifice, which many politicians brandish in their public speeches but few adhere to. The squatters also talked about ideals of moral perfection and of sacrifice for the sake of national goals, although in practice they were rather practical and opportunistic.

A large number of squatters viewed the political parties also as modern channels of communication with the government (Table 8.6). In fact, a large segment believed that one could not communicate with the government without political parties. Other squatters, however, named a number of alternative channels to reach the government.

Table 8.6. *Forms of communication with government* (*in percentages*)

	Men	Women	Unmarried
Through political parties only	48	35	36
Through the press	3	5	13
Through *muhtar* and the police	17	24	12
Through *vali* and *kaymakam* (administrative heads)	5	6	2
Through municipality	3	5	2
By personal, oral demand	9	15	11
By written petition	12	8	20
Through organizations	1		
Other means	2	2	4
Total	100	100	100

Most of these alternative channels had been used, in fact, to reach the governments prior to the advent of multiparty democracy in the late 1940s. In the villages the *muhtar* is still the chief agent of communication with the government.[7] The same can be said about the *muhtar* in the cities, although his role is more technical and administrative. In cities and towns, the *karakols* (police stations in districts), besides their main responsibility to maintain security, are still used as a channel of communication, often to convey demands and grievances to the central government. Some of those who thought of directly addressing the government in person or in writing were probably still under the influence of the petition system, constituted the backbone of the redress mechanism open to subjects during Ottoman rule. It is on the basis of these individual or group requests or complaints, whatever the case may be, that the Sultan issued his *adaletname* (order to redress wrong). However, the answers to questions about voting behavior and party affiliations, and especially about politics at the local level, leave little doubt that the political behavior of the squatters has been conditioned primarily by contemporary issues and practical interests, usually revolving around the *gecekondu*.

The squatters' political behavior in national elections seemed to be influenced essentially by the interests of the *gecekondu* as a whole, but also by national issues and ideas.[8] The political parties exposed the *gecekondu* to constant propaganda and pressure under the assumption that the squatters' votes might be easily won with various promises of reward. The candidates, usually accompanied by party members from the settlement, addressed the dwellers repeatedly. An overwhelming majority of the residents – that is, 88, 84, and 91 percent of the men, women, and unmarried – were aware of the visits made by the party candidates and many reported listening to their speeches. However, actual membership in political parties was limited: only 14 percent of 381 male respondents and 3 percent of 406 female respondents (Table 8.7). The number of votes cast for various parties, however, reached significant proportions. The squatters referred to the elections of 1968, for senate and local officials. (The results of national elections of 1969 have been taken from official records.) The reported distribution of votes among parties is shown in Table 8.8.

Voting behavior

An overwhelming majority of the *gecekondu* residents reported voting for the ruling Justice party. The reported distribution of votes among the political parties was confirmed by the official results at three polling stations where most of the *gecekondu* voters cast their ballots in the national elections of 1965 and 1969 (Table 8.9). It is interesting to note that the percentage of votes received by the socialist Labor party in the *gecekondu* was higher than its national average. It received 2.7 percent of the total electorate vote in 1969 as against 9 percent in the *gecekondu*. The same is true for the liberal Justice party (JP), whose country average was 46.5 percent in 1969 but 61 percent in the *gecekondu*. In the same elections, the leftist-statist RPP drew less support in the *gecekondu* than in the country at large. This is indeed surprising since a majority of squatters voted for the RPP while in the village, as shall be discussed later.

Concerns about material welfare seemed to predominate in the choice of a party in the elections of 1968. A breakdown of the reasons offered by the voters for choosing a party is shown in Table 8.10. It suggests that while the men were influenced by pragmatic concerns in voting for a party, the women generally followed the advice of their husbands and relatives.

Table 8.7. *Party membership*

	Men		Women		Total	
	No.	%	No.	%	No.	%
Justice (JP)	32	60	8	73	40	62
Republican People's (RPP)	17	32	2	18	19	30
Nation (NP)						
New Turkey (NTP)	1	2			1	2
Republican Peasants' National (RPNP)						
Reliance (RP)						
Labor (TLP)	2	4			2	3
Unity (UP)	1	2	1	9	2	3
Total	53	100	11	100	64	100

Table 8.8. Gecekondu *vote distribution in the local elections of 1968*

Party	Men		Women	
	No.	%	No.	%
JP	189	60	148	62
RPP	75	24	64	27
NP	9	3	5	2
NTP	1			
RPNP				
RP	1		2	1
TLP	35	11	17	7
UP	5	2	2	1
Independent	1			
Combined	1			
Total	317	100	238	100

Note: In Tables 8.7 and 8.8 bachelors are excluded; because of their young age, only a fraction of them can become party members and vote.

The men registered and voted for a party mainly as a result of information received during political campaigns and, less often, through newspapers. For the women, the information supplied by

Table 8.9. *Election results at polling stations in Rumelihisar* (*where most squatters cast their votes*)

	Station number 5		Station number 10		Station number 12
	1965	1969	1965	1969	1965[a]
Registered voters	300	315	283	282	295
Actual votes cast	170	202	195	150	213
Valid votes	166	190	190	145	201
JP	75	83	84	86	121
RPP	61	73	81	28	56
TLP	21	13	13	4	6
NP	6	3	5	4	11
NTP	2	12	3	4	2
UP		3		9	
RP		0		7	
RPNP/NAP	1	3	0	3	0
Independents	0	0	4	0	5

Sources: 1950–1965 Milletvekili ve 1961, 1964 Cumhuriyet Senatosu Üye Seçimleri Sonuçları (State Institute of Statistics), Ankara, 1965; *12 Ekim 1969 Milletvekili Seçimi Sonuçları* (State Institute of Statistics), Ankara, 1970.
[a] This polling station was in Rumelihisar in 1965, and in 1969 it was located in Emirgân.

relatives provided an alternative source (Table 8.11).

The results also indicate that political parties were able to penetrate into the smallest settlements and mobilize individuals directly. Indeed, political parties played a major role in increasing awareness among the lower classes about their place in society and their political rights. The fact that the political parties were seeking votes and not sociopolitical awareness does not alter the outcome of this process of politicization. Moreover, the results presented above suggest that oral communication and personal relations played a major part in spreading information and in facilitating the *gecekondu* dwellers' choice of a political party. This observation leads to a discussion of the squatters' perception of party "activists."

Table 8.10. *Reasons determining choice of party (in percentages)*

	Men	Women
Beneficial to country	18	8
Useful to *gecekondu*	15	16
Provides employment	14	8
Affinity with squatters and all people	9	5
Care for the poor	8	9
Most popular party (everybody votes for it)	8	7
Good party leaders	7	7
Established, rooted organization	7	3
Trustworthy promises	3	2
Class affiliation	3	2
Other (feeling of obligation, advice of relatives)	8	19
Spouse's advice		14
Total	100	100

Note: The unmarried are excluded because only a small fraction of them were of voting age.

Table 8.11. *Sources of information about parties (in percentages)*

	Men	Women
Election speeches by candidates	28	17
Party propaganda, pamphlets, contacts	25	9
Newspapers	23	6
Information supplied by members (father, husband)	7	41
Information supplied by relatives	7	17
Record of achievement	3	
Other	7	10
Total	100	100

Note: The unmarried are excluded because only a small fraction of them were of voting age.

Political preferences

The Turkish political parties maintain permanent organizations and have a number of members who are constantly active. These party "activists" play an important part in recruiting followers and voters for their party. The squatters were asked to identify the party activists to whom they felt very close and those to whom they felt very distant and to explain the reasons for these attitudes (Table 8.12). The unmarried, who generally did not vote because of age, nevertheless had their own opinions about these activists, proving once more the relatively high level of political awareness in the *gecekondu*.

A comparison of election results (Tables 8.8 and 8.9) with the party affiliations of the activists toward whom the squatters expressed affinity (Table 8.12) indicates that more people voted for the JP than felt close to its activists. This is so probably because the JP was the ruling party at the time and promised to issue deeds to the land. The same is true for the RPP, which is the oldest political party in Turkey. On the other hand, more people felt close to the TLP activists than voted for TLP. If the TLP had not deviated to leftist extremism, its chances of success in the long run would probably have been enhanced.

The reasons cited by the *gecekondu* residents for their support or rejection of party activists (Tables 8.13 and 8.14) were rooted either in concrete events or in the traditional political culture. For instance, squatters who said that they liked a politician because he had "deep roots" probably had in mind the politicians who belong to well-established families and had been long associated with power and position. This type of politician generally belonged to the RPP. It is interesting to note that the squatters who emphasized "deep roots" as determining their choice of leaders came from the two oldest age groups; evidently, they regarded established position as more important than personal qualifications. On the other hand, ideological consciousness, which can be considered a modern concept in Turkish politics, is inversely related to age. Nine percent of the total number of answers given by the oldest age group are related to ideological affinity; the percentages are 14, 17, and 18, respectively, as age groups get younger. Men in the 26 to 35 and 36 to 45 age groups, especially the latter, supported the JP most

Table 8.12. *Squatters' feelings about party activists* (*in percentages*)

	Men		Women		Unmarried	
	Close	Distant	Close	Distant	Close	Distant
JP	44	9	47	18	37	26
RPP	19	12	28	20	30	15
TLP	15	31	10	17	19	26
NP	2	5	2	6	2	6
RP	1	6		3		4
RPNP/NAP			1			
UP	1	5	1	3	5	6
NTP	1					
All parties	6	9	2	4		2
None	11	13	9	25	7	4
Other		10		4		11
Total	100	100	100	100	100	100

enthusiastically. Interviews indicated that among these men, those who still remembered the one-party rule played a major role in keeping the opposition toward the Republicans alive, and thus helped to increase the support for the JP.[9] The JP politicians were appreciated for their pragmatic outlook and informal ways in dealing with the *gecekondu* residents. The reason for the increased support for the RPP politicians among the youngest men can be attributed to the "left of center," or welfare state policy, adopted by this party in 1965. The TLP was accepted or rejected strictly for ideological reasons.

The squatters' opinions about the national political leaders deviated from their views of the local and regional party politicians or activists (Table 8.15). Inönü, the chairman of the RPP at the time, was considered to be, by far, the most reliable national leader, although his party did not receive a majority of votes either in the *gecekondus* or the country at large. In fact, as mentioned, the percentage of votes received by the RPP in the *gecekondus* was lower than its national average. It appears that some squatters regarded Ismet Inönü as the embodiment of the state, a dominating father figure much in the manner of Atatürk and perhaps the old sultans. Inönü's past as military leader, president, and premier stood as the

Table 8.13. *Reasons for supporting certain party activists (male respondents only)*

	Age 16–25			Age 26–35			Age 36–45			Age 46–			Total	
	JP	RPP	TLP	JP	RPP	TLP	JP	RPP	TLP	JP	RPP	TLP	No.	%
The ruling party	1			3			7			1			12	4
Knows how to spread its views	1			11		2	5	1	1	2			23	9
Helps the *gecekondu*			2	3			5		1	2			13	5
Uses simple language						1	2		1				4	2
Promises are trustworthy		2		5	2		6	2		2			19	7
Dedication to work for the country	2	2	2	15	2	2	8	1	1	1	3	1	40	15
Cares for the poor	2			3	4	4	2		1	1		1	18	7
Does not oppress the people				2			1			1			4	2
Promises employment	2		2	5	1	1	2		1	1			15	6
Ideologically close	2	2	5	7	2	9	8	1	2	3			41	16
Deep roots, known family							1	2			5		8	3
Promise of social equality			2		3				3				8	3
Recommended by friends, relatives, spouses	2	1	1					2		1	1	1	9	3
Admires party leaders		4			1		2	4			2		13	5
Religious preference				2						2			4	2
No knowledge	1												1	
Other	2	4		7	7	2	4	1	1	2	1		31	11
Total No.	15	15	14	63	22	21	53	14	12	19	12	3	263	100

Table 8.14. *Reasons for rejecting party activists of parties different from one's own (in percentages)*

	Men	Women	Unmarried
Leftists and communists	23	12	14
Does not trust them personally	12	14	15
Cannot understand them	10	6	3
Useless and impractical	9	16	15
Unreliable promises	10	13	6
Undecided policy	5	1	8
Rejected by the nation	5	2	
Inexperienced	2		3
Rightist ideology	3		2
Dislike for top leaders	3	4	
Antireligious	4		2
Loyalty to one's own party	3	17	2
Does not know leaders	4	1	3
Other	7	14	27
Total	100	100	100

best ultimate guarantee for the safety and survival of the state. Inönü's single-handed defiance of military groups as well as politicians who threatened the democratic regime in Turkey tended to justify the squatters' confidence in him. However, at the same time, the squatters felt that such a man could be obeyed, followed, and perhaps idealized but could not be made party to petty but useful bargainings, as was the case with other politicians.

Indeed, it seems that party politics in the *gecekondus,* if not in Turkey in general, is not determined by the charisma of the old leaders, but rather by a series of practical matters debated and settled by ordinary people at local and regional party organizations. The contradictions between the squatters' rather noble professed

Table 8.15. *Turkey's most reliable and trustworthy political leaders (1968)*

	Men		Women		Unmarried	
	No.	%	No.	%	No.	%
Ismet Inönü (chairman of RPP at the time)	192	50	84	20	47	39
Süleyman Demirel (chairman of JP)	53	14	60	14	16	13
Cevdet Sunay (president of Turkey at the time)	12	3	5	1	5	4
Mehmet Ali Aybar (chairman of TLP at the time)	11	3	4	1	5	4
Bülent Evevit (secretary general of RPP at the time; now its chairman)	10	3			8	7
Osman Bölükbaşı (chairman of NP at the time)	9	2	2	1	7	6
Adnan Menderes (chairman of DP, hanged in 1961)	8	2	2	1		
Çetin Altan (a leftist journalist)	5	1			3	3
Alparslan Türkeş (chairman of RPNP/NAP)	4	1				
Nobody	58	15	19	5	4	3
Does not know	4	1	227	54	21	18
Other	19	5	14	3	3	3
Total	385	100	417	100	119	100

political attitudes and their expediency in practical matters mirrors the preoccupation of the Turkish political parties with local issues and their inability to provide a true national leadership in this crucial period of Turkey's transition from an agrarian to a semi-industrialized existence. The effects of this transition are observable in the differences in the political behavior of the rural migrants before and after they have settled in the *gecekondu*.

Change in political behavior: shifts in party loyalty

Party affiliation and voting patterns observed among the *gecekondu* dwellers seem to have undergone a sharp change from their voting behavior in the village, where 44 percent of the men said that they voted for the RPP and 54 percent either for the DP or the JP. Because of substantial continuity in membership between the two parties, despite the name change, it is evident that some of the respondents voted for the DP in 1946 and 1960, and for the JP in 1961 and 1969. On the other hand, a large percentage of the migrants who voted for the RPP in their village switched their votes to the JP and the TLP in the city. Indeed, 39 percent of the men reported that they switched parties after settling in Istanbul. This is supported by the actual number of votes received by the RPP in some of the migrants' villages in the national elections of 1965 and 1969. The official statistics show that the RPP was still well ahead of all parties in the six villages from which almost half of the migrants came, as shown in Table 8.16.

The shift in migrants' votes in favor of the JP in the city was the consequence of political bargaining between the ruling party and the squatters. This party had the means to grant economic advantages such as the title to the house and to improve the quality of life in the *gecekondu* by installing amenities such as water and electricity in exchange for votes. Yet, it must be stressed that bargaining was preceded by considerable debate and organizational work by the squatters themselves. The shift in votes indicated that the squatter was able to break away from the pressure of his elders, from traditional ties and loyalties, and to vote according to his individual preferences and interests.

Some RPP spokesmen claimed that many Alevis, especially those in the central and northeastern part of the country supported the RPP because of its secularist policies, which compelled the Sunnites (orthodox Muslims) to lift pressure off the Alevis. The idea that party affiliation and voting in the squatters' original villages and provinces was influenced by the Alevi-Sunnite rivarly is not supported by facts. For instance, the Birlik Partisi (UP, the Unity, or Union, party), established by Alevi leaders, did not even enter elections in the provinces of Giresun and Gümüşhane, which are inhabited by large numbers of Alevis. However, the UP entered the elections in the adjoining province of Sivas also inhabited by sizable groups of Alevis and did well, chiefly to the detriment of the secularist RPP and of the JP. Sivas had been a stronghold of the RPP in the past. In the 1969 elections the UP received 16.7 percent, the RPP 30.8 percent, and the JP 29.3 percent of the votes

Table 8.16. Results of national elections in selected squatter villages in northeastern Anatolia

Squatters' original village	Election year	Eligible votes	Votes cast	Valid votes	JP	UP (only 1969)	RPP	RP	NP	RPNP/ NAP	TLP	NTP	Independents
Kırıntı	1965	328	220	201	79		83					15	24
(Şiran-Gümüşhane)	1969	337	197	196	86		103	6	1				
Yeniköy	1965	158	158	106	11		84					2	9
(Şiran-Gümüşhane)	1969	145	101	101	28		69				3	1	
Kayacık	1965	104	104	102	29		39		32	1	1		
(Alucra-Giresun)	1969	79	49	49	4		8		2	1	1		34
Yeni Yol	1965	224	159	152	106		13		12	8	7	6	
(S. Karahisar-Giresun)	1969	223	146	142	122		4	6	1	5	3		1
Düzyayla	1965[a]	210	165	153	35		33		40	27	6	12	
(Hafık-Sivas)	1969	415	274	233	56	17	23	10	31	12	8	5	
Gökçekent	1965	222	168	159	6		22		3		2		132
(Suşehri-Sivas)	1969	223	184	183			170		3	5	2		

Sources: 1950–1965 Milletvekili ve 1961, 1964 Cumhuriyet Senatosu Üye Seçimleri Sonuçları (State Institute of Statistics) Ankara, 1965; *12 Ekim 1969 Milletvekili Seçimi Sonuçları* (State Institute of Statistics), Ankara, 1970.
[a] Only one ballot box, which corresponds roughly to 50 percent of the eligible votes.

cast in the province of Sivas.[10] On the other hand, despite the presence of a large bloc of Alevis in the Baltaliman and Nafibaba *gecekondus* (probably 300 voters), the UP received only 12 votes in the two polling stations used most frequently, but not exclusively, by the squatters in the elections of 1969 (Table 8.9). These official results were also supported by interview results; only five people declared that they actually voted for the UP candidates in the municipal elections of 1968.

The shift of votes in favor of the JP in the *gecekondus,* resulting from practical motives, indicates a trend to break from the influence of the old type of traditional leaders. In areas of the country where communal organizations dominated by religious leaders, tribal leaders, or rich landowners prevail, the votes were mobilized generally as a bloc. In the past the RPP usually benefited from the support of such blocs because of the close association, established during the one-party period, between the leaders of such traditional groups and the party. It must be stressed that the Alevi communities, although more democratic and egalitarian at least in some sections of Turkey (notably in Giresun and Gümü-şhane provinces), are often religiously oriented and conservative in their own way. These groups, like many other similar traditional organizations, initially provided the framework for internal solidarity, cohesion, and opportunity for mutual assistance to rural migrants in the city, but tended to disintegrate over time under the impact of industrialization and urban culture.

The party politics in the *gecekondu* revolving around rationally determined goals enabled the migrants to break away from a party loyalty dictated in part, at least, by communal and traditional forces. The urban environment, including the orientation of the *gecekondu* toward a rationally organized form of group action, has compelled the migrant to develop new political loyalties accordingly. Thus, politics played a major role in speeding the squatters' integration into the city by sharpening their consciousness of self, place, and role in society. It also increased their communication with city and national party leaders. On balance, the impact of the new forces seems to have prevailed over old attachments, despite the survival of the latter under a variety of forms. The sharp rise in the level of aspiration and the high degree of individualization, manifest in the squatters' growing confidence in their own ability to achieve higher goals, best symbolize the fact that the migrants' personality has been transformed in line with the achievement-oriented urban technological environment. The belief that higher economic and social status can be achieved by political action coupled with ability and effort indicates that the old belief in the immutability of the social arrangement and ascribed social positions prevailing among the lower classes in Turkey has been drastically undermined.

The elections of October 14, 1973, support these views. In the elections the Rumelihisar district, which included the Nafibaba and Baltaliman settlements, voted about 60 percent in favor of the RPP, nearly double the votes received nationally (33.3 percent) by this party. The votes received by the JP, on the other hand, dropped to about 17 percent in Rumelihisar compared with 29.8 percent in the nation (see Table 8.17).[11]

The election results actually reflected the changes in the composition of the *gecekondus,* their numerical growth, and the shifts in national politics. By 1973, the two squatter districts of Nafibaba and Baltaliman grew and merged fully. According to some figures obtained informally, at the end of 1973, the combined population of the two squatter settlements consisted of 6,798 people and the old district of Rumelihisar of 3,346, or a total population of 10,144 people. The number of balloting stations went up from 6 in 1969 to 15 in 1973; the number of registered voters rose from 1,926 to 4,243, the increase being mostly in the squatter settlements. The combined population of the squatter settlements in 1973 was twice that of the old Rumelihisar district and caused a fundamental change in their relations, as shall be explained in the section dealing with the election of the *muhtar.* The outcome of the general elections in 1973 was essentially conditioned by national events.

The JP, ousted from power by the military in 1971, did not have the power any longer to grant concessions to the *gecekondus.* On the other hand, the old preoccupation with the *gecekondu* interests was partly replaced by a concern for national welfare since the fate of the first was linked to the country as a whole, especially after the *gecekondu*'s survival seemed assured. This resulted from a series of events that helped integrate the *gecekondu* into the city. In 1971 the *gecekondu* was declared an *islah* (improvment) area

Table 8.17. *Election results in Rumelihisar (1973)*

Ballot box number	Number of voters	Votes cast	Valid votes	JP	RPP	RRP	DP	NP	NAP	NSP	UP	Independents
1	275	181	170	42	101	7	8	3	1	6	1	1
2	298	177	172	44	101	3	13		1	7	1	2
3	330	238	231	55	133	9	19		2	6	6	1
4	278	185	179	30	113	2	12		4	16	1	1
5	211	79	77	19	42	7	2			4	2	1
6	254	165	160	12	108	3	8		10	13	6	
7	291	155	149	34	70	2	19	1	6	16	1	
8	360	228	212	28	113	3	28		1	25	7	
9	319	154	152	34	78	13	12		2	8		5
10	316	225	208	14	155	4	17		2	11	5	
11	277	187	177	31	127	5	4	1		9		
12	288	199	194	68	94	12	3	2	4	6	2	3
13	290	181	178	40	87		21		1	28	1	
14	248	188	182	7	134	3	21	1	3	1	10	1
132	209	128	127	32	43	3	15	5	10	17	1	1
Totals	4243	2670	2568	490	1499	76	202	13	47	173	44	16

Source: 14 Ekim 1973 Milletvekili Seçimi Sonuçları (State Institute of Statistics), Ankara, 1973.
Note: Squatters from Nafibaba and Baltaliman cast approximately 65 percent of the votes; Mereysitesi, 5 percent. Deputy elections only. Eight undecided votes were omitted.

– that is, suitable for rehabilitation and improvement by municipal authorities. This official act guaranteed the survival of the *gecekondu* and permitted it to acquire electric and water facilities. Inflation and a series of other economic difficulties, including a rise in unemployment, undermined the *gecekondu* faith in private enterprise and compelled it to look on the social democracy promoted by the RPP as a better political alternative. The trend toward the RPP was strong among lower urban classes and some peasant groups, in large measure because of the successful populist image this party was able to assume. Finally, the fact that a growing number of squatters identified themselves with the urban-national culture, because of their longer stay in the city and younger age, was responsible for the *gecekondu*'s vote shift in favor of the RPP. The results of the political survey in 1968 and 1969 already indicated the existence of a trend among the young toward identification with ideological parties. The fact that the RPP succeeded in assuming a leftist ideological stand attracted many of the young as well as those who had sided with the Marxist Labor party of Turkey, which was banned in 1971. That political ideology was important and effective in the *gecekondu* is clearly indicated by the fact that at least five young people from the settlement were jailed in 1972 and 1973 for participation in radical militant political activities, a trend deserving further study.

The "gecekondu" in local politics

In politics the main problem for *gecekondu* leaders was to convince the dwellers to vote in common as a bloc for a specific party or a candidate. The problem of voting in a united front was relatively more important in local than in national elections: water, electricity, sewage, and other amenities needed by the *gecekondus* could only be provided by the local government, consisting of the municipality and the *muhtarlık,* the main channel of communication with higher government authorities.

The *muhtar,* his council, and the *belediye reisi* (mayor) of the city are the most important leaders of local government. Their prestige and influence have been greatly enhanced by the multiparty system since 1946 and by the constitution of 1961. Local government offices, therefore, have acquired a vital importance for each community in particular and for the political parties in general as bases for building good will and popular support. As will be seen below, the candidates' personal abilities rather than their party affiliation determine the outcome of the local elections for both *muhtar* and mayor. Hence political parties seek the most qualified candidates to fill these positions.

All *gecekondus* are attached to the nearest *muhtarlık*, which is the smallest unit of both the central and the local governments. The *muhtar* provides the basic channel of communication between the precinct and the provincial and municipal authorities. If a *gecekondu* grows large enough it may be recognized as an independent precinct; otherwise it functions as part of an old precinct. The *gecekondus* of Nafibaba and Baltaliman were attached to the precint of Rumelihisar and participated in the elections of its *muhtar*. The settlement in Celâlettin Paşa was part of a different precinct, which bears its own name. According to the tabulation of votes in the national elections of 1969, 1926 people voted in the Rumelihisar district. Of this total, approximately 850 voters resided in the Nafibaba and Baltaliman settlements. It is obvious that these people and their relatives who resided in the old section of Rumelihisar formed a powerful voting bloc. Their votes were decisive in the local elections and consequently each candidate for the position of *muhtar* had to take into account the needs and opinions of the *gecekondu* dwellers.[12]

A detailed study of the *muhtar* elections of 1968 in Rumelihisar shows the *gecekondu* political impact at the local level. There were four major candidates for the office of *muhtar:* Kemal Sir, who was supported by the JP; Can Dümencioğlu, the former *muhtar,* who ran as an independent, although he was a member of the New Turkey party; Mahmut Harmancıoğlu, a founder of the Nafibaba settlement and owner of a coffeehouse there, who ran as an independent; and Faruk Çapa, the candidate of the RPP. Kemal Sir won with 490 votes; the others received, 452, 268, and 170 votes, respectively. (The figures were obtained from the candidates themselves since official figures were not available.) The votes did not follow party lines. The total number of votes cast for the Republican party in the national elections of 1969 was higher than the votes received by the *muhtar* candidate of the same party:

416 votes were cast for the party in 1969; only 170 votes were cast for its candidate for *muhtar* in 1968.

The precinct elections generally reflect the interplay of local interests. This was observed in the *gecekondu* under study. The winner, Kemal Sir, was considered an educated man, for he held a technical degree and knew how to plan sewer and water lines. He had, moreover, the manners of the city elites, as well as an established position in the old community of Rumelihisar. Thus, in his dealings with the city and government authorities, he could represent his community, including the *gecekondu*, without social and intellectual handicaps. Anticipating his own candidacy, and though an outsider to the *gecekondu*, Kemal Sir had assumed the chairmanship of the *Gecekonduyu Güzelleştirme Derneği* (Association for Settlement Improvement) earlier and strived to prove himself a friend of the *gecekondu*.

The squatters did not vote for the former *muhtar* Can Dümencioğlu, despite an open expression of gratitude for his past services, chiefly because he lacked social, intellectual, and political influence outside the Rumelihisar community. The fact that he was an Armenian and a Christian does not seem to have played an important part in his defeat, despite a few opinions to the contrary. He had been elected *muhtar* previously with a relatively large number of votes, and since the number of non-Muslim voters in Rumelihisar is only about 200, allegations of religious discrimination cannot hold true. The *gecekondu* community did not support its own candidate, Mahmut Harmancıoğlu, either, since he was considered even less qualified than the other two candidates to represent the precinct as a whole. During the 1968 elections the chief goals of the *gecekondu* residents were to qualify the settlement as an *islah* area and to improve its situation by integrating it fully into the community of Rumelihisar. It was deemed that these could be achieved best by a leader who belonged to the established order but had the interest of the *gecekondu* at heart. That leader seemed to be Kemal Sir.

Kemal Sir, though a good *muhtar*, did not fulfill the *gecekondu*'s expectations, largely because of the rapid growth of the settlement from 1969 to 1971. Consequently, the *gecekondu* leaders began to think of fusing the two settlements into one and renaming it

Hisarüstü mahallesi (quarter of Hisarüstü), which conveyed a better image and a sense of a new urban identity. The leaders thought first to detach the settlement from Rumelihisar, to which it had been tied administratively since its inception, and establish it as an independent *muhtarlık*. In other words, Hisarüstü – that is, the former *gecekondus* of Nafibaba and Baltaliman – wanted to choose its own *muhtar* and administer itself independently. Already it had acquired its own *karakol* (police station) with three regular city policemen and eight *bekçi*, or night guards, chosen from among the residents, who work as auxiliaries of the regular police. The residents agreed to build themselves the police station, which in view of their experience, seemed an easy task. But the higher authorities, in order to prevent the settlements from acquiring too much power and from remaining isolated from the city, did not accept the plan for a new *muhtarlık*, and consequently the settlements remained attached to Rumelihisar. In reaction to this situation the *gecekondu* residents concentrated their efforts on acquiring control of the *muhtarlık*. The elected *muhtar*, Kemal Sir, according to some *gecekondu* residents, allegedly used the office to promote his own political career; in case of dispute he tended to side with the established residents of Rumelihisar and even tried to undermine the unity of the settlement by inciting an Alevi-Sunni rivalry.

In reality the *muhtar*, unable to dominate the *gecekondu* because of the strong Alevi leadership of the Kırıntı group, decided to undermine it by inciting the Sunni majority to break away and assert its own power. He used the mosque issue to win his point. Allegedly posing as a very religious man, he told the Sunnis that they should build a mosque, without taking into consideration the fact that the Alevis wanted to build first a school and then a mosque. The Sunnis, in fact, had used a house in the settlement for prayer while building a mosque just at the entrance to the *gecekondu*. On the other hand, the *muhtar* had initiated steps to build a school in the settlement and played some part in bringing in electricity. But his greatest political mistake was to join the DP, an organization newly formed by dissidents from the ruling JP. Meanwhile, the influx of new people into the settlement broke down the internal unity among the relatively tight group of Alevis as well as their control of the *gecekondu* votes. The arrival of additional Alevis from the Sivas province, which belonged to another group and had a different regional leader, caused some friction with the Alevis from Kırıntı-Kayacık villages. The solution to the resulting conflict was to deemphasize the Alevi allegiance and emphasize the idea of secular Turkish national identity. Thus, some squatters from Kırıntı continued to extol the virtues of the Alevi sect; others claimed that "these old beliefs and traditions have lost their meaning, besides we have more important problems to solve in the city than fight over these superstitions." All these internal developments created a new sense of identity and purpose that superseded the old religious and regional allegiances. Consequently, in the election for *muhtar* in 1973, all the *gecekondu* dwellers united to elect a new *muhtar,* Mehmet Başkaya, a resident of the settlement. The old mayor, Kemal Sir, although supported by residents from the old district of Rumelihisar and a few well-to-do dwellers living in Baltaliman, was defeated, as was Can Dümencioğlu, a perennial candidate for *muhtar.*

The new *muhtar,* a driver by profession, belonged to one of the smallest groups originating in the province of Kastamonu. He had no large group of relatives or *hemşeris* to support him. He was elected solely because of his leadership abilities and prior achievements. Mehmet Başkaya was about 32 years old, intelligent, aggressive, but also extremely balanced in his views and acts. He had firsthand knowledge of conditions in the *gecekondu* and an excellent understanding of city and party politics, as well as a keen knowledge about various bureaucratic formalities related to land deeds and other technical matters. His dress, manners, and general behavior were not different from those of established city dwellers, whom he treated as equals. The seat of the *muhtarlık,* a one-room office, was located now in the squatter settlement. As though paying homage to the victor, the established residents of the old district of Rumelihisar grudgingly climbed the hill to see the new *muhtar* in the *gecekondu* despite the existence of an old *muhtarlık* office in the Rumelihisar. The new *muhtar* in a gesture of good will – one would say the magnanimity of the victorious leader – eventually decided to work one or two days in the old office to save the old Rumelihisar residents time and effort. There was no doubt that power in Rumelihisar was in the hands of the *gecekondu* dwellers. They had come a long way. Though ignored and despised by the old Rumelihisar residents, they established a firm foothold in the area; and then gradually manipulating the political apparatus, they captured the chief political office in the district. They called themselves now not *gecekondu* dwellers, but residents of Rumelihisar in Istanbul. The integration of migrants and squatters into city – in other words, their urbanization – was an accomplished fact.

Conclusion

The three squatter settlements in Istanbul studied in this work appear, on the one hand, as the by-product of rural migration and, on the other, as a self-devised solution by the migrants to the shortage of housing in the city. They are also part of a broader process of urbanization. Consequently, two sets of interrelated conclusions can be drawn from this study: one regarding the nature of the squatter community and its integration into the city, and the other regarding the practical policies connected with low-cost housing, land zoning, and other problems necessary to solve the squatter problem.

The squatter settlements appear as transitional communities between the village and rural town and the city. In the rural areas, their inhabitants are idle or marginally employed, attracted to the city by opportunities of employment, higher pay, and better living conditions. The newcomers are usually unskilled workers, who take low-paying jobs and engage in all kinds of occupations and individual enterprises. Low income coupled with high rents and lack of low-cost housing in the city compel the migrants to build their own dwellings wherever possible. The shacks thus built can be transformed within a short period of time, if conditions permit, into acceptable living places. Thus, the *gecekondus* increase the real estate value in the city. The migrants' life in the city, at least during the early stages of their urban existence, centers around the family and community. Consequently, the shack and the settlement acquire a central position in the migrants' personal life as a home and as a community with all the attachments and sense of belongingness and identity they entail.

The *gecekondu* residents retain some of the social values, attitudes, and organizational patterns prevailing in villages and rural towns; they appear at the same time predisposed toward integrating themselves into the city through the adoption of urban physical amenities and through social and cultural identification. While the communal culture prevailing in the settlement gradually loses its intensity, it provides, nevertheless, a common ground for achieving internal group solidarity, mutual assistance, protection, a sense of belongingness, and a basis for common political and civic action to secure the settlement's physical survival. The settlement's survival, in turn, is a guarantee for maintaining the family as a unit and for safeguarding the squatters' investment in land, building materials, and labor; their shacks, however modest, are a form of economic security and a potential source of income, as well as a symbol of higher social status gained through urban achievement. The attachment to the communal culture, the sense of belongingness stemming from it, and the security achieved through ownership prevent the squatters' psychological disintegration and alienation, and indirectly facilitate their integration into the urban environment. The existence of a relatively general national culture and language, represented by the ruling political structure, the adoption of which the squatters regard as a necessary step toward upward mobility, further facilitates the squatters' urban integration, provided that the action and goals of the ruling groups are congruent with the squatters' socioeconomic condition and aspirations, and vice versa.

But the *gecekondu* residents, despite the persistence of natural attachments to the village, do not regard the rural and communal culture as a permanent and superior form of belief system. On the contrary, they tend gradually to change, discard, or reinterpret their original village culture as the practical circumstances warrant, with a view of adapting themselves to urban life. Urban life, because of cultural values rooted in history, is considered a higher form of human organization. In this process of urbanization, the squatters develop a more rational and individualized concept of rights and freedoms, a keener sense of individual achievement and higher aspirations.

The squatter settlements, inadvertently perhaps, give a new shape and new characteristics to the traditional city by infusing it with a dynamic and democratic spirit inherent to the natural folk culture prevailing in the countryside. All this contributes new elements to the emerging national culture. Finally, rural migration plays a significant role in easing the population pressure in rural areas and places the squatter in a position to provide financial assistance to the village and to act as a channel of communication between the city and the countryside.

It has been noted that the availability of employment in the city, job mobility, and higher income are instrumental in raising the squatters' living standards in the city and in inducing them to adopt urban patterns of consumption. All this gives the squatters an optimistic outlook on life and a willingness to accept the existing sociopolitical order as ideal, as well as to develop confidence that their living conditions will improve further in the future. The sense of material well-being and the psychological satisfaction deriving from the existence of a relatively integrated family and community appear to have enhanced among squatters a dynamic, creative, and innovative attitude that can be maximized and perpetuated as a permanent feature of the new urban growth. However, should economic development stagnate and the political system's ability to answer demand erode, the squatters' optimism may fade away, their sense of alienation may increase and turn them into a formidable radical force, as happened in North Africa after World War II. However, within the conditions of the Turkish *gecekondu* today, the dwellers' philosophy, despite some political polarization, may be still defined as conservative middle-of-the-road.

The changes that occurred in the three *gecekondus* between the time the major survey was conducted in 1968 and the last visit in the summer of 1974 tend to support the above conclusions, especially those regarding urbanization. The three settlements have expanded and consolidated, especially after their survival was assured, and have integrated themselves into the old city districts around which they were established. The settlements of Nafibaba and Baltaliman in particular have combined into one district (Hisarüstü). Meanwhile, their population came to exceed the total population of the old district of Rumelihisar by a margin of almost three to one. Consequently, they captured the major political office there, the *muhtarlık,* and were able to set the course of local politics. Yet instead of forcing the district of Rumelihisar to adapt itself culturally and socially to their own pattern and organization, the two settlements strived to conform to the mode of life prevailing in that old district since it represented in their view a superior urban form of existence. In other words, the squatters gallantly accepted the mode of life of their defeated opponents in Rumelihisar, despite the latter's contemptuous treatment in the past, simply because they had reached, formally at least, their initial urban goal of being accepted as part of the city.

Now the settlements of Nafibaba and Baltaliman have water, electricity, bus transportation, and relatively usable roads. Job mobility and income have definitely increased. More than one hundred business establishments of all kinds, including a shop that sells expensive electrical gadgets and musical instruments, as well as official establishments (a post office, a police station), and a dentist's office, have sprung up there. Businessmen from the older sections of Istanbul have invested large sums of money in business ventures there. Cars and taxis move people continuously to and from the settlement without causing comment, and almost everyone wears normal city dress. The sense of community and solidarity that prevailed at the beginning has not disappeared but has changed considerably since the once-homogenous community has grown too big now and has broken down into several subcommunities, each one representing a specific *mahalle* in the settlement. At the same time people in each subcommunity seem to have intensified their relations with the city people. Crime in the settlement seems to be also rising, despite the greater income and more comfortable life, as indicated by the growing number of cars, TV sets, recorders, and other "modern" gadgets. Yet the settlements are not fully integrated into the ctiy. Whether or not they will fully integrate and how they accomplish this must be a subject of research for another study.

The squatters' full integration into the city appears to be the first major objective for any realistic policy maker; the success of such a policy depends on fully understanding the nature of the squatter settlements. It is obvious that the positive aspects of rural migration and the squatter settlements greatly overbalance their negative aspects. In fact, the negative view derives from an impressionistic and subjective attitude on the part of a small urban minority and their spokesmen in the press and universities, who, acting as self-appointed defenders of the urban culture, albeit an ossified traditionalist culture, have given the squatter settlements a bad name. Nevertheless, the squatter settlements in Turkey and elsewhere in the world remain the most important urban problem. The policy toward the *gecekondus* in Turkey and similar settlements throughout the world must begin by regarding them as key factors of development and by maximizing their role in urbanization as well as village development whenever possible. It seems that priority should be given to a proper land zoning and housing construction policy, not only to speed up the squatters' integration into the city but also to provide for an orderly migration and harmonious urban growth.

Some of the practical steps necessary to deal with the squatter problem in Turkey, and possibly elsewhere in the world, are the following:

1. The establishment of a national agency to deal with squatter settlements in the framework of rural migration, urbanization, and housing.

2. The establishment of a national and eventually international typology of squatter settlements according to their origins, organization, building patterns, and other relevant criteria, which may be used to devise corresponding international programs and projects of rehabilitation.

3. The preparation of inventories concerning the type of material and construction plans utilized by squatters in building their dwellings. It should be noted that the squatters have firsthand practical knowledge and experience about the least expensive local construction materials and about their suitability to the geographic and climatic conditions of the area. These are, in fact, "self-help," "low-cost housing projects" adapted to local conditions and could provide useful information for devising inexpensive national housing programs.

4. The adaptation of precise, simple, and easy-to-carry-out regulations concerning property rights, including rapid acquisition of legal titles to the land and dwelling. Similarly, standard legal provisions should be drawn for the swift expropriation of lands suitable for construction in zones designated for this purpose around urban areas. It must be stressed that the urban expansion in Turkey has caused a high rise in land values and has created a class of rich but unproductive rentiers who have engaged in land speculation and have opposed the adoption of low-cost housing and settlement projects.

5. The adoption of a modern housing policy concomitant with the citizens' need for shelter. Housing should be defined as an area of public policy and treated accordingly. All land around cities

should be classified and priced according to their suitability for various types of construction. Presently the municipalities and the governments tend to act as though they are avaricious landlords defending their property against rural invaders.

6. The adoption of housing and settlement policies fully cognizant of the need and standards of life but also of the capabilities of the incoming migrants. In other words, these policies should not take as a goal the creation of dwellings similar to those in the developed countries in the West, with emphasis on capital intensity, but proceed to develop these dwellings according to the availability of local resources and explore the ways to make the best use of the available manpower in the village and city. It has been noted that the squatters have improved and made usable by personal effort and ingenuity lands officially deemed unsuitable for house construction. For instance, some expensive housing projects in Istanbul and Ankara were developed only after the squatters successfully proved their usefulness as construction sites. Indeed, Ankara is expanding eastward and southward into former squatter areas.

7. The establishment of training courses to provide information and plans for house building and the development of sewage and draining systems. Lack of plans for such facilities is one of the major shortcomings of the Turkish squatter settlements, which gives place to heavy expense once the settlements are declared rehabilitation areas and are improved according to urban standards.

8. The easy availability of credit to squatter settlements designated for rehabilitation as well as to the new settlers who observe the regulations concerning land, buildings, and properties. Since most of the migrants settle around the work places, it is imperative to involve the concerned enterprises in the planning and financing of low-cost houses developed in their vicinity.

9. The incorporation of squatter settlements into the nearest established administrative unit rather than allowing them to develop into independent administrative centers. Such a policy may, if carried out without discrimination on the part of old city residents, speed up the squatters' integration into the city and discourage political bargains whereby the vote of the squatter community as a whole is delivered to a party in exchange for practical benefits. This policy in turn may have an indirect effect in preventing the

proliferation of squatter settlements, especially during election time.

10. The adoption of a proper tax policy in order to secure the squatters' participation in municipal expenditure and thus increase their sense of participation and belongingness to city life.

11. The establishment of a program of urban education designated to intensify communication between squatters and the old-time city residents and increase the level of mutual acceptance.

Notes

Chapter 1. The "gecekondu" in comparative perspective

1 Gerald Breese, *Urbanization in the Newly Developing Countries*, p. 3. For the Turkish case, see Orhan Turkay, *Türkiye' de Nüfüs Artışı ve İktisadi Gelişme.*

2 John F. C. Turner, *Uncontrolled Urban Settlement*. See also "Lima's Barriadas and Corralones."

3 A large percentage of the squattertown population of India, Pakistan, and some of the Arab countries is made up of refugees whose political orientation, background, and goals differ sharply from those whose migration was caused by internal factors. For instance, Palestinian refugees in Jordan, Lebanon, and Syria, who are a separate group, desire to go back to their original places in Palestine (Israel). The Biharis in Bangladesh live as aliens in shantytowns and cannot integrate into the city. In Turkey, until the early 1950s a considerable percentage of migrants consisted of refugees and expellees from the Crimea and the Balkan countries. However, today, despite the existence of some shantytowns populated by migrants from abroad, mostly in Istanbul and Izmir, the bulk of the population, possibly 90 percent of the total number of squatters, comes from villages and towns in the interior. The refugees from abroad constitute an insignificantly small group in Latin America.

4 Some of the major works providing material for comparative studies of migration and squatter settlements are the following: Aprodicio A. Laquian, ed., *Rural-Urban Migrants and Metropolitan Development;* William Mangin, ed., *Peasants in Cities,* to be mentioned hence as *Peasants*. Works of synthesis include William Mangin, "Latin American Squatter Settlements"; Joan M. Nelson, *Migrants, Urban Poverty, and Instability in Developing Nations*. See also note 16 below.

5 United Nations, *Report on World Social Situation*, p. 114. In the period from 1941 to 1951 in Venezuela alone the urban population increased by 71 percent, in Colombia (1938–51) by 68 percent, in Brazil (1940–50) by 49 percent, and in Chile (1940–52) by 47 percent. Nearly all of it was attributed to migration. See José Balista, *Aspectos Humanos de la Vivienda*, p. 58; Chi-Yi-Chen, *Movimientos Migratorios en Venezuela*, Caracas, 1968.

6 The United Nations estimated that the population of developing countries grows at 2 to 3 percent annually, whereas many cities grow at 6 percent. Slums and squatter settlements grow at rates of 12 percent

and sometimes exceed 20 percent (United Nations *Report* A/8037, p. 21).

7 *Problems of Urban Housing*, p. 139; see also *Slum Clearance in India.*
8 *Levantamento da populaçao favelada de Belo Horizonte*, pp. 4–7.
9 Carlos Alberta de Medina, *A Favela E O Demagogo*, pp. 26–44. On Brazil, see also G. De Menezes Côrtes, *Favelas;* and E. Fischlowitz, "Internal Migration in Brazil." The New York *Times* (January 25, 1971) reported that the *favelas* of Rio were disappearing after having served as "way stations for migrants from mud and grass huts in the interior of Brazil on their way to what they hope will be the greater comforts of urban living." The *favelas* were gradually transformed into neat houses through the combined effort of National Housing Bank and city authorities. Yet in 1971, Rio still had 500,000 dwellers living in some 27 shantytowns. It must be noted that the shantytown population was not moved out of Rio but into better quarters closer to the accepted city standards. However, the slum clearance effort in Brazil did not succeed very well. A number of squatters did not want to move to a low-cost housing project because they could not afford it or liked their current place. However, as a whole, Brazil's Popular Housing Agency, established to cope with the squatter problem, is one of the best of its kind in the world (New York *Times*, December 29, 1974). The United Nations reports supply extensive information to the effect that squatter areas occupy a significant portion of cities in the developing nations (United Nations *Report* A/8037, pp. 21–23). See also United Nations, *International Social Development Review;* the first issue was dedicated entirely to "Urbanization: Development Policies and Planning." For a recent report on Turkey, see the New York *Times*, July 12, 1975.
10 Cevat Geray, "Urbanization in Turkey," *Siyasal Bilgiler Fakültesi Dergisi*, 4, (1970), 158–59.
11 Ministry of Reconstruction and Settlement, *13 Büyük Şehirde Gecekondu*, pp. 5–6, tables 1 and 2. Detailed information on Turkish squatters' homes is provided in the next chapters.
12 Edith Abbott, *The Tenements of Chicago*, pp. 9–10. The same problems of overcrowding and housing occurred in socialist countries during industrialization. In the Soviet Union, it was reported that the occupancy per room went up from 2.60 in 1923, to 4.02 in 1950 but has improved since. In 1925, during the early stages of industrialization, the housing shortage in the USSR was so acute that workers in the Donetz Basin "lived in dugouts on the outskirts of the city" (Declaration in Central Executive Committee; Timothy Sosnovy, *The Housing Problems in the Soviet Union*, pp. 47, 108.
13 Julie Cotler and A. A. Laquian, "Lima," p. 115.
14 Laquian, *Rural-Urban Migrants*, p. 98.
15 Andrew Pearse, "Some Characteristics of Urbanization in the City of Rio de Janeiro," p. 194.
16 Bharat Sevak Samaj, *Slums of Old Delhi*, p. 23; also *Slum Clearance in*

India. See also Charles Abrams, *Housing in the Modern World,* pp. 12–24; United Nations, *Report* A/8037, p. 21, n. 4. For extensive bibliographies on the squatter settlements in addition to the works cited in this study, see Turner, *Urban Settlement,* pp. 106–12; United Nations, *Improvement of Slums and Uncontrolled Settlements,* pp. 184–89.

17 Medina, *Favela,* pp. 18–20. By 1890, Rio already had 18,338 families living in 1,449 tenements. *Favela* is the name given to a stinging plant that covered a hill on which war veterans seeking pensions established their tents and founded the first squatter settlement.

18 Robert Descloitres et al., *L'Algerie des bidonville,* pp. 95–97.

19 The Turkish administration brought to the Middle East a concept of land property and usage that admirably suited the climatic and social conditions of the area. The *mülk,* or private property, was subject to Shariat laws. The *miri* (state), *vaqf* (foundation), *metruke* (communal or public), and *mevat* (unproductive) lands were subject to public, religious, or customary law and were administered as collective, indivisible holdings. The French and British destroyed it. Only the Israelis have retained many of the principles of the old Ottoman land code.

20 Robert Montagne, ed., *La naissance du proletariat Morocain,* pp. 80–130.

21 The Youssoufia-Takaddoum settlement in Rabat, Morocco, was established in 1920 by migrants expelled from Agdabal and Souissi in the south. It eventually became the fourth district of the city and then expanded as a *bidonville,* and residential quarters were built for city officials. See Marie Renée Chene, *Marges Citadines à Rabat-Sale.* This is one of the most insightful studies of the squattertowns. The author has spent most of her adult professional life working in the Rabat settlements.

22 Elliott P. Skinner, "Labor Migration Among the Mossi of the Upper Volta," pp. 60–63.

23 Kemal H. Karpat, "Social Effects of Farm Mechanization in Turkish Villages."

24 This view finds increasing acceptance in the relevant literature, especially in the third world. The review *Demografia y Economia,* published in Mexico, is specifically interested in studying the interrelation among social structures, population, and socioeconomic development in the third world. See also Gaetano Ferro, *Cittá e campagna in Italia,* p. 11. The author considers the movement between village and city an aspect of the population mobility and finds the difference between the two to be of degree rather than substance since people have lived in both of them in constant economic, social, political, and historical relationships. A very useful source, both as information and as bibliography, is the *Peasant Studies Newsletter,* published by the University of Pittsburgh. It has been used with profit in this study. See also U. Toschi, *La Cittá.*

25 William Mangin, "Similarities and Differences Between Two Types of Peruvian Communities," pp. 20–29; and Paul L. Doughty, "Behind the Back of the City," pp. 30–46.

26 For instance, individual settlements in Kuala Lumpur, despite the presence of large groups of Malays, Chinese, Indians, and other groups, are rather homogeneous; see Enche Ali Bin Esa, "Kuala Lumpur," pp. 93–110.

27 This view is found in T. G. McGee, *The Southeast Asian City;* Philip M. Hauser, ed., *Urbanization in Asian and the Far East Cities,* 1967; and somewhat in Horace Miner, ed., *The City in Modern Africa.*

28 Some see both the rural and the urban situation in the third world, notably in Latin America, as a situation specific to dependent economies and arising from underdevelopment. Dependence here is regarded as the result of external trade and the incapacity of the national economy to compete externally rather than being a system of dependent capitalism. See Rodrigo Parra Sandoval, "Marginalidad y Subdesarollo," in Cardona Guttierrez, *Las Migraciones Internas,* pp. 223ff.

29 Raanan Weitz, ed., *Urbanization and the Developing Countries,* pp. 4, 112.

30 Ethel Rodriqueuz-Espada, "La incorporación de los migrantes a la estructura economica y social de la ciudad de Bogotá," p. 195.

31 For instance, in Ciudad de Dios, Lima, Peru, it was found that 28 small enterprises had a capital or initial cost of 1,000 to 8,000 soles, and 66 enterprises 190 to 980 soles; Mar, *Estudio de las Barriadas,* pp. 78ff.

32 Rodriqueuz-Espada, "La incorporación," p. 190.

33 Jorge Balán, "Migrant-Native Socio-Economic Differences in Latin American Cities," pp. 3–29. Balán applies the same approach to developing and stagnant villages and towns to determine the outflow of migration.

34 Actually T. G. McGee speaks about the peasant and his economic system as being different from socialist and capitalist systems. The peasant supposedly maintains his "economic system" in the city. I believe that indeed the squatters in the city do fit in the mold of a traditional economy and often give the appearance of having occupations different from the normal city occupations. This is a temporary situation arising from the nature of the urban occupational structure – that is, its underdevelopment and dependency as well as lack of technology – rather than a permanent "peasant enclave." Industrialization eventually ends this dichotomy. See McGee, *The Urbanization Process in the Third World;* see also "Peasants in the Cities," pp. 135–42; B. L. Isaac, "Peasants in Cities," pp. 251–57; and McGee's reply, pp. 258–60.

35 David R. Hunter, *The Slums,* p. 12. On slums, see also Charles J. Stokes, "A Theory of Slums"; Edward C. Banfield, *The Case of the Blighted City;* Hunter, *The Slums,* pp. 38–39; George S. Odiorne, *Green Power;* Harvey Warren Zorbaugh, *The Gold Coast and the*

Slum, Chicago, 1961; Oscar Lewis, *The Children of Sanchez.* See also
the bibliography in Mangin, *Peasants,* p. 39.

36   John R. Seeley, "The Slum," pp. 8–9.
37   Herbert J. Gans. *The Urban Villagers.*
38   Seeley, "The Slums," pp. 10–11.
39   Gerald D. Suttles, *The Social Order of the Slum.*
40   William Mangin, "Latin American Squatter Settlements," p. 65. See
also his "Squatter Settlements," pp. 21–27. For a view of the African
shantytown as not a slum, see Regina M. Solzbacher, "East Africa's
Slum Problem," pp. 45–51.
41   A *katra* (in Delhi) is a group of usually single-room tenements constructed in rows within a compound or an enclosure, with a common
entrance, water faucets, and latrines. It has an inner court called
pucca. Katras are usually old. Those of Delhi were 50 to 100 years old.
For instance, Delhi had 1787 dwellings classified as "slums." Of these,
1726 were *katras* and 61 *bastis,* or squatter settlements. Yet, of the
total population, 47.5 percent lived in *bastis* and 52.5 percent in
katras. Only 3 *bastis* were older than 50 years. The remaining were
10 years or less, created after World War II. The average land per
basti was 30.577 square yards, but only 453 square yards per *katra.*
Samaj, *Slums,* pp. 11, 17, 19, 23, 191.
42   Some of the *fondouks* of Rabat, Morocco, were built in the seventeenth
century by migrants from Andalusia and resemble the Western cloisters
of the Roman period; they are classical in style. At the time of their
building, they were regarded as excellent living quarters and were
described by contemporaries with admiration. Built as hotels in rec-
tangular form with columns, the *fondouks* were pious foundations
serving travelers. Some of the *fondouks* of Rabat are still the property
of *habous* (*vaqf*). According to Chene, in the medinas of Rabat and
Sale there were a total of 57 *fondouks* with 1550 pieces, in which
lived 759 families, or 3033 people; Chene, *Marges Citadines,* pp. 60,
73–76.
43   For examples in Latin America, see Cotler and Laquian, "Lima,"
p. 114; Douglas S. Butterworth, "A Study of the Urbanization Process
Among Mixtec Migrants from Tilantongo in Mexico City," p. 101; and
especially, Robert V. Kemper, "Rural-Urban Migration in Latin
America." See also Chapter 3 in this study for further references.
44   The origin of the inhabitants of squattertowns varies. In general, the
largest group of shantytown dwellers originate in villages and rural
towns. In the Middle East and North Africa, the rural migrants,
peasants, and tribesmen formed the overwhelming majority of inhabitants in the squattertowns, whereas in Latin America the ratio of
migrants from towns was relatively higher than those from villages. In
Rabat, for instance, at least 60 percent of the city population came
from southern villages and steppes; Chene, *Marges Citadines,* p. 85.
Some of the squatters originated, as mentioned before, in the poorer
districts of the city. However, a relatively high percentage of these were

born in villages and lived in the low-cost rent areas in the city until
economic necessity and favorable conditions allowed them to build their
own dwelling in a shantytown. In some cases, they were responsible for
planning and developing the settlement because of their intimate
knowledge of city politics and legal procedures.

45   The Ankara *gecekondus,* according to one study, had 3.7 children per
family. See Ibrahim Yasa, *Ankara'da Gecekondu Aileleri,* pp. 3, 37.
The national average of children per rural family in Turkey, according
to another study, was 3.9; *Türk Köyünde Modernleşme Eğilimleri
Araştırması,* p. 111. In the three *gecekondus* surveyed in this study, the
average number of children per family appeared to be only 2.8, due
mostly to the young age of the parents. In Chile (Santiago) there were
4.5 children per mother; Mangin, "Latin American Squatter Settlements," p. 72. For Rabat, Morocco, see Chene, *Marges Citadines,*
p. 173.

46   The information on causes of migration is based on the following
sources: William Flinn, "The Process of Migration to a Shantytown in
Bogotá, Colombia," paper read through the courtesy of the author;
Noel F. McGinn and Russell G. Davis, *Build a Mill, Build a City,
Build a School,* p. 5; Ruth Hurtado et al., *Estudio Sobre Barrios de
Caracas,* p. 57; John F. C. Turner, "Housing Priorities, Settlement
Patterns, and Urban Development in Modernizing Countries"; Thomas
P. A. Borges, "Relationship Between Economic Development, In-
dustrialization and the Growth of Urban Population in Brazil," pp. 149–
170; Richard M. Morse, "Urbanization in Latin America," pp. 35–72;
José M. Mar, "The 'Barriadas' of Lima," pp. 170–90. See also Hassan
Awad, "Morocco's Expanding Towns," pp. 114–21. Cotler and
Laquian indicate as reasons for moving to the shantytown (Pueblo
Jovene) of El Agostino in Lima, Peru, the following: economic, 19.2
percent; high rent, 4.1; family reasons, 31.5; land acquisition, 13.7;
better housing, 9.6; other, 21.9. Laquian, *Rural-Urban Migrants,* p. 115.

47   It must be mentioned also that the city in the third world, in addition
to the economic opportunities offered, has been regarded traditionally
as a superior form of existence. The high status attached to life in
the city – *şehir, madina, polis,* or *urbanismo* – is a deeply engrained
element in the cultures of Asia, Africa, and Latin America. The term
madaniyyat – that is, civilization – in the Muslim culture derives from
madina, or city. It stands, in fact, as an independent cultural variable
responsible for rural migration into cities. Most of the Turkish squatters
studied in this work came from the Black Sea region located nearly
800 miles from Istanbul. They did not stay in Ankara, another major
squatter area only 500 miles away from their villages, partly because
they followed some of their ancestors who had set a precedent by
coming to work seasonally in Istanbul during the earlier centuries. For
the tendency of some inhabitants from distant provinces to migrate to
Istanbul despite long distance, see John R. Clark, "City Size and Choice

of Destination by Turkish Migrants," paper presented at MESA meeting, Toronto, 1969. The Tepoztecans living in Mexico City adapted themselves to city life better than the migrating American farm families. This was facilitated not only by the proximity of the migrants' original place to the city, but also by the fact that Mexico City had been an important political, economic, and religious center for Tepoztecans since pre-Hispanic times. The communications established then in the context of Indian culture with Mexico City continued in modern times. See Oscar Lewis, "Urbanization Without Breakdown," p. 41.

48 Andrei Simič, *The Peasant Urbanites*, pp. 102ff.

49 For examples, see Mangin, "Latin American Squatter Settlements," pp. 68–69; also the New York *Times* (September 24, 1968) for a case in Lima, Peru. In Turkey invasions take place mostly around election time when the government seeks to avoid a show of force.

50 This explains why some squatter settlements are formed by people from one region, often related to each other, as was the case in Nafibaba in Istanbul and in the Isla Maciél settlement in Buenos Aires. For the latter, see Gino Germani, "Inquiry into the Social Effects of Urbanization in a Working Class Sector of Greater Buenos Aires," pp. 206–33.

51 In Lima, Peru, squatters built 100,000 housing units, whereas the low-cost housing authorities were able to build only 31,000 units from 1950 to 1968. (New York *Times*, September 24, 1968). In Ankara it had been estimated that a *gecekondu* replacement project built only 700 units in three years, whereas the squatters built at least 15,000 units during one year. For an excellent study on low-cost housing, see Robert North Merrill, *Toward a Structural Housing Policy*.

52 Chene divided the *bidonvilles* of Rabat into hygienic, anarchistic, and *briquette* villages. The last is the best dwelling and costs $10, or 50 *dirhams,* the square meter. The *briquetteville* is regarded as a transitional settlement between the shantytowns and the urban districts. Chene, *Marges Citadines,* pp. 56–58, 80.

53 For a detailed survey of crime in the Turkish squatter settlements surveyed in this study, see Chapter 5. Montagne notes that in the Algerian *bidonville* there was a low crime rate. Montagne, *La Naissance,* pp. 241–44. See also the works dealing with Latin America cited earlier.

54 Louis Wirth, "Urbanism as a Way of Life," pp. 1–24.

55 This view is defended in part in a series of articles in Mangin, ed., *Peasants*. See Janet L. Abu-Lughod, "Migrant Adjustment to City Life," pp. 22–23. See also works cited in note 34 above.

56 Writing on urbanization in the Middle East is rather limited. A partial bibliography has been provided in Kemal H. Karpat, "The Background of Ottoman Concept of City and Urbanity." See also A. H. Hourani and S. M. Stern, eds., *The Islamic City;* Janet Abu-Lughod, *Cairo;* L. Carl Brown, ed., *From Madina to Metropolis;* and Dale F. Eickel-

man, "Is There an Islamic City?" pp. 274–94. A relevant publication is *La Ville Balkanique, XVe–XIXe SS.*, number 3 of *Studia Balcanica* (Sofia, 1970).

57   For a detailed study, see Kemal H. Karpat, "The Economic and Social Transformation of Istanbul in the Nineteenth Century."

58   B. F. Hoselitz, "Generative and Parasitic Cities"; Robert Redfield and Milton Singer, "The Cultural Role of Cities."

59   Descloitres et al., *L'Algerie*, p. 35.

60   Oscar Lewis, "Urbanization Without a Breakdown." Sunderland, on the northeastern coast of England, is an ideal example of a city that went through various stages of the industrial revolution, steel and steam engineering, shipbuilding, and so on, by preserving the community and its spirit through an enlightened understanding of home and house. See Norman Dennis, *People and Planning*, London, 1970.

61   According to an extensive survey, 84.2 percent of the villagers interviewed in Turkey stated that they would like to settle in the city. I strongly suspect that cultural and social considerations played some part in this answer; *Türk Köyünde Modernleşme Eğilimleri Araştırması*, p. 105. For Yugoslavia, see Simič, *Peasant Urbanites*, p. 79. Changes in dress among migrant Indians in Mexico City are common; see Butterworth, "Urbanization Process," p. 111.

62   For Mexico, see Butterworth, "Urbanization Process," p. 105. The migrants in Morocco (Rabat-Sale) shantytowns regard the city as a "choice place where one finds comfort, modernity of living, elegance of clothing, distinction of language, the spirit of finesse or literally where there is spirit." Chene, *Marges Citadines*, p. 199.

63   Hurtado, *Estudio*, p. 66; Talton F. Ray, *The Politics of the Barrios of Venezuela*, p. 156. For Africa, see Marc Howard Ross, *The Political Integration of Urban Squatters*.

64   Frank Bonilla, "Rio's Favelos," p. 80.

65   Chene, *Marges Citadines*, p. 201.

66   Edward M. Bruner, "Medan," pp. 122–34.

67   Butterworth, "Urbanization Process," pp. 103ff.; Hans C. Buechler, "The Ritual Dimension of Rural Urban Networks," pp. 62–71. See also Sydney W. Mintz and Erik R. Wolf, "An Analysis of Ritual Co-Parenthood (*Compadrazzo*)," pp. 174–99.

68   Paul J. Magnarella, "Descent, Affinity and Ritual Relationship in Eastern Turkey," pp. 1626–33. See also Ayşe K. Sertel, "Ritual Kinship in Eastern Turkey," pp. 37–50.

69   Simič points out that Serbian migrants to the city hold the view that rural ties are an insurance against misfortune, that visits to village levels differences between villagers and town people and allows migrants to retain some relation to the village corporate establishment. "Problems of alienation on the part of the migrant are balanced by continuing participation as part of a village-based kinship network, while new ties are gradually created in the urban community." Simič, *Peasant Urban-*

ites, pp. 113–150; for quotation, see p. 151. These observations are valid also for Turkey, as will be shown in the next chapters.

70 Mangin, *Peasants,* p. xx.

71 Leonard Plotnicov, "Nigerians," p. 170. See also, John C. Caldwell *African Rural-Urban Migration.*

72 A few years ago, I visited in Cairo the so-called Nasser City built by the government for squatter residents. When regarded from a distance, the impressive buildings turned out to house a dismal gathering of people with little in common. The buildings were dirty and decaying, reminding me of some of the worst tenement houses in industrial cities. These had become slums because community spirit and solidarity had seemingly disappeared.

73 Cotler and Laquian, "Lima," p. 129.

74 Chene, *Marges Citadines,* p. 29.

75 Harold A. Gould, "Some Preliminary Observations Concerning the Anthropology of Industrialization," p. 139. Cotler notes, for instance, that in a group of Peruvian migrants employment in agriculture dropped from 39.5 to 1.2 percent after migration; Mangin, *Peasants,* p. 120.

76 On occupational changes see E. Wilbur Beck and S. Iutaka, "Rural-Urban Migration and Social Mobility: The Controversy in Latin America," *Rural Sociology,* 34, 3, 343–355. For the supposed exception in South Asia, see note 34 above.

77 On employment, see Mar, "Barriadas," p. 178; Germani, "Social Effects," p. 220; Medina, *Favela,* pp. 57–66; Mangin, "Latin American Squatter Settlements," p. 75; Samaj, *Slums,* pp. 89–90; Descloitres et al., *L'Algerie,* p. 225. Ibrahim Yasa, who studied the *gecekondus* in Ankara, gives the rate of unemployment among family heads as only 6.41 percent; *Ankara,* p. 46. Unfortunately, Hauser's study in *Urbanization in Latin America,* despite its excellence, reflects some old myths about the squatter settlements, including a rather distorted view of employment; see, for instance, p. 56. Hurtado gives the percentage of unemployment in Caracas as 50.2 percent, but this derives from lumping men and women together; *Estudio,* p. 63. For other employment figures, see Pedro Susa Franco, "Caracas," p. 47, and p. 118 for Lima, Peru.

78 In Calcutta (1958–59), the wards of Cossipore and Sinthi had 13,588 people of all ages. Of this total 6,631 were classified as earners. Their occupational distribution was the following: ordinary labor, 1471; sales, 1397; handicrafts, 1282; small owners-managers, 664; professionals, 216; clerks, 311; and the rest distributed among other occupations. *Report on the Bustee Survey in Calcutta, 1958–59,* p. 11. For Rabat see Chene, *Marges Citadines,* pp. 118–38.

79 *Slums of Delhi,* p. 135; in Ahmedabad 59,968 families, or 78.7 percent, of a total of 76,192 families surveyed earned up to 175 rupees a month. *Problems of Urban Housing,* pp. 141–150.

80   The monthly income in *dirhams* – 5 *dirhams* to the dollar – for squatters in Rabat was as follows (Source: Chene, *Marges Citadines,* p. 118):

Income	Number of people	Percentage of interviewed
Unemployed	155	20.7
0–100	19	2.5
101–200	234	31.2
201–300	257	34.4
301–400	59	7.9
401–500	16	2.1
501 and above	9	1.2

81   On these points, see Joseph A. Kahl, "Some Social Concomitants of Industrialization and Urbanization," pp. 53–74; also *Social Implications of Industrialization and Urbanization in Africa, South of the Sahara;* B. F. Hoselitz and Wilbert E. Moore, eds., *Industrialization and Society;* R. B. Textor et al., *The Social Implications of Industrialization and Urbanization.*

82   A comparative study conducted in Ankara among 25 women in a *gecekondu* (Altındağ) and 25 women in a middle-class suburb (Yeni Mahalle) showed that the nuclear family prevailed in 88 percent of the *gecekondu* and 68 percent of the suburb. Thirty-two percent of the lower classes and only 8 percent of the middle classes eloped to marry. On the other hand, 56 percent of the middle classes and 32 percent of the lower classes decided to marry with the consent of their parents. Those girls who were married without their own consent were 24 and 28 percent, respectively. The bride price was not a factor in marriages. See Serim Gülsüm Yurtören (Timur), *Fertility and Related Attitudes Among Two Social Classes in Ankara,* pp. 50–52. For Morocco, see Chene, *Marges Citadines,* pp. 107–8.

83   It was reported that women in the *bidonvilles* in Morocco remarried frequently, in the Ben Misk area about 50 percent of the women married two or more times, and elsewhere there was a certain amount of sexual freedom – all of which is unusual in Muslim countries. Montagne, *La Naissance,* pp. 242–44.

84   Butterworth, "Urbanization Process," p. 110.

85   "Certainly" writes Chene, about Moroccan squatter religious attitudes, "he is very believing; his faith in the unique God, in His generosity, compassion, justice is evident many times in the interviews. But he is aware of his religious ignorance. His fervor to attend the *baraque-*mosque and participate in ritual prayers, the assiduous interest in Koranic schools he demands from his children are the manifestations of

his desire to integrate himself in the world of citizens or at least, that of the traditionalist citizens. Islam, the national religion, is very certainly the most important factor of unity among all citizens regardless of the social status to which they belong." Chene, *Marges Citadines,* p. 164.

86 Buechler, "Ritual Dimension," p. 69.

87 Doughty, "Back of the City," pp. 41–42.

88 Doughty notes that 25 years ago it was commonplace for highlanders arriving in Lima to reject their traditions. Today, with the big wave of migration, highland culture has become more respectable. Many are startled not by anomie but by the fact that families and individuals can reorganize their lives in meaningful fashion by retaining their old integrative structures. Doughty, "Back of the City," p. 32. For Mexico, see Butterworth, "Urbanization Process," p. 105.

89 A series of local traditions specific to an ethnic or linguistic group are also revived but within the context of a natural culture rather than a divisive nationalistic factor. See Chapters 5 and 6.

90 Chene reports that if in Rabat the migrants felt marginal to city residents "That was because they preserved an accent in speech and village manners . . . one lived [thus] in the city without quite belonging to it." Otherwise, there were not cultural differences between them. "I do not hesitate to conclude on the basis of this work," writes Chene, "that the former peasants and especially the young, regardless of whether or not they inhabit the marginal quarters, are the most active elements of the Moroccan society on their march towards modernity. And if there are really marginal groups in Rabat-Sale, I would be tempted to discover them in the privileged and closed circles who inhabit the rich villas in the residential quarters of Agdal and Souissi." Chene, *Marges Citadines,* pp. 199, 206, 293.

91 Doughty, "Back of the City," pp. 35–43.

92 Cotler and Laquian, "Lima," p. 120.

93 Wayne A. Cornelius, "Urbanization and Political Demand Making," pp. 1125–46 and bibliography. Also David Collier, *Squatter Settlement Formation and the Politics of Co-optation in Peru;* R. R. Fagen and W. S. Tuehy, *Politics and Privilege in a Mexican City,* Stanford, Calif., 1962.

94 The nature of the needs and the political action used to satisfy them has been studied among Mexican migrants; see Cornelius, "Urbanization," pp. 1128–29. For a detailed study of Turkish squatters' political behavior, see Chapter 8.

95 Some students of Latin American settlements have noted repeatedly the cooperative work undertaken by squatters in building schools, sewage systems, and so on; others have claimed that the squatters are not interested in self-help projects. The Turkish squatters, despite occasional practice of *imece,* a rural form of collective work, are quite deficient in this respect. This may be attributed to traditions of strong government that inhibit individual initiative.

96 Ray, *Politics,* pp. 36, 103; Medina, *Favela,* pp. 36–80; Mangin, "Latin

American Squatter Settlements," p. 82. The attempts by the Movimiento de Izguierda Revolucionaria in Venezuela to use the *barrios* were unsuccessful since the organizers seemed to have been guided by their own theories rather than the realities of the *barrio;* Ray, *Politics,* pp. 129–130. During the last days of our survey, the University of Istanbul underwent one of its periodic student upheavals. Since some of the members of the research team were students or recent graduates, a few squatters became uncooperative and one of them called the interviewers "bolsheviks," who came to stir up trouble in the settlement.

97 Nelson, *Migrants.*
98 Mangin, "Latin American Squatter Settlements," p. 84. Mangin believes that to work hard for one's own interest and save money while dealing mostly with one's own family members and voting conservatively are the characteristics of this ideology.
99 Roger Le Tourneau, "Social Change in the Muslim Cities of North Africa," p. 533.
100 A good account of this migration is in Montagne, *La naissance.*
101 See J. Buy, "Bidonville et ensemble moderne," pp. 71–121; André Adam, "Le Bidonville de Ben Msik," pp. 61–199, and "La Population Musulmane de l'Algerie." Several publications in this series provide excellent background information on population problems in North Africa; see also Descloitres et al., *L'Algerie,* pp. 63, 80; Pierre Nora, *Les Francais d'Algerie;* Marcel Egretaud, *Réalité de la Nation Algerienne.*
102 Le Tourneau, "Social Change," p. 532.
103 Montagne, *La naissance,* p. 248.
104 Frantz Fanon, *The Wretched of the Earth,* p. 129. See also Irene L. Gendzier, *Frantz Fanon.*

Chapter 2. Historical roots of migration and the "gecekondu" in Turkey

1 For an extensive study of population movements in the Ottoman State in the nineteenth and twentieth centuries based on archival materials, see Kemal H. Karpat, *Migration and Its Effects in the Ottoman State in the Nineteenth Century,* paper submitted to Conference on Economic History and Population, Princeton University June, 1974; and "Ottoman Immigration Policies and Settlement in Palestine" in I. Abu-Lughod and Baha Abu-Luban, eds., *Settler Regimes in Africa and the Arab World,* Wilmette, Ill. 1974, pp. 57–72.
2 On the historical background of migration and settlement, see Ömer Lutfi Barkan, "Osmanlı Imparatorluğunda bir iskân ve kolonizasyon metodu olarak sürgünler," *Istanbul Universitesi Iktisat Fakültesi Mecmuası,* 13 (1951–52), 15 (1952–54); Oğuz Arı, *Bulgaristanlı Göçmenlerin Intibakı,* Ankara, 1960; Ahmet Refik [Altınay], *Anadolu'da Türk Aşiretleri,* Istanbul, 1960; Wolfram Eberhard, "Nomads and

Farmers in the Southeast Turkey," *Oriens,* 6 (1953); Encyclopaedia of Islam (Turkish edition), under "Göç"; A. C. Eren, *Türkiye'de Göç ve Göçmen Meseleleri, Tanzimat Devri,* Istanbul, 1966; Z. F. Fındıkoğlu, Türkiye'de Muhaceret meselesi ve bibliografik kaynaklar," *İş* (September 1, 1954), pp. 13–16; Cevat Geray, "Turkiyeden ve Türkiye'ye Göçler ve Göçmenlerin Iskânı," *Siyasal Bilgiler Fakültesi Dergisi* (January, 1962); Tayyib Gökbilgin, *Rumeli'de Yörükler, Tatarlar ve Evlad-ı Fatihan,* Istanbul, 1957; Huseyin Raci Efendi, *Zağra Müftüsünün Hatraları,* Istanbul, 1973; Hue L. Kostanick, *Turkish Settlement of Bulgarian Turks,* doctoral thesis, University of California, Berkeley, 1957; Kostanick, "Turkey's Resettlement of Refugees from Bulgaria, 1950–1953," *Middle East Journal* (Winter, 1955); Cengiz Orhonlu, *Osmanlı Imparatorluğunda Aşiretleri Iskân Teşebbüsü, 1691–1696,* Istanbul, 1963; Bilal N. Şimşir, *Rumeliden Türk Göçleri,* 2 vols., Ankara, 1968, 1970; Ziya H. Ülken, "Un aperçu bibliographique du problème des refugiés en Turquie," *Sosyoloji Dergisi,* 10–11 (1955–56); Sabahattin Zaim, "Yugoslavya'dan Türk muhaceratı," *Türk Yurdu,* 11 (1959).

3 The Ministry of Reconstruction and Settlement was established on May 14, 1958, through Law § 7116. There had been a similar organization in the 1920s. See *Les fonctions, l'organisation et les activités du Ministère de la Reconstruction et du Reetablissment,* Ankara, 1966.

4 Wolf-Dieter Hütteroth, *Ländliche Siedlungen im südlichen Inneranatolien in den letzten vierhundert Jahren,* Göttingen, 1968. The historical background to population movements is in Kemal H. Karpat, *An Inquiry into the Social Foundations of Nationalism in the Ottoman State: From Social Estates to Classes, From Millets to Nations,* Princeton, 1973.

5 Üner Turgay, "The Development of Trabzon in the Nineteenth Century," doctoral dissertation, University of Wisconsin, Madison, forthcoming in 1976.

6 For a history of the town, see Hasan Tahsin Okutan, *Şebinkarahisar ve Cıvarı, Cografya, Tarih, Kultür, Folklor,* Giresun, 1949. For the economic and political relationship between the old Muslim town and village, see A. H. Hourani and M. Stern, eds., *The Islamic City,* pp. 14ff.

7 For instance, the village of Yeniyol was called Anna in the past allegedly because it was founded under a Greek princess ruler by that name. We did find in the ruins of an old church some coins bearing the figure of a woman. It is possible that the name relates to Anna Comnena, the queen of Trebizond, who married the king of Georgia, Bagrat V, and was captured by Tamerlane in 1386. Greeks left the village to settle in towns along the sea.

8 Great Britain, the House of Commons, *Parliamentary Papers,* 60 (1868–69), 431–32.

9 The Ottoman census of 1831 shows the provinces of Sivas and Trabzon, which covered our area of study, as having 270,820 and 125,119 male

Muslims and 49,543 and 11,431 male Christians, respectively. See E. Z. Karal, *Osmalı Imparatorlugunda Ilk Nüfus Sayımı, 1831*, Ankara, 1943, pp. 152–53, 177–78, 210, and 213–14; and Fazil Akbal, "1831 tarihinde Osmanlı Imparatorlugunda idari taksimat ve nüfus," *Belleten* (Türk Tarih Kurumu), 15, 60 (Ankara, 1951), 622, 626, and 628.

10   The information that is oral history is fully supported by research; see Charles Issawi, "The Tabriz-Trabzon Trade, 1830–1900, Rise and Decline of a Route," *International Journal of Middle East Studies*, 1 (1970), 18–27.

11   Great Britain, the House of Commons, *Parliamentary Papers*, 66 (1874), 1077–78.

12   Ibid., 71 (1878–79), 1027.

13   Ibid., 60 (1868–69), 433–34.

14   Ibid., 71 (1878–79), 1023–24.

15   According to Munis Sayılgan of Şebinkarahisar, who was a soldier in the local police unit at the time, the town merchants consisted of Armenians and some Greeks. They brought from Istanbul steel (imported from abroad), cotton, and clothes, and collected wax, hides, and eggs from the local Turkish peasants and sent them to Malatya, Elaziğ, Diyarbakır, and other cities. Armenians were engaged in the mulberry brandy and alum businesses. The trade route crossed the mountains to the seaport of Giresun. Mules were used for transportation. The Armenian merchants, who had organized themselves, gave the signal for a local uprising in 1915. This resulted in the burning of the town since the rebels, although a minority, occupied the citadel overlooking the town and fired indiscriminately on the town population.

16   The members of the leftist group in the first National Assembly, as well as the leaders of the Green Army, supposedly representing a religious-social revolutionary movement in 1920, found considerable support in this area. Possibly they were seeking a change of regime to remedy their own economic problems

17   *Gurbet* means also "away from home" or figuratively "a wanderer in foreign lands." It is an important subject and deserves more attention than can be given in this study.

18   A former *gurbetçi* described the situation as follows: "What destroyed us was the fact that we married at the age of 15. As soon as we marry we are forced to leave the parental home. If we ask our father how we are going to make a living he points to a small piece of land and says 'till and sow it and God will take care of you.' By the time we are 25 we are crushed by the burden of 6–8 children. My view now is that a man should not marry until he can make a decent living."

19   The late Zihni Yılmaz, the colorful septuagenarian in the village of Yeniyol, who fought in the War of Liberation in 1920–22, and against the Kurdish revolt of Sheikh Sait in 1925, was wounded twice and decorated. He had in his room large pictures of Atatürk and Ismet Inönü to whom he referred as "my commanders"; he did not permit anyone to criticize them.

20 This problem has been discussed in Kemal H. Karpat, *Turkey's Politics,* Princeton, 1959; and "Social Effects of Farm Mechanization in Turkish Villages."

21 From 1955 to 1965 about 25,000 tractors, 31,000 cultivators, and 7,000 combined thrashers were introduced, accounting for 50 to 220 percent increase in this type of machinery. See Ministry of Agriculture, *Tarım Istatistikleri Özeti, 1966,* Ankara, 1967.

22 These are observations made in some villages in 1970. The custom of sharing one's income with all relatives, at least by supporting them, seemed to be losing its former power.

23 The farm mechanization in 1952 and 1953 had little impact in parts of our research area since the scarcity of land and the rough terrain makes the use of the tractor impossible, especially in the Şebinkarahisar area. It did have some impact in the Suşehri and Hafik districts, where terrain conditions permit the use of machines.

24 Ibrahim Yasa, *Ankara'da Gecekondu Aileleri,* p. 46.

25 The figures have been compiled from official statistics that appeared in a publication related to the total quantitative transformation of Turkey. Kemal H. Karpat, *Social Change and Politics in Turkey.*

26 *25 Ekim 1970 Genel Nüfus Sayımı* (State Office of Statistics), Ankara, 1970, p. 6. Statistical information on the village urban shift of population for 1927–65 may better illustrate the situation.

	Urban population	Rural population	Total population of Turkey
Population increase 1927–65 (percentage)	227.44	98.92	130
Total population in 1927	3,301,046	10,347,224	13,648,270
Total population in 1965	10,808,869	20,582,338	31,391,207

Source: Ministry of Reconstruction and Settlement, *Türkiye'de Şehirleşme ve Konut Durumu,* Ankara, 1966, pp. 33.

For population growth, see also J. C. Dewdney, "Turkey: Recent Population Trends," in J. I. Clarke and W. B. Fisher, eds., *Populations of the Middle East and North Africa,* London, 1972, pp. 40ff.

27 Sami Öngör, "1950–1960 devrinde Türkiye'de iç göçler," *Ankara Universitesi Siyasal Bilgiler Fakültesi Dergisi,* 17, 3–4 (1962), 320; and Cevat Geray, "Urbanization in Turkey," 159ff. See also Ministry of Reconstruction and Settlement, *Türkiye'de Şehirleşme ve Konut Durumu – Şehirleşme, Gecekondular ve Konut Politikası* Ankara, 1966; Mahir Gencay, *Gecekondu Problemi* Ankara, 1962. The related studies are mentioned in the general bibliography.

28 Chief publications on the Turkish *gecekondu* are the following: Ibrahim Yasa, *Ankara.* This is a study based on interviews with 1000 heads of

gecekondu families in Ankara. It deals extensively with the sociological aspects of squatter settlements. Another rather unsatisfactory study commissioned by the Istanbul Chamber of Trade was carried out by Charles W. M. Hart, *Zeytinburnu Gecekondu Bölgesi*, and deals with Zeytinburnu, a rather old squatter area of Istanbul. A good study is Granville H. Sewell's *Squatter Settlements in Turkey*. It deals with the Aktepe settlement in Ankara and makes a number of interesting points. Among the government publications Turhan and Ayda Yorükhan, *Gecekondular ve Gecekondu Bölgelerinin Sosyo-Kültürel Özellikleri*, Ankara, 1968, has useful social and cultural data. Kemal H. Karpat, *Gecekondu Sorunu Uzerine*, includes seven talks on the subject. See also Ned Levine, *Rural-Urban Migration and Its Effects on Urbanization over the Next Fifty Years*, a paper presented to the conference on Turkish development organized by Hacettepe and Wisconsin universities, June, 1974. See also a request by the Turkish government for assistance addressed to the United Nations, the first country to do so in accordance with ECOSOC resolution 1224 (Ankara, 1971). It includes excellent information. There are also a series of unconcluded surveys of *gecekondus* undertaken at Hacettepe University and Middle East Technical University in Ankara, which may be published in the future. These were consulted for the present study and some of them are mentioned in appropriate places.

29　Ministry of Reconstruction and Settlement, *Ankara Gülveren-Çınçınbağları ve Topraklık Gecekonduları*, p. 12. Yasa found that only 17 heads of family of a total of 916 had come from abroad; Yasa, *Ankara*, p. 262.

30　Ministry of Reconstruction and Settlement, *Izmir Gürceşme Gecekondu Araştırması*, p. 9.

31　Hart, *Zeytinburnu*, p. 126, table 4. Possibly only Taşlıtarla, a squatter district in Istanbul, has predominantly foreign-born residents.

32　*Millet Meclisi Tutanak Dergisi*, session 2, vol. 5, p. 584. The Minister of Reconstruction and Settlement, Haludun Menteşeoğlu, attributed the rise of the *gecekondu* to unemployment in villages and to lack of "civilized means of existence," that is, lack of "social and cultural facilities." Ibid., vol. 2, p. 665 (debate of April 7, 1966).

33　Ibid., p. 589.

34　The date is taken from official parliamentary records. Ibid., pp. 568–95; vol. 6, pp. 106–10; vol. 7, pp. 620–22; debates of March 24 to July 11, 1966. Text of law in *Resmi Gazete*, No. 12362 (July 30, 1966).

35　These laws are numbers 1580, 2290, and especially 5218, 5228, 5431, 6188, 7367, and 327. After the 1960 revolution the laws were renumbered. Actually as early as 1943, when Turkey underwent some limited industrialization mostly in the area of textile and household goods, there was some movement toward cities. The ruling Republican party suggested through a commission that the government enterprises – most of the heavy industry was state owned – provide housing for its personnel and that some provisions for low-cost housing be made. The vacant lots were to be reserved to this purpose. However, no concrete and wide-scale action was undertaken. When the migration began to accelerate late in the 1940s, laws 5218 and 5228 were passed in order to sell public land to cooperatives so as to provide dwellings for those who did not own houses. The beneficiaries of this law were almost exclusively the salaried groups and not the rural migrants. Anyway, the *gecekondu* had not yet become a major problem. When it became so in 1953, a law was passed that eased the acquisition of title by the established *gecekondus*. However, alarmed by the mushrooming of the *gecekondus*, the government began to adopt restrictive measures. It instituted legal procedures for demolishing the dwellings and prohibited the introduction of utilities into the *gecekondu* (Law 6188). See Yasa, *Ankara*, pp. 35–39, and Sewell, *Squatter Settlements*, pp. 55–57.

36 *MMTD*, session 2, vol. 5, pp. 541–42 (Ihsan Kabadayı, Republican party deputy of Konya). *Uygarlık*, or *medeniyet*, which means civilization, is often used in Turkish as synonymous with technological advancement and the comforts derived from it.

37 The cause of migration in the village of Kayacık was bureaucratic blunder. The landless peasants of Kırıntı asked Atatürk in the 1920s to permit them to settle in this village, which had been populated by Greeks. Hınzırı, the old name of Kayacık, was the only village inhabited by Greeks among the 32 villages attached to the district seat of Mindeval. It was thus settled by 140 people who received 10 *dönüms* (about 2 acres) per capita. However, the new settlers could not receive the title to the land, despite the central government's decision, because of the opposition of a businessman, Tevfik Ekmen, in the town of Alucra, who wanted the land for his own "poor" kin. Eventually, the deeds were issued in 1958, but at a total cost of 240,000 liras, or about $26,000. Unable to pay for the land the villagers migrated to Istanbul. The village had only 8 families at the time of the visit in 1968, and only one man left in 1974. Ten years earlier the population consisted of 60 families, or about 300 people. If the terms of land payment were eased the villagers thought that it could flourish rapidly.

In the Şebinkarahisar area, the village of Turupçu or Turupçular was settled in 1926 by 200 Turkish exchangees families from the village of Katranza, district of Kayalar, in the province of Salonica, which was left to Greece. Some of the exchangees sold their land to people from Alucra and went to live in other towns. Apparently, the tensions between the migrants from abroad and the local people, which occasionally gave place to serious clashes, was one of the causes of migration on the part of some migrants from abroad. This village, however, boasts 90 percent literacy and is one of the most advanced in the area.

38 Some of the squatters from Kırıntı, Yeniköy, and Kayacık were briefly studied in 1964 as an extension of the village in the city; see Peter Suzuki, "Peasants Without Plows": and "Encounters with Istanbul."

39 The surveyed villages and towns account for 45 percent of the squatters in the three settlements in Istanbul. The villages (41 percent) are Kırıntı, Yeniköy, Yukarı, Görede, Tatar, Düzyayla, Kayacık, Yeniyol,

Tosunlu, Koyuncular, Kahraman, and Yağmurlu; the towns (3.9 percent) are Şiran, Suşehri, Koyulhisar, Alucra, Şebinkarahisar, Araklı, and Sürmene. These villages and towns are in the provinces of Sivas, Giresun, Gümüşhane, and Trabzon; 63 percent of the people of the three *gecekondus* surveyed come from these provinces.

40 Evliya Celebi, *Seyahatnamese*, Istanbul, 1970, vol. 3, 196–98; vol. 4, 80–86.

41 The families of Bal, Coşkun, and Günel in Kırıntı had 12, 24, and 27 representatives among the squatters interviewed. The Coşkun family, once called Sofular, apparently took its present name after the secularist reforms of 1923–35, in order to avoid the stigma of conservatism and religiosity that Sofu (pious) carried. The village of Yeniköy was formed by four families who left Kırıntı after one of the old established families, old nomad stock, broke a marriage promise. The village has four *mahalles*, or quarters, each one inhabited by one extended family: Güner, Kara, Şahintaş, and Selvi. Their representation in the squatter settlement was 7, 13, 10, and 3 people, respectively. Interestingly enough, the Selvis, who are the least numerous family in the village, have the smallest number of representatives in the *gecekondus*.

42 See M. B. Kiray, "Squatter Housing, Fast De-peasantization and Slow Workerization in Underdeveloped Countries," paper presented at the 7th World Congress of Sociology, Varna, 1970.

43 Some verbatim expressions taken directly from the questionnaires describe the agricultural situation in a clear and dramatic fashion typical of the Turkish villager's mode of talk: "The land was poor. There was no work. All the village land could barely feed 15 families. We did not even have pasture lands. We took the beasts into the pastures of other villages. Even on the mountains the herds could not stay longer than 40 days. The wood, oil, cheese in the village costs just as much as in the city, so why stay there? Land was insufficient. Even those who had enough land escaped the village in order to avoid being shot." (This last statement comes from a squatter from the village of Tosunlu – Trabzon – where local rivalries reached an unusually high tension.) "The production of the land and of the beasts has diminished. I knew that the land was to be divided among my 5–6 brothers, so I left before it was too late." "The land is not really scarce but it is thoroughly unproductive. We hear that in the past the land was more productive and there were fewer people." "I just cannot figure out why productivity had decreased. Land is insufficient and poor. Very little crop is sold to outside. Besides everybody is raising the same crop and so there is no market for it in the village. If it rains we have some crop, if it does not we do not. Land is scarce everywhere. We gathered money in the village and sent a man to look for land to Siirt and Doğu Beyazit [southeastern Turkey] but could not find. So we all migrated." "We worked the land, cut and sold wood and still we did not make enough. So the village remained backward. My father did not have land. He was making a living by using his mules for transportation. The new [mechanized] transportation made it useless."

44 A sample study for the entire country indicates that villagers migrating from forest areas settle in the next town (58 percent), whereas villagers located near and outside forests (71 percent) settle mostly in cities and the metropolis (Istanbul, Ankara, Izmıt). The three largest cities attracted 22, 30, and 33 percent of the migrants departing from the three type of villages. T. Yurt, G. Erzil, and H. T. Sevil, *Orman Köylerinin Sosyo-Ekonomik Durumu*, p. 71, table 59. This study of two types of villages located in forest areas indicates as cause of migration the availability of employment opportunities in the city (47 and 40 percent), poverty in the village (11 and 13 percent), landlessness (4 and 7 percent), lack of educational facilities (1 and 2 percent), and other causes. Ibid., p. 74, table 62.

45 It is interesting to note that the desire for higher education among Turkish squatters was less important than in Latin America, probably because in the 1960s higher education in Turkey was monopolized by city dwellers, sons of bureaucrats, and upper-class villagers and townsmen.

Chapter 3. The establishment and growth of the "gecekondu"

1 The dwellers, some of whom are Alevis, insisted in calling the settlement Nafibaba, possibly in deference to the Bektashi "saint" by that name buried on the hill top overlooking their site. Lately they seem to prefer the name Hisarüstü.

2 W. L. Flinn, "Rural and Intra-Urban Migration in Colombia," in F. F. Rabinovitz and F. M. Trueblood, eds., *Latin American Urban Research*, vol. 1, 1971, p. 85. A study dealing with migrants in Turkey found that migrants from all over the country showed a preference for Istanbul regardless of distance, whereas in other cities distance was important in determining the place of destination. See John R. Clark, *City, Site and Choice of Destination by Turkish Migrants*, paper presented at the Middle East Studies Association meeting, Toronto, November, 1969.

3 Verbatim excerpts from questionnaires may supplement the information concerning the roles of relatives and *hemşeris*
Women on housing and jobs: "My relatives went to visit the village so we stayed in their home." "My husband built the house three weeks before I arrived." "We stayed with my husband's brother." "We set up a tent and stayed there." "We all stayed in my husband's room. He worked as a gardener for a family at Baltaliman. Then we heard that houses were built here and came too so as not to pay the rent." "We stayed with my in-laws for almost ten years, and then built our own house." "For one year I could not work because I had a child. Then I decided to work and found employment in one week."
Men on housing and jobs: "I stayed with my uncle without paying him rent. I stayed in the construction site even in the winter time." "I stayed a few days at the hotel and then started this house." "I stayed with the relatives of my wife." "I stayed two years with my aunt." "I stayed with relatives but paid rent." "I stayed with my friends; we worked and ate

together and then departed." "I found work before I came." "I found work immediately after I came through a friend." "My uncle was working in an enterprise. After the Revolution (1960) they were afraid of sabotage so they added new guards, so he told me about it and I went there and was hired." "I spent a month or so looking around. Then I went to a factory and asked if they needed workers. They said yes." "For three months I could find nothing. I went back to the village and then returned to the city and found work." "I went and found the job by myself. I lifted bags of 300 pounds so that I could take care of my children. I would be ashamed to hear that I could not take care of my children." "First, I found the first job in 2–3 days. Then I found this present job and moved to it." "I used to come and work every summer in the malaria control campaign. Now I am on the permanent staff." "The director of the plant lay sick in the hospital where my father worked. It is through him that my father arranged for my employment."

4   I watched for days a young squatter in the Celâlettin Paşa settlement remove a rock inch by inch with a bare chisel and an ordinary hammer in order to add one room to his house. He had worked all day in the shipyards but the idea of improving "his" house gave him, as he explained it, boundless energy.

5   It was reported that the Turkish workers rejected plans for a housing project identical to one built in Germany because it limited living space to 1 or 2 bedrooms. They wanted houses with at least 3 or 4 living rooms.

Chapter 4. The social and economic structure of the "gecekondu"

1   F. C. Shorter and B. Güvenç, eds., *Turkish Demography*, p. 159. The population studies of Hacettepe University in Ankara provide extensive data on the size and birth and death rates in Turkish families.

2   Emre Kongar, *Survey of Familial Change in Two Turkish Gecekondu Areas*, table 1.

3   Kongar reports that in Izmir 62.5 percent of the *gecekondus* had nuclear families, as against 63.6 percent in the city; whereas in Ankara *gecekondus* the percentage of nuclear families was 72 percent. Ibid., table 2. See also Kongar, *Izmirde Şehirsel Ailenin Bazı Nitelikleri*.

4   Forty-nine percent of the men and only 24 percent of the women who could not pursue further studies cited poverty as the main reason; 31 percent cited the lack of schools as the cause. On the other hand, only 2 percent of the men, but 25 percent of the women, cited the parents' opposition and village traditions as the chief impediment to attending school or pursuing studies beyond elementary level. It is interesting to note that 46 percent of the unmarried cited poverty as the chief obstacle to higher education, whereas 14 percent confessed that they failed in the city schools because of personal deficiency or low IQ. The percentage of men and women who cited personal deficiency as the impediment to further education was 2 and 1 percent, respectively. On the other hand,

about 11 percent of the men, and slightly over 10 percent of the women said that they were orphans and had to care for younger brothers and sisters and could not attend school. This was the toll of *gurbetçilik*. For another view of migrants in the city, see Oguz Arı, *Istanbulda Göç ve Çalışma Hayatına Intibak Araştırması*, Istanbul, 1968.

5 A similarly high degree of freedom to choose professions prevailed in Ankara *gecekondus*; 87.6 percent of those interviewed in a survey said that they will allow their boys to freely choose a profession but only 25.2 percent will permit the girls to do so. Kongar, *Survey of Familial Change*, table 4.

6 Joan M. Nelson, *Sojourners vs. New Urbanites: Causes and Consequences of Temporary vs. Permanent Cityward Migration in Developing Nations*. Paper read through the courtesy of the author.

7 J. Hindernik and M. B. Kiray, *Social Stratification as an Obstacle to Development*.

8 In the questionnaire we used the word *güveniyorsun*, with the connotation of trust. During talks we discovered that in the squatters' understanding *güven* implied reliance more than trust.

Chapter 5. Association and leadership in three "gecekondus"

1 I believe that the high percentage of Alevi squatters in the three settlements studied is rather an exception, despite the fact that another study claims that the Alevis formed a high percentage of migrants and squatters in Ankara. See Granville Hardwich Sewell, *Squatter Settlements in Turkey*. The Alevis in the three settlements in Istanbul belonged to the Kızılbaş (red hat) group. The name was assumed by the Alevi Turkoman nomad tribes late in the fifteenth century and preserved as such even after they became sedentary. The migrants in the settlement belonged to the Tahtacı and Cepni branches of the Kızılbaş and are more traditionalist, community-oriented, and, in a way, secular than others. On the other hand, the Bektashis, another branch of the Alevis, came to represent the Alevis, including the Janissaries until their abolition in 1826, in towns. The difference between the rural and nomad Kızılbaş and urban Bektashis has widened considerably during the past four centuries, despite the fact that doctrinally they were identical. One was a folk religion; the other became an urban, unorthodox order. Formally, in the town of Hacı Bektaş where the founder of the order was buried, the Kızılbaş were represented by a Çelebi, whereas the Bektashis had a *baba*. The standard book on the order is J. K. Birge, *The Bektashi Order of Dervishes*. For a general view on Alevis see also, A. Gölpınarlı, *Alevi-Bektaşi Nefesleri*, Istanbul, 1963; J. M. Erişen and K. Samancıgil, *Hacı Bektaş Veli, Bektaşilik ve Alevilik Tarihi*, Istanbul, 1966; S. V. Ornek, *Sivas ve Çevresinde Hayatın Çeşitli Safhalarile Ilgili Batıl Inançlar ve Büyüsel Işlemlerin Etnolojik Tetkiki*, Ankara, 1966. The attitude of the migrant Kızılbaş toward the Bektashis is mentioned further in this chapter. It

would be interesting to find out whether indeed a substantial part of rural migrants in Turkey consisted of Alevis. One fact is certain: The Alevis inhabit the eastern mountainous and poorest sections of Turkey and are more predisposed toward migration than other relatively well-to-do villagers.

2 The leader, somewhat afraid that his highhanded rule in the *gecekondu* may be publicized, tried to incite the residents against the research team. He called the interviewers, all students or university graduates, political agitators bent on creating trouble. The students at Istanbul University were engaged at the time in one of their customary political actions. I admonished one man who referred to the researchers as "bolsheviks" and who asked his friends not to cooperate with them. Fortunately, all this happened during the last days of the survey and did create an unpleasant situation, possibly, also because of the intervention of higher government authorities whom I informed about the incident.

3 One of the important members of the Coşkun family suffered a mild heart attack early in 1974. When I visited the village of Kırıntı in the summer of 1974, his relatives all inquired about his health and I had to pay a special visit to the house of his brother and drink one glass of *ayran* (watered yogurt) as a sign of special deference to their social position.

4 Yasa took *namaz* (prayer) and *oruç* (fasting) as indicators of religious observance in the *gecekondus* of Ankara. He found that 30 percent of family heads – that is, men – prayed regularly, 40 percent irregularly, and 83 percent fasted regularly; 44 percent of the women prayed regularly, 33 percent irregularly, and 84 percent fasted. Yasa, *Ankara*, p. 222, table 106. These figures refer usually to older people since Yasa interviewed only family heads. I have a strong suspicion that those who said they prayed occasionally actually did not pray at all. Fasting – that is, abstaining from eating, drinking, and smoking – from sunrise to sundown is observed throughout Turkey largely because of its health value.

5 The Turkish sociologist Ziya Gökalp, inspired partly by Durkheim's collectivist views, formulated the ideology of Turkish nationalism on the basis of community and all it entailed. To him the nation was a community that acquired political consciousness. He was belittled and dismissed as a reactionary by many Western scholars and their Turkish counterparts. Contemporary research in sociology and social psychology indicates that Gökalp had much more insight than his critics into the nature of his society and the forms it assumed under the impact of modern forces. Some excellent insights into the political transformation of the villagers in the Balkans, with some relevance to Turkey, may be found in Mehmet Begiraj, *Peasantry and Revolution*, Ithaca, N.Y., 1966.

6 Sewell, *Squatter Settlements*, p. 178, n. 17.

7 Ibid.

8 William Mangin reports that the Indian migrants from the Peruvian coastal cities, who fixed the *barrio* roads on Sundays, claimed that they worked in Minga groups just like their Inca ancestors. Most of them had never heard of the Minga until they read about it in the newspapers; "Latin American Squatter Settlements," p. 82. The Turkish Alevis immigrants apparently learned their history and doctrine in the city.

9 At one point an Alevi leader in the community became very much incensed because a youth from the Black Sea village had approached an Alevi girl in impolite fashion. He cursed all the people from the region and called them Laz (a minority ethnic group from the extreme northeastern region). This caused a reaction among the youth from the Black Sea villages, who organized themselves in order to seek revenge and satisfaction. The uproar was quelled easily after the leaders intervened and calmed all parties. But one man was still offended by the incident and said that he "hated" the Alevis because they did not follow orthodox rites and thus were not good Muslims. But the same man was instrumental in arranging a marriage between a Sunni boy and an Alevi girl who had fallen in love with each other but were meeting with some opposition from their parents.

10 The *gecekondus* of Ankara showed the same conservatism toward women; 63 to 78 percent of the husbands did not approve of their wives going outside the house without covering their head, wearing short-sleeved dresses, going out without stockings, cutting their hair, or doing their nails. On the other hand, 64 percent of the husbands were against women wearing the veil. Yasa, *Ankara,* p. 217, table 105. It must be pointed out that 26 percent of those interviewed by Yasa had been in Ankara 11 to 20 years and 25 percent 21 to 40 years – that is, they moved in when Ankara was still a provincial town and the settlement stayed segregated from Yenişehir, or the new city, which is the modern section. It is only in the last 10 years or so, because of the rapid growth of Ankara, that intensive social mobility and its modernizing impact was felt in the *gecekondu*. For squatters' length of stay in Ankara see Yasa, *Ankara,* p. 74.

11 In addition to Turkish, 7 men and 5 women spoke Kurdish or Laz (the last related to Georgian), and 2 men spoke Arabic, which may indicate their ethnic origin; 5 men and 1 woman (all migrants from abroad) also spoke Balkan languages, though they were of Turkish origin. On the other hand, 21 men (usually of younger age, a few of whom had worked in Germany), 5 women, and 30 unmarrieds claimed to speak Western languages, possibly very poorly. Actually, these referred to language courses taken in school. A few *gecekondu* dwellings located farther on the hill north of Celâlettin Paşa were inhabited by Kurds, "who did not mix with anybody because they wanted to establish a Republic of their own." One may assume that this was hearsay since the Kurds, all recent arrivals, had hardly time to become politically conscious of their ethnic differences. (The question of Kurds in Turkey

is very different from that in Iraq and Iran. A proportion of Kurds in Turkey are Shiites or Alevis. They were originally Turkish-speaking Alevi Turkomans who rebelled against the central Ottoman government in the fifteenth and sixteenth centuries. Faced with military and political pressure, they took refuge in the domains of the feudal Kurdish lords, who were recognized local autonomy by the Sultan. Gradually the Turkoman groups acquired the Kurdish language but remained closer in outlook to the Turkish Alevi groups.

12   Brian W. Beeley, "The Turkish Village Coffeehouse as a Social Institution," pp. 475–93.

13   I had to go to each major coffeehouse before interviewing the squatters and explain the purpose of the survey. While answering questions in the coffeehouse then and on many other occasions, I had to drink many cups of strong tea, as anyone working with squatters or villagers would have to do.

14   A study shows that about 64 percent of the villagers interviewed in a study showed the *muhtars* to be the most influential men in villages. I. Yurt, G. Ergil, and H. T. Sevil, *Orman Köylerinin Sosyo-Ekonomik Durumu*, p. 94, table 84.

15   Richard B. Scott, *The Village Headman in Turkey*.

16   See, for comparison, Gilda Echeverria Alarcón, "Las Organizaciones Informales y la Difusion de la Informacion en los Sectores Marginales Urbanos," in Cardona Guttierrez.

17   Some village professions survived also in the *gecekondu* although this was a rare exception. The zurna, an old type of flute that belonged to the family of Kara in the village of Yeniköy, was still played by a member of the same family during holidays and wedding festivities.

18   Economic activities and occupations are occasionally monopolized by squatters from one region; one factory in Istanbul employed workers only from the employer's own region since he trusted them and had faith in their ability.

Chapter 6. The urbanization of the "gecekondu"

1   The need for an integrative theoretical framework had been signaled and partially satisfied by Leo Jakobson and Ved Prakash, eds., *Urbanization and National Development*, Beverly Hills, Calif., 1971, pp. 17ff.

2   A collective work undertaken by the Ankara Chamber of Architecture defines the city as a "special human settlement which can assume specific features in time and space" and urbanization as "the transformation of the city in a specific direction" subject to a series of variables whose relations may vary. The chief variables of urbanization are heterogeneity, action, competition, anonymity, division of labor, concentration, specialization, differentiation, and so on. *Türkiyede Kentleşme*, Ankara, 1971, pp. 4–5; Ruşen Keleş, *Türkiyede Şehirleşme, Konut ve Gecekondu;* and Turhan and Ayda Yörükhan, *Urbanization, Squatter Houses and Housing Policy*, Ankara, 1966. Also see, Emel

Barışçı, *Şehirsel Toplum Kalkınması Açısından Ülkemizde Şehirleşme Hareketleri,* (prepared for State Planning Organization), Ankara, 1966. The same distinction between the study of cities and urbanization – the latter being a "phenomenon describing a process of change in the situs of population due to changing conditions in society at large" – is provided by Jakobson and Prakash, *Urbanization,* p. 15.

3 I have known quite well and had intensive communication with the Balkan peasants notably in Romania and Bulgaria, whose languages I speak. These villagers had higher standards of education and life and were better organized than the Turkish villagers. Yet their feeling about the city and their relations with it, at least until the 1950s were marked by deep antagonism and mistrust, as though they were two completely different worlds. The Turkish peasant, however, has a positive view toward the city and regards it, though inaccessible and ready to exploit him at times, as part of his own world. The universal suffrage and the dominant role played by peasant votes in national elections contributed in developing a positive view of the city.

4 According to Allan Schnalberg, the determining factor in modernization is the nature of the community of early residence – that is, acceptability of what he called modernism – rather than the time of migration. Though this study follows Sorokin, Zimmerman, and Sjoberg and postulates on the differences between urban and rural organization, it nevertheless indirectly stresses the impact of modernism on urbanism. The criteria of modernism according to this study was involvement in a broad information network, freedom from extended family ties, involvement in an egalitarian conjugal union, freedom from intensive religious involvement, adaptive relation to an environment beyond the local community, and involvement in a suprafamilial, economic system. Schnalberg, "Rural-Urban Residence and Modernism," pp. 71–85.

5 An average of 84 percent of villagers living in or near forested areas said that if it were possible they would like to settle in a city. When asked whether their friends and relatives who had migrated and settled in cities were satisfied with their urban life, an average of 83 percent of the same villagers said that they were indeed happy to live in the city. An average of 80 percent also said that the migrants in the city earned well. A very high percentage also thought that the children of the people who migrated to cities had better opportunities, that they were not lonely, that their morality was high, and that they had a good time there. I. Yurt, G. Ergil, and H. Sevil, *Orman Köylerinin Sosyo-Ekonomik Durumu,* pp. 76, 79, 80; tables 67, 69, 75.

6 Ned Levine, "Old Culture – New Culture," p. 357. Levine's study was based on interviews with 400 *kapıcı,* or caretakers – maids who take care of apartment buildings. They do not form a homogeneous community but live dispersed in basement rooms. One assumes that their contacts with the city and acculturation was bound to be greater than these living in the *gecekondus* because of their intensive exposure to contact with city residents.

7 The dress reforms of Atatürk from 1925 to 1935 were criticized by native conservatives as a blow to Turkish cultural identity. Then the sophisticated Westerners criticized him as having adopted the rather shallow forms of modernity. Finally, the Turkish radical left has criticized the dress reform as another proof of Atatürk's intention to create a Turkish society according to the model of a "corrupt imperialistic West." Actually Atatürk, who had an intuitive knowledge of the society's own methods of change, initiated the dress reform in order to undermine the social inertia and opened the way to other changes in society. It must be remembered that it was during Atatürk's time that the first organized efforts were made to develop an authentic Turkish national culture based on folklore and the vernacular.

8 This attitude cannot be attributed to fatalism, long associated with Muslim culture, since the very move into the city and the relative welfare achieved there showed that one's fate was not decided in advance but conditioned by objective factors. The old fatalism, if it really existed at all, was the consequence of limited economic opportunity and lack of social mobility.

9 Gossiping about women's infidelity is one of the most dreaded aspects of family life in villages. This is a form of social pressure against the temptation of the outside world, especially with regard to women whose husbands are working away. There are cases in which unscrupulous men, notably from towns, exploit this situation and delegate henchmen to procure from the villages the wives of the seasonal workers. I learned personally of a case while visiting a village in the Black Sea region. A young woman whose husband was working in Istanbul and who had only very few relatives in the village was abducted by four armed men and taken to Samsun to a rich man. She was returned to the village only because she was *dolu,* or pregnant.

10 I have witnessed one case in which three men tried to study algebra and geometry by consulting with each other in order to take examinations and qualify as certified masons and mechanics. Unfortunately the intellectuals, still subject to their elitist philosophies and preoccupations with total solutions to the country's problems, had no time to educate these aspiring *gecekondu* residents.

11 Frederick Frey reports that 12 percent of the village population had no radios and 53 percent had a total of 1 to 9 receivers. The radio situation in villages has changed drastically since Frey conducted his research in 1961. Frey, *The Mass Media and Rural Development in Turkey,* Cambridge, Mass., 1966, pp. 28, 44. Granville Sewell also reported a sharp increase in the use of radios in the *gecekondus, Squatter Settlements in Turkey,* pp. 316–17.

12 Some townspeople tend to think of the villagers as being naive, ignorant, but also full of guile. There are stories of bridges, streetcars, and squares in the city sold to villagers by smart townsmen.

13 Another survey of migrants in Ankara showed that squatters were willing to expose themselves to urban behavior but lack of income

inhibited them. The effect of education was higher in achieving urban participation even than in finding jobs and securing higher income. Ned Levine, "Value Orientation Among Migrants in Ankara, Turkey," p. 56.

14 The case of E. G. is a good example. Aged 17 when interviewed, she was born to a very poor family of sharecroppers in the region of Suşehri. Some relatives helped raise her and her sister, and eventually brought them to Istanbul in order to prevent their impoverished father from marrying them off for some meager *başlık*. The two girls lived in Istanbul with an aunt. Both found jobs and eventually built a *gecekondu* dwelling for themselves. Meanwhile E. G. fell in love with a married man. Aware of the impossibility of uniting with her beloved without breaking his marriage, she decided to forget her love. Meanwhile her aunt and parents, sensing her problem, forced her – in fact, engaged her – in absentia to a young man who came from a nearby village. E. G. was so angry that she fought with her aunt and tried to convince her that a marriage with a freely chosen and loved man would be a happy one. She complained bitterly that village girls were not free to choose their husbands and criticized her mother "who should have given birth not to six children but only two, and should have raised them properly and sent them to school." E. G. denounced the *başlık* as a kind of treatment resembling the sale of animals. Her aunt listened and, with complete confidence in the wisdom of the elder, passed the ultimate judgment: "Büyükler herşeyin iyisini bilir" (The elders know the best for everything).

15 Emre Kongar, *Survey of Familial Changè in Two Turkish Gecekondu Areas,* and *Izmirde Şehirsel Ailen in Bazı Nitelikleri.*

16 Even some professionals still persist in seeing the problem solely in terms of land and housing. See Sadık Gökçe, "Gecekondu," *Milliyet* (August 31–September 2, 1973).

17 Some excerpts from the interviews are typical: "If a man has no brains neither money nor education will help. If you have it, however, then you can use money to educate yourself." "This nation is being awakened. Nobody will stop our children from going high according to their ability. Even in villages men who were rich men's shepherds have become *muhtars.*" "Education, money and ability complement each other." "You may go up by nepotism for a while but at the critical moments you are lost. Suppose you give me a university diploma now, what can I do with it?" "If Turkey is ruled by a Republican regime you can become president." "A man with ability can rise under any conditions." "According to Europeans we are not educated. Without education your ability is valueless." "Ability is above everything else." "If you have ability and education money is a natural result." Those who defended the opposite viewpoints were equally emphatic: "You cannot reach the highest position in Turkey without the support of the powerful." "You cannot go anywhere without money. Even if you had some you could not go anywhere since the city people back only each other." "The poor children cannot enter the university because they

have no backing." "Everything in the country is on the rich man's side." "In Turkey you cannot go up without backing, and that is what keeps the country underdeveloped." "Everything is money. If you have it you can do all you desire and become anything you want."

18   The respondents most liked this and the next question and took visible pleasure in describing their aspired positions. Obviously many had hoped at some point in their lives to achieve higher status than the present one. Random excerpts from many squatters follow: "I can be a doctor or engineer." "I like to be an entrepreneur and employ many people who would make a decent living." "I would like to be a high school teacher." "I would like to have a position which would enable me to order around." "I would like to be a Vehbi Koç [the richest industrialist of Turkey] to open factories and help the poor." "I would like to be a high official to work for the country and also promote Islam." "I could be even a professor." "If I had the opportunity I could become anything I wanted. Those who have better skills and positions than me were not born with them. We all spent nine months in the mother's womb and are equal." "I would like to become a star soccer player." "I would like to be a foreign ministry official to travel around the world." "Napoleon said that in order to win the war you need three things: money, money, and money." "I would like to be a general and have for ten days absolute authority to end all evil." "You must tell lies in order to reach the highest positions. I cannot lie so I cannot go high." "I would like to drive a car like other women in the city, they show that we women can do it too." "I [a woman] would like to be functionary to sit at a table and deal with everybody." "I cannot think of anything because I do not have the ability." "I was so eager to study that I surely would have become a great man if I could have completed my studies." "If I [a woman] studied I might have become another Şule Hanım [a unique Muslim woman preacher]." "I would like to be a man because there is no life for women." "I could become a deputy." "The president is a man like you and me. If I had what he had I would be in this place." "I could become a deputy, I know so well the villagers' problems that I would solve them."

Chapter 7. "Gecekondu" – village relations and rural change

1   The lengthy debates about the true meaning of "modernization" have reached the point where one cannot define it at all. My definition is an eclectic one, adopted merely to illustrate the migrants' role in the village change.

2   In Turkish these are named *amca* and *hala* (uncle and aunt from the father's side); *dayı* and *teyze* (uncle and aunt from the mother's side).

3   The idea of receiving some income from inheritance is one of the most deeply rooted traditions in Turkish-Muslim culture. I know of a case in which a man, though very poor himself, worked and saved 500 liras to pay his sisters their share in the parental house some 30 years after the house had been torn down. The sisters had no claim to the house. He

said he lived in the house longer and as an elder brother it was his responsibility to give his sisters their due share—*hakkını vermek.*

4　I am using the concept of empathy not only as part of the process of integration into the city and national life, as did Daniel Lerner in *The Passing of the Traditional Society,* but also as the migrant's ability to develop a new understanding of the village and the villagers, and eventually raise their living standards. The idea of the development envisaged by the squatter as well as his sense of responsibility toward his village was determined mostly by urban models and modern social ideas. Blood relations served to help establish a basis for action and, in some cases, economic ventures.

5　Some excerpts from interviews may be relevant here: "I found the dialect so strange." "I visited the forest and fields and found all sunk in mud and asked myself what was I doing there." "I was born and raised in the village but I found myself alien there and realized that I was used to the city." "I felt very uneasy with my parents and with their authority over me." "I realized that I did not know how to cultivate the soil." "The village is no longer my home so I do not want it." "We feel like aliens in the village."

6　See Chapter 6, note 5, on urbanization.

7　The main subdivisions of Kavaklı were Abbaslı, Gövceli, Kılbacakgil, Hasanlıderesi, Mullahabib, and Palatcılar. Those of Orta mahalle were Hamzalı, Kösehasangil, and Deredam; Yukarı mahalle, Kocaömergil-mahalle; Pınarönü mahalle, Buluş, Mehmetli, Seyranlıgil Sandalcı, Kepekçigil, and Abazaoğulları.

8　Similar developments have been noticed elsewhere. Jan Hindernik and Mubeccel Kiray, *Social Stratification as an Obstacle to Development.*

9　The most recent and comprehensive study of this subject is Suzanne Paine, *Exporting Workers: The Turkish Case.* Pages 54–55 list the main works on the subject. Several other studies on Turkish labor migration abroad are being prepared.

Chapter 8. Politics and party affiliation in the "gecekondu"

1　Portions of this chapter were presented at a conference organized at Princeton University May, 1972. The proceedings appeared in E. Akarlı, ed., *Political Participation in Turkey: Historical Perspectives and Present Problems,* Istanbul, 1975.

2　For the conceptualization of the squatters' politicization, I am grateful to the work of Wayne A. Cornelius, "The Local Urban Community as an Arena of Political Learning," and "Urbanization and Political Demand Making"; and Marc H. Ross, *The Political Integration of Urban Squatters,* and a number of other studies cited in Chapter 1.

3　For a study among peasants see Frederick W. Frey, "Socialization to National Identification Among Turkish Peasants," pp. 934–65.

4　The squatter's integration here is not taken in the sense of forming a new community but rather moving from a marginal position to a strategic one to become capable of influencing urban, regional, and national centers of decision making. In the process he assumes, partly or totally, their methods of political action, organization, and work and develops a sense of identification with the values shared by them.

5   Quotations from several squatters may be useful in evaluating the interest in voting: "It allows for the selection of best ideas." "It expresses our problem." "No matter what party you vote for, what is important is to vote and that the vote is secret." "If I do not vote and elect leaders, who is going to administer the country?" "We vote in order to help the people who protect us." "If voting were not useful it would not have been invented." "If you vote, your party wins and you benefit." "There was no voting in the past. The *padişah* ruled the country, Atatürk introduced the vote and it is the last and the best way." "I feel it is useful but I do not know how to explain it." "We are under [state's] authority and must show our allegiance, May God protect it but also preserve us from being totally dependent on it." "One single vote may help win the election so I vote." "God helps the government so must we." "I vote in order to elect *muhtar* whomever I want. It is good for our settlement. I do not know anything about national elections."

6   A series of excerpts from the respondents' comments in favor of political parties may illustrate the point better:

"Parties oppose dictatorship and religious rule." "There should be three parties: one good, one bad, and one average." "Two parties are useful, the rest are unnecessary." "They are good for the villagers' progress." "Parties come to village and find out the country's situation. Without parties there will be no government." "I vote for parties because it is for the country and my personal gain." "They provide competition so the best prevails." "The nation has a chance to select the best." "Parties ought to be useful since the government permits them to function." "Each party provides a new idea so they help good ideas to prevail." "The parties criticize the government in the parliament and we hear it over the radio and this is good for us the workers." "Those who rule us at the top are made cautious." "One single party leads to dictatorship. Better to have only two." "The parties allow us to select our own leaders." "Parties are means of political control." "They are useful in foreign relations." "Parties work to develop the country." "They are [apparently] useful since there are so many of them and they still survive." "They tell the country what is wrong." "It is good to have different opinions expressed." "Parties can show alternative ways of development." "They prohibit the rule of a single group." "We need political ideas and the parties provide them." "Difference of opinions produces good results." "One party is not sufficient for Turkey because there are people with many different ideas." "I hope God never leaves us without political parties."

There were also views against political parties:

"Parties are not needed if the nation is good." "Parties divided the nation." "They promote their own interest." "Parties fight with each other and have no time to deal with national problems." "They behave well until they secure our vote." "One small party can produce order and quiet instead of the chaos we now have." "Parties merely deceive us and work for their own good." "We had a more orderly existence during Atatürk's time [when there was but one-party rule]." "Parties are good for the rich but not for the poor." "If a boat has more than one captain it sinks." "We are left on our own with all these parties and feel disoriented." "You cannot figure out what is right when there are too many ideas around." "If the government knew our wants there would be no need for partisanship."

7 See Richard B. Scott, *The Village Headman in Turkey.* See also Chapter 6.

8 The party initials to be used henceforth are JP: Adalet Partisi (Justice party), the ruling party from 1965 to 1971, is the successor of the Demokrat Parti (Democrat party), or DP, of Adnan Menderes, ousted by the military in 1960. It is a liberal party favoring free enterprise. Until 1970 it was supported by villagers and lower classes. RPP: Cumhuriyet Halk Partisi (Republican People's party) ruled the country as a single party from 1923 to 1950. It is a leftist-statist and democratic party supported mostly by intellectuals, bureaucrats, and other hetero-geneous groups. NP: Millet Partisi (Nation party) is a small regional party with liberal views. NTP: Yeni Türkiye Partisi (New Turkey party) represents some sectional groups that supported the Democrat party. It merged with JP in 1973. RPNP: Cumhuriyetçi Köylü Millet Partisi (Republican Peasants' National party), which recently became NAP (Millî Hareket Partisi; National Action party), is a rightist na-tionalist party. TLP: *Türkiye İşçi Partisi* (Turkish Labor party) was a marxist party beset by internal strife and was supported chiefly by intellectuals. It was banned in 1971. UP: Birlik Partisi (Unity, or Union, party) supposedly established by Alevis (Shiite, or nonorthodox, Muslims) has social democratic views. RP: Güven Partisi (Reliance party), established by dissidents from the Republican People's party, has a middle-of-the-road nationalist democratic philosophy. The RP and the splinter Cumhuriyetçi Parti (Republican party) combined in 1973 to form the Cumhuriyetçi Güven Partisi (Republican Reliance party), or RRP. The recently formed Demokratik Parti (Democratic party), a dissident group from JP, figures only in Table 8.17. Of all these parties, only JP and RPP qualify as major parties. Together they received about 70 percent of the total votes cast in 1965 and 1969.

9 The political views and careers of two men who supported JP are rele-vant: O. O. related: "I used to vote for Bölükbaşı (NP). He is the most outspoken among politicians. But he never wins. So now I vote for JP." Explaining why he did not vote for RPP he continued, "When I was a small boy, I went once with my father to sell our quota of grain to the government. [During war years grain was sold to the government.] They made us wait a long time. Then my father sent me to the government official. 'Go!' he said, 'you are a child and they

will have mercy if you told them that we have been waiting in hardship for three days here.' I went and pleaded with the official. But he called me 'son of a donkey' and started slapping me [for daring to ask to expedite matters], and called the gendarmerie to 'take away this dog!' I still carry the pain in my heart." The specter of oppressive bureaucratic rule was revived after the military takeover in 1960: "It was after the revolution, I went by Tophane and noticed that everybody was like me and you, and so I decided to stay. I thought that the party had changed [its oppressive mentality]. Then a woman speaker appeared, a member of the Beyoğlu [the most fashionable district of Istanbul] Women's Branch. She said, 'We buried the Koran in the ground but these people [Democrat party] unearthed it, so we shall have to put it back [into the ground].' Upon hearing all these I said to myself that these [RPP] will close the mosques and install a regime of oppression if they could come to power."

The political career of H. K., who was a longtime resident of Istanbul, is rather different: "During the war I came to Istanbul with the first boat which left the Black Sea ports. I worked as gardener and finally opened a small grocery store in Emirgan. The baker in Emirgan offered me 20 cents profit for the bread I sold. But I bought the bread in Ortaköy because I could make more profit. The baker in Emirgan was angry, so he induced the municipality police to give me a fine. In the end I had to sell everything. In 1946, when DP was established I went with an Armenian who lives in Rumelihisar to see a professor who was in charge of the organization. [This was Professor Kenan Öner, the head of the first DP organization in Istanbul. In 1948 he left the party and along with others established the Nation party.] He gave us the job of organizing the entire area between Rumelihisar and Emirgan. We worked hard and contributed to the success of our party in the elections of 1950. I am mad at RPP not only because they closed my grocery store but also for the fact that they paid such a low price for the grain I cultivated on the land lying in front of my house. In 1954, I left DP because it deviated from its original program. I understand nothing about 'socialism' or 'rightists and leftists' that you hear about so much these days. Why don't they speak in an intelligible fashion? I get mad at TLP. They address us as *emekçi* [laborer] although we have the word *işçi* [worker] in our language. Radio Moscow also uses the same word *emekçi*."

10 The shift in support from the RPP to JP, reported by the migrants, is indirectly substantiated by the actual election results in the provinces of origin – namely, Giresun, Gümüşhane, and Sivas. The performance of the RPP in these provinces was better than it was nationally: 30.7 percent of the votes in the three provinces combined, compared with 28.7 percent of the national vote in 1965; and 28.2 percent compared with 27.4 percent in 1969. A similar comparison for the JP shows that it obtained 45.2 percent of the votes in these three provinces compared with 52.9 percent of the national vote in 1965; and 35.6 percent com-

pared compared with 46.5 percent in 1969 (*12 Ekim 1969 Milletvekili Seçimi Sonuçları*, State Institute of Statistics, Ankara, 1970, and *1950–1965 Milletvekili ve 1961, 1964 Cumhuriyet Senatosu Üye Seçimleri Sonuçları*, State Institute of Statistics, Ankara, 1965). See also Paul J. Magnarella "Regional Voting in Turkey," *Muslim World* 57, 3–4 (1967), 224–34, 277–87,

11 For the full names of these parties, see note 8 above. The new party in 1973 was the National Salvation party (Mili Selâmet Partisi), or NSP.

12 See Chapter 6 for additional information on the *muhtars*, as well as Paul J. Magnarella, *Tradition and Change in a Turkish Town*, pp. 148ff.

Bibliography

Abadan-Unat, N. "Turkish External Migration and Social Mobility." In Benedict et al., eds., *Turkey.*

Abbott, E. *The Tenements of Chicago: 1908–1935.* Chicago, 1936.

Abou El-Ezz, M. S. "Some Aspects of Migration in Cairo." *Bulletin de la Société de Geographie d'Egypte,* 32 (1959), 121–42.

Abrams, C. *Housing in the Modern World.* London, 1966.

Abu-Lughod, J. L. *Cairo: 1001 Years of the City Victorious.* Princeton, N.J.; 1971.

"Migrant Adjustment to City Life: The Egyptian Case." *American Journal of Sociology,* 67, 1 (July, 1961), 22–32.

"Tale of Two Cities: The Origins of Modern Cairo." *Comparative Studies in Society and History,* 7 (July, 1965), 429–57.

"Urban-Rural Differences as a Function of Demographic Transition: Egyptian Data and an Analytical Model." *American Journal of Sociology,* 69 (March, 1964).

"Varieties of Urban Experience: Contrast, Coexistence and Coalescence in Cairo." In Lapidus, ed., *Middle Eastern Cities,* pp. 159–87.

Adam, A. "Le Bidonville de Ben Msik." *Annales de l'Institut d'Etudes Orientales* (Algiers), 8 (1949–50).

"La Population Musulmane de l'Algerie." *Cahiers Nord-Africains,* 2 (Paris, ESNA, 1956).

Akçura, T. "Ankara et ses Fonctions Urbains." *La Vie Urbaine* (January–March, April–June, 1960).

Altuğ, S. M. "Le Problème des émigrations turques des Balkans." *Integration,* 6 (1959), 182–89.

Anderson, N. *The Urban Community: A World Perspective.* New York, 1959.

Arı, O. *Bulgaristanlı Göçmenlerin Intibakı.* Ankara, 1960.

"1950–1951 senelerinde Bulgaristandan tehcir edilen Türk Göçmenleri." *Istanbul Universitesi Iktisat Fakültesi Mecmuasi,* 20 (1960), 1–4.

and Tutengil, C. O. "Adapazarı'na Göç ve Çalışma Hayatına Intibak Araştırması." *Sosyoloji Konferansları, 1966–1967.* Istanbul, 1968.

Asika, U. "Rehabilitation and Resettlement." Paper given at the Conference on National Reconstruction and Development in Ibadan, Nigeria (March, 1969).

Asma, T. *Rural-Urban Migration: "Night Squatter" Communities of Istanbul and Ankara.* Master's thesis, University of Wisconsin, Milwaukee, 1970.

Awad, H. "Morocco's Expanding Towns." In Mangin, ed., *Peasants,* pp. 114–21.

Balán, J. "Migrant-Native Socio-Economic Differences in Latin American Cities: A Structural Analysis." *Latin American Research Review,* 4, 1 (Spring, 1969).

Balista, J. *Aspectos Humanos de la Vivienda.* Buenos Aires, 1965.

Banfield, E. C. *The Case of the Blighted City.* Chicago, 1959.

Barkin, R., et al. *Şehirlere Akın ve Mesken Davası,* Ankara, 1959.

Barringer, H. R., Blanksten, I., and Mack, R. W., eds. *Social Change in Developing Areas: A Reinterpretation of Evolutionary Theory.* Cambridge, Mass., 1965.

Bascom, W. "Urbanism as a Traditional African Pattern." *Sociological Review,* n.s. 7, 1 (July 1959), 29–44.

Bauer, R. A., ed. *Social Indicators.* Cambridge, Mass., 1966.

Becker, H. S. "Personal Change in Life." *Sociometry,* 27, 1 (1964).

Beeley, B. W. "The Turkish Village Coffeehouse as a Social Institution," *Geographical Review,* 60 (October, 1970).

Beijer, G. *Rural Migrants in Urban Settings.* The Hague, 1963.

Benedict, P. et al., ed. *Turkey: Geographic and Social Perspectives.* Leiden, 1974.

Benet, F. "The Ideology of Islamic Urbanization." *International Journal of Comparative Sociology,* 4 (September, 1963), 211–26.

Berelson, B., and Steiner, G. A. *Human Behavior: An Inventory of Scientific Findings.* New York, 1964.

Berg, E. J. "The Development of a Labor Force in Sub-Sahara Africa." *Economic and Cultural Change,* 13 (July, 1965).

Berque, J. "Medinas, villeneuves et bidonvilles." *Les Cahiers de Tunisie,* 6 (1958), 5–42.

Bhagwati, J. *The Economics of Underdeveloped Countries.* New York, 1966.

Birge, J. K. *The Bektashi Order of Dervishes.* Hartford, 1937.

Black, C. E. *The Dynamics of Modernization: A Study in Comparative History.* New York, 1966.

Bock, E. W., and Iutaka, S. "Rural-Urban Migration and Social Mobility: The Controversy in Latin America." *Rural Sociology,* 34 (September, 1969), 343–54.

Bonilla, F. "Rio's Favelas: The Rural Slum Within the City." In Mangin, ed., *Peasants,* pp. 72–84.

Borges, T. P. A. "Relationship Between Economic Development, Industrialization and the Growth of Urban Population in Brazil." In Hauser, ed., *Latin America,* pp. 149–70.

Braibanti, R. J. D., and Spengler, J. eds. *Traditions, Values and Socio-Economic Development.* Durham, N.C., 1961.

Breese, G. *Urbanization in the Newly Developing Countries.* Englewood Cliffs, N.J., 1966.

⸻ ed. *The City in Newly Developing Countries: Readings on Urbanism and Urbanization.* Englewood Cliffs, N.J., 1969.

Brown, L. C., ed. *From Madina to Metropolis.* Princeton, 1973.

Bruher, E. M. "Medan: The Role of Kinship in an Indonesian City." In Mangin, ed., *Peasants,* pp. 122–34.

Buechler, H. C. "The Ritual Dimension of Rural-Urban Networks: The Fiesta System in the Northern Highlands of Bolivia." In Mangin, ed., *Peasants,* pp. 62–71.

Butterworth, D. S. "A Study of the Urbanization Process among Mixtec Migrants from Tilantongo in Mexico City." In Mangin, ed., *Peasants,* pp. 98–113.

Buy, J. "Bidonville et ensemble moderne: approche sociologique de deux populations de Casablanca." *Bulletin Economic et Social du Maroc,* 28 (1966).

Caferoğlu, A. "The Migration of the Caucasian Peoples in the last 150 Years." *Integration,* 6 (1959).

Caldwell, J. C. *African Rural-Urban Migration: The Movement to Ghana's Towns.* New York, 1969.

Cardona Guttierrez, R., ed. *Las Migraciones Internas.* Bogotá, 1971.

Celasun, M. *Prospective Growth of Non-Agricultural Employment in Turkey.* State Planning Organization, Ankara, July, 1970.

Chance, N. A. "Acculturation, Self-Identification, and Personality Adjustment." *American Anthropologist,* 67, 2 (1965), 372–93.

Chene, M. R. *Marges Citadines à Rabat-Sale.* Thesis presented to Ecole Pratique des Hautes Etudes, Paris, February, 1971.

Clark, J. B. "Measuring Alienation within a Social System." *American Sociological Review,* 24 (1959), 849–52.

Collier, D. *Squatter Settlement Formation and the Politics of Co-optation in Peru.* Doctoral dissertation, University of Chicago, 1971.

Cornelius, W. A., "Political Learning Among the Migrant Poor: The Impact of Residential Context." *Sage Professional Papers in Comparative Politics.* Vol. 3 (Spring, 1973).

"Urbanization and Political Demand Making: Political Participation among Migrant Poor in Latin American Cities." *American Political Science Review,* 68 (September, 1974).

Côrtes, G. de M. *Favelas.* Rio de Janeiro, 1959.

Costa, E. "Manpower Mobilization in Economic Development in Tunisia." *International Labour Review,* 93 (January 1966).

Cotler, J., and Laquian, A. A. "Lima." In Laquian, ed., *Rural-Urban Migrants.*

Davis, K. "The Origins and Growth of Urbanization in the World." *American Journal of Sociology,* 60 (March, 1955), 429–37.

Dawson, J. "Urbanization and Mental Health in a West African Community." In Ari Kiev, ed., *Magic, Faith, and Healing: Studies in Primitive Psychiatry Today.* New York, 1964.

Dennis, N. *People and Planning: The Sociology of Housing in Sunderland.* London, 1970.

Desai, A. R., ed. *Essays on Modernization of Underdeveloped Societies.* Bombay, 1971.

Descloitres, R., et al. *L'Algérie des bidonvilles; le Tiers Monde dans la cité.* Paris, 1961.

Deutsch, K. W. "Social Mobilization and Political Development." *American Political Science Review,* 55 (September, 1961), 493–514.

Doughty, P. L. "Behind the Back of the City: 'Provincial' Life in Lima, Peru." In Mangin, ed., *Peasants,* pp. 30–46.

Egretaud, M. *Réalité de la Nation Algérienne.* Paris, 1961.

Eickelman, D. F. "Is There an Islamic City? The Making of a Quarter in a Moroccan Town." *International Journal of Middle East Studies,* 5 (June, 1974), 274–94.

Eisenstadt, S. N., ed. *Comparative Social Problems.* New York, 1964.

Eldridge, R. H. "Emigration and the Turkish Balance of Payments." *Middle East Journal,* 20 (1966), 296–316.

Elkan, W. "Circular Migration and the Growth of Towns in East Africa." *International Labour Review,* 96 (December, 1967), 581–89.

Migrants and Proletarians: Urban Labor in the Economic Development of Uganda. London, 1960.

Eren, A. C. "Die Bedeutung des Flüchtlingsproblems in der Türkei." *Integration,* 6 (1959), 167–77.

Ergil, G. *Köylerimizde Yapılan Araştırmalarla İlgili İzahı Bibliyografya.* Ankara, 1968.

Erinç, O. "250 yıl Önce İstanbulda Gecekondu Sorunu." *Belgelere Türk Tarihi Dergisi,* 12 (September, 1966).

Esa, E. A. B. "Kuala Lumpur." In Laquian, ed., *Rural-Urban Migrants.*

Fanon, F. *The Wretched of the Earth.* New York, 1968.

Ferro, G. *Città e campagna in Italia.* Rome, 1969.

Fischlowitz, E. "Internal Migrations in Brazil." *International Migration Review,* 3 (Summer, 1969), 36–45.

Flinn, W. L. "Rural and Intra-Urban Migration in Colombia: Two Case Studies in Bogota." In Rabinovitz, F. F. and Trueblood, F. M., eds. *Latin Urban Research.* Vol. I. 1971.

Forde, D., ed. *Social Implications of Industrialization and Urbanization in Africa South of the Sahara.* UNESCO, Paris, 1956.

Foster, G. M. *Traditional Cultures and the Impact of Technological Change.* New York, 1962.

Franco, P. S. "Caracas." In Laquian, ed., *Rural-Urban Migrants.*

Frey, F. W. "Socialization to National Identification Among Turkish Peasants," *Journal of Politics,* 30 (1968).

Gans, H. J. *The Urban Villagers: Group and Class in the Life of Italian Americans.* New York, 1962.

Geertz, C. *Social Development and Economic Change in Two Indonesian Towns.* Chicago, 1963.

Gendzier, I. L. *Frantz Fanon: A Critical Study.* New York, 1973.

Geray, C. *Büyük Belediyelerde Şehirleşme Sorunları Konferansı.* Ankara, 1968.

"Gecekondu Sorununa Toplu Bir Bakış." *Amme İdaresi Dergisi,* 1, 2 (1968), 11–28.

Türkiye'de Kendi Evini Yapana Yardım. State Planning Organization, Ankara, 1967.

"Urbanization in Turkey." *Siyasal Bilgiler Fakültesi Dergisi,* 24, 4 (1970).

Germani, G. "Inquiry into the Social Effects of Urbanization in a Working Class Sector of Greater Buenos Aires." In Hauser, ed., *Latin America.*

Gibbs, J. P. "Measures of Urbanization." *Social Forces,* 45, 2 (December, 1966), 170–77.

Goode, W. J. *The Family.* Englewood Cliffs, N.J., 1964.

World Revolution and Family Patterns. New York, 1963.

Goodenough, W. H. *Cooperation in Change: An Anthropological Approach to Community Development.* New York, 1963.

Gould, H. A. "Some Preliminary Observations Concerning the Anthropology of Industrialization." In Mangin, ed., *Peasants,* pp. 137–49.

Gözaydın, E. F. *Kırım Türklerinin Yerleşme ve Göçmeleri.* Istanbul, 1948.

Graves, T. D. "Alternative Models for the Study of Urban Migration." *Human Organization,* 25, 4 (1966), 300–7.

Gulick, L. *Tripoli: A Modern Arab City.* Cambridge, Mass., 1967.

Gürsen, C. T., and Neyzi, O. *Istanbulda Rami Gecekondu Bölgesinde Çocuk Sağlığı Konusunda Araştırmalar.* Istanbul, 1966.

Hagen, E. E. *On the Theory of Social Change: How Economic Growth Begins.* Homewood, Ill., 1962.

Hamurdan, Y. O. "Surplus Labor in Turkish Agriculture." State Planning Organization, Ankara, July, 1970.

Hart, C. W. M. *Zeytinburnu Gecekondu Bölgesi.* Istanbul, 1969.

"Peasants Come to Town." *Social Aspects of Economic Development.* Istanbul, 1963.

Hauser, P. M., ed. *Urbanization in Asian and the Far East Cities.* New York, 1967.

Urbanization in Latin America. UNESCO, Liège, 1961.

and Schnore, L., eds. *The Study of Urbanization.* New York, 1965.

Hindernik, J., and M. Kiray. *Social Stratification as an Obstacle to Development.* New York, 1970.

Horowitz, I. L. *Three Worlds of Development: The Theory and Practice of International Stratification.* New York, 1966.

Hoselitz, B. F. "Generative and Parasitic Cities." *Economic Development and Cultural Change,* 3 (April, 1955).

ed. *The Progress of Underdeveloped Areas.* Chicago, 1952.

Sociological Aspects of Economic Growth. Glencoe, Ill.; 1960.

and Moore, W. E., eds. *Industrialization and Society.* Paris, 1965.

Hourani, A. H., and Stern, S. M., eds. *The Islamic City.* Oxford, 1970.

Hunt, C. L. *Social Aspects of Economic Development.* New York, 1966.

Hunter, D. R. *The Slums: Challenge and Response.* New York, 1964.

Hurtado, R. et al. *Estudio Sobre Barrios de Caracas.* Caracas, 1968.

Imoagene, S. O. "Mechanisms of Immigrant Adjustment in a Western African Urban Community." *Nigerian Journal of Economic and Social Studies,* 9, 1 (1967), 51–66.

Isaac, B. L. "Peasants in Cities: Ingenious Paradox or Conceptual Muddle." *Human Organization*, 33, 3 (1974), 251–57.

Jenkins, G. D. "Africa as It Urbanizes: An Overview of Current Research." *Urban Affairs*, 2 (1967).

Kabusan, V. M. "La Colonisation Paysanne de la Cote Nord de la Mer Noire (Novorussie) de 1719 a 1857." *Annals de Demographie Historique*. La Haye, 1971.

Kahl, J. A. "Some Social Concomitants of Industrialization and Urbanization." *Human Organization*, 18, 2 (Summer, 1959), 53–74.

Karpat, K. H. "Social Effects of Farm Mechanization in Turkish Villages." *Social Research*, 20, 7 (Spring, 1960), 83–103.

Social Change and Politics in Turkey: A Historical-Structural Analysis Leiden, 1973.

Political and Social Thought in the Contemporary Middle East. New York, 1968.

"The Background of Ottoman Concept of City and Urbanity." *Structures Sociales et Développment Culturel des Villes Sud-Est Européennes et Adriatiques*. Bucharest, 1975, 323–40.

"The Economic and Social Transformation of Istanbul in the Nineteenth Century." Paper delivered at the South East European Studies Association Conference on Istanbul, Istanbul, October, 1973. Forthcoming.

"Gecekondu meselesi." *Milliyet* (June 15–30, 1969).

Gecekondu Sorunu Uzerine, Middle East Technical University Publication, Ankara, 1973.

Keleş, R. "Turkiye'de Işçi Konutları Sorunu." *Sosyal Siyaset Konferansları*, 19 (1968), 17–34.

Eski Ankara'da Bir Şehir Tipolojisi. Ankara, 1971.

"Türkiyede Şehirleşme Eğilimleri." *Siyasal Bilgiler Fakültesi Dergisi*, 25 (Aralık, 1970) 41–83.

Turkiyede Şehirleşme, Konut ve Gecekondu. Istanbul, 1972.

Kemper, R. V. "Rural-Urban Migration in Latin America: A Framework for the Comparative Analysis of Geographical and Temporal Patterns." *International Migration Review*, 5 1–4 (Spring, 1971), 36–47.

Kiray, M. *Ereğli-Ağır Sanayiden Önce bir Sahil Kasabası*. Ankara, 1964.

"Values, Social Stratification and Development." *Journal of Social Issues*, 24, 2 (1968), 87–101.

Kolars, J. H., and Malin, H. J. "Population and Accessibility: An Analysis of Turkish Railroads." *Geographical Review*, 60 (April, 1970), 229–46.

Kolodny, Y. "Données recentes sur la population urbaine de la Turquie." *Méditerranée*, 9 (1968), 165–80.

Kongar, E. "Altındağ Gecekondu Bolgesi." *Amme Idaresi Dergisi*, 6, 3 (September, 1973).

"Altındağ'da Kentle Bütünleşme." *Amme Idaresi Dergisi*, 6, 4 (December, 1973).

Izmirde Şehirsel Ailenin Bazı Nitelikleri (unpublished monograph). Ankara, 1969.

278 *The Gecekondu*

Survey of Familial Change in Two Turkish Gecekondu Areas. Paper submitted to the Social Anthropological Conference, Nicosia, September, 1970.

Kostanick, H. L. *Turkish Settlement of Bulgarian Turks, 1950–1953.* Doctoral dissertation, University of California, Berkeley, 1957.

Kuper, H., ed. *Urbanization and Migration in West Africa.* Berkeley, 1965.

Kuznets, S., and Thomas, D. "Internal Migration and Economic Growth." *Selected Studies of Migration Since World War II. Milbank Memorial Fund Quarterly,* 33 (July, 1955).

Lapidus, I., ed. *Middle Eastern Cities: A Symposium on Ancient, Islamic, and Contemporary Middle Eastern Urbanism.* Berkeley, 1969.

Laquian, A. A., ed. *Rural-Urban Migrants and Metropolitan Development.* Toronto, 1971.

Slums and Squatters in Six Philippine Cities. Report to Asia Society, New York, 1972.

La Ville Balkanique, XVᵉ–XIXᵉ SS. Studia Balcanica, 3. (Sofia, 1970).

Lee, E. S. "A Theory of Migration." *Demography,* 3 (1965), 47–57.

Lerner, D. *The Passing of Traditional Society: Modernizing the Middle East.* Glencoe, Ill., 1958.

Le Tourneau, R. "Social Change in the Muslim Cities of North Africa." *American Journal of Sociology,* 60, 6 (May, 1955), 527–35.

Levantamento da populaçao favelada de Belo Horizonte. Department of Housing of Minas Gerias, Belo Horizonte, 1966.

Levine, N. "Old-Culture, New-Culture: A Study of Migrants in Ankara, Turkey." *Social Forces,* 51, 3 (March, 1973).

"Value Orientation Among Migrants in Ankara, Turkey: A Study." *Journal of Asian and African Studies,* 8, 1–4 (1974).

Lewis, O. *The Children of Sanchez: Autobiography of a Mexican Family.* New York, 1963.

"Urbanization Without Breakdown: A Case Study." *Scientific Monthly,* 75 (July, 1952), 31–41.

Lipset, S. "Research Problems in the Comparative Analysis of Mobility and Development." *International Social Service Journal,* 16, 1 (1964).

Little, K. *West African Urbanization: A Study of Voluntary Associations in Social Change.* London, 1965.

Maboqunje, A. L. "Urbanization in Nigeria: A Constraint on Economic Development." *Economic Development and Cultural Change,* 13, 4, pt. 1 (July, 1965).

Magnarella, P. J. "Descent, Affinity and Ritual Relationship in Eastern Turkey." *American Anthropologist,* 75, 5 (October, 1973).

"From Villager to Townsman in Turkey." *Middle East Journal,* 24 (Spring, 1970), 229–40.

Tradition and Change in a Turkish Town. New York, 1974.

Mangin, W., ed. *Peasants in Cities: Readings in the Anthropology of Urbanization.* Boston, 1970.

"Latin American Squatter Settlements: A Problem and a Solution." *Latin American Research Review,* 2, 3 (Summer, 1967).

"Mental Health and Migration to Cities." *Annals of the New York Academy of Sciences,* 84, art. 17 (December, 1961).

"Similarities and Differences between Two Types of Peruvian Communities." In Mangin, ed., *Peasants,* pp. 20–29.

"Squatter Settlements." *Scientific American,* 217 (October, 1967), 21–27.

Mar, J. M. "The 'Barriadas' of Lima: An Example of Integration into Urban Life." In Hauser, ed., *Latin America,* pp. 170–90.

Estudio de las Barriadas. Limenas, 1966.

Urbanizacion y barriadas en America del Sud. Lima, 1968.

Mayir, P. *Tribesmen or Townsmen, Conservatism and the Process of Urbanization in a South African City: Capetown.* London, 1962.

McGee, T. G. "Catalysts or Cancers? The Role of Cities in Asian Society." Jakobson, L., and Prakash, V. eds. *Urbanization and National Development.* I, Beverly Hills, Calif., 1971.

"Peasants in the Cities: A Paradox, a Paradox, a Most Ingenious Paradox." *Human Organization,* 32, 2 (1973), 135–42.

"The Rural-Urban Continuum Debate: The Preindustrial City and Rural-Urban Migration." *Pacific Viewpoint,* 5, 2 (1964), 159–82.

The Southeast Asian City: A Social Geography of the Primate Cities of Southeast Asia. London, 1967.

The Urbanization Process in the Third World: Explorations in Search of a Theory. London, 1971.

McGinn, N. F., and Davis, R. G. *Build a Mill, Build a City, Build a School: Industrialization, Urbanization and Education in Ciudad Guayana.* Cambridge, Mass., 1969.

Medina, C. A., de. *A Favela E O Demagogo.* Sao Paulo, 1964.

Merrill, R. N. *Toward a Structural Housing Policy: An Analysis of Chile's Low Income Housing Program.* Latin American Studies Program, Dissertation Series 22, Cornell University, Ithaca, N.Y., 1971.

Miner, H. ed. *The City in Modern Africa.* New York, 1967.

"The Folk-Urban Continuum." *American Sociological Review,* 17 (October, 1952), 529–37.

Ministry of Reconstruction and Settlement (Imar ve Iskân Bakanliği). *Konut Özel Ihtisas Komisyonu (1971) Gecekondu Raporu.* Ankara, 1974.

50 Yılda Imar ve Yereşme, 1923–1973. Ankara, 1973.

Ankara-Cıncınbağları Gecekondu Araştırmaları. Ankara, 1965.

Ankara-Esat-Çankaya ve Dikmen Gecekonduları. Ankara, 1965.

Ankara-Gülveren-Cıncınbağları ve Topraklık Gecekonduları. Ankara, 1965.

Ankara-Gülveren Gecekondu Araştırması. Ankara, 1965.

Ankara-Topraklık Gecekondu Araştırması. Ankara, 1965.

Izmir-Gürceşme Gecekondu Araştırması. Ankara, 1965.

Şehirleşme, Gecekondular ve Konut Politikası. Prepared by T. and A. Yorukan. Ankara, 1966.

13 Büyük Şehirde Gecekondu. Ankara, 1965.

Imar Kongresi. Ankara, 1963.

Mintz, S. W., and Wolf, E. R. "An Analysis of Ritual Co-Parenthood (*Compadrazzo*)." In J. M. Potter, ed. *Peasant Society*. Boston, 1967, pp. 174–99.

Moller, H., ed. *Population Movements in Modern European History*. New York, 1964.

Montagne, R., ed. *Naissance du prolétariat Morocain*. Paris, 1952.

Moore, W. E. *Social Change*. Englewood Cliffs, N.J., 1963.

Morse, R. M. "Urbanization in Latin America." *Latin American Research Review*, 1 (Fall, 1965).

Musgrove, F. *Youth and the Social Order*. Bloomington, Ind., 1965.

Naciri, M. "Quelques examples d'evolution de douars à la péripherie urbaine de Sale." *Revue de Geographie du Maroc*, 8 (1965).

Nelson, J. M. *Migrants, Urban Poverty and Instability in Developing Nations*. Harvard University Center for International Affairs, Cambridge, 1969.

Nora, P. *Les Francais d'Algerie*. Paris, 1961.

Odiorne, G. S. *Green Power: The Corporation and the Urban Crisis*. New York, 1969.

Ogretmen, I. "Ankara'da 158 Gecekondu." *Ankara Univ. Siyasal Bilgiler Fakültesi Dergisi*, 1 (1957).

Okun, B., and Richardson, R. W. "Regional Income Inequality and Internal Population Migration." In Friedmann, J., and Alonso, W., eds. *Regional Development and Planning*. Cambridge, Mass., 1964, pp. 303–20.

Öngör, S. "1950–1955 devresinde Türkiye'de iç göçler." *Türkiye Cografya Dergisi*, 21 (1961).

Paine, S. *Exporting Workers: The Turkish Case*. London, 1974.

Pearse, A. "Some Characteristics of Urbanization in the City of Rio de Janeiro." In Hauser, ed., *Latin America*.

Peasant Studies Newsletter. Pittsburgh, University of Pittsburgh Press, 1957.

Planhol, X. de. "Les migrations du travail en Turquie." *Revue de Geographie Alpine*, 40 (1952).

The World of Islam. Ithaca, N.Y., 1959.

Plotnicov, L. "Nigerians: The Dream Is Unfulfilled." In Mangin, ed., *Peasants*, pp. 170–74.

Problems of Urban Housing. Indian Institute of Public Administration, Bombay, 1960.

Ray, T. F. *The Politics of the Barrios of Venezuela*. Berkeley, 1969.

Redfield, R. *The Little Community*. Chicago, 1960.

Peasant Society and Culture. Chicago, 1956.

The Primitive World and Its Transformation. Ithaca, N.Y., 1953.

and Singer, M. "The Cultural Role of Cities." *Economic Development and Cultural Change*, 3 (October, 1954).

Report on the Bustee Survey in Calcutta, 1958–59. Vol. 5. Alipore-West Bengal, 1963.

Reverdy, J. C. *Habitations nouvelles et urbanization rapide: conditions écologigues de l'adaptation au logement en Algérie*. Aix en Provence, 1963.

Robinson, R. D. "Turkey's Agrarian Revolution and the Problem of Urbanization." *Public Opinion Quarterly*, 22 (Fall, 1958), 397–405.

Rodriqueuz-Espada, E. "La incorporación de los migrantes a la estructura economica y social de la ciudad de Bogotá." In Cardona Guttierrez, ed., *Migraciones*.

Rogers, E. M. *Modernization among Peasants: The Impact of Communication*. New York, 1969.

Rose, A., and Warshay, L. "The Adjustment of Migrants to Cities." *Social Forces*, 36 (1957).

Rosenmayer, L. "Towards an Overview of Youth Sociology." *International Social Science Journal*, 20 (1968), 286–315.

Ross, M. H. *The Political Integration of Urban Squatters*. Evanston, Ill., 1973.

Samaj, B. S. *Slums of Old Delhi: Report of the Socio-economic Survey of the Slum Dwellers of Old Delhi*. Delhi, 1958.

Sandoval, R. P. "Marginalidad y Subdesarollo." In Cardona Guttierrez, ed. *Migraciones*.

Santos, M. *Les Villes du Tiers Monde*. Paris, 1971.

Schaw, L. C. *The Bonds of Work: Work in Mind, Time and Tradition*. San Francisco, 1968.

Schnalberg, A. "Rural-Urban Residence and Modernism: A Study of Ankara Province, Turkey." *Demography*, 7, 1 (February, 1970).

Some Determinants and Consequences of Modernism in Turkey. Unpublished dissertation, University of Michigan, 1968.

Scott, R. B. *The Village Headman in Turkey*. Ankara, 1968.

Seeley, J. R. "The Slum: Its Nature, Use and Users." *Journal of the American Institute of Planners*, 26 (February, 1959), 7–14.

Seguin, G. A. "Migration and Psychosomatic Disadaption." *Psychosomatic Medicine*, 18, 5 (1956).

Sen, N. *Plan ve Yapı Bakımından Gecedonduların Incelenmesi* (*ITU Yayimi*). Istanbul, 1966.

Sencer, M. *Türkiye'de Köylülüğün Maddi Temelleri*. Ankara, 1970.

Sertel, A. K. "Ritual Kinship in Eastern Turkey." *Anthropological Quarterly*, 44, 1 (1971), 37–50.

Sewell, G. H. *Squatter Settlements in Turkey: Analysis of a Social, Political and Economic Problem*. Doctoral dissertation, MIT, 1964.

Siegel, B. J. "The Role of Perception in Rural-Urban Change: A Brazilian Case Study." *Economic Development and Cultural Change*, 5, 3 (April, 1967), 244–56.

Shorter, F. C., and Güvenç, B., eds., *Turkish Demography: Proceedings of a Conference*. Hacettepe University Publication Number 7. Ankara, 1969.

Simič, A. *The Peasant Urbanites: A Study of Rural-Urban Mobility in Serbia*. New York, 1973.

Skinner, E. P. "Labor Migration Among the Mossi of the Upper Volta." In Kuper, ed. *Urbanization*.

282 *The Gecekondu*

Slum Clearance in India. Ministry of Information and Broadcasting, Delhi, 1958.

Social Implications of Industrialization and Urbanization in Africa, South of the Sahara. UNESCO, Paris, 1956.

Solzbacher, R. M. "East Africa's Slum Problem: A Question of Definition." In Gugler, J., ed. *Urban Growth in Subsaharan Africa.* Makerere Institute of Social Research, Kampala, 1970.

Songu, C. *Aras Problemi ve Alınması Düşünulen Tedbirler.* Ministry of Reconstruction and Settlement, Ankara, 1962.

Sosnovy, T. *The Housing Problems in the Soviet Union.* New York, 1954.

Southall, A. W., ed. *Social Change in Modern Africa.* London, 1961.

Stokes, C. J. "A Theory of Slums." *Land Economics,* 38 (August, 1962), 187–98.

Suttles, G. D. *The Social Order of the Slum: Ethnicity and Territory in the Inner City.* Chicago, 1968.

Suzuki, P. "Ecounters with Istanbul: Urban Peasants and Village Peasants." *International Journal of Comparative Sociology,* 5 (September, 1964), 208–16.

"Peasants Without Plows: Some Anatolians in Istanbul; Anatolians' Transition from Rural Life to Metropolitan Life." *Rural Sociology,* 31 (December, 1966), 428–38.

"Village Solidarity Among Turkish Peasants Undergoing Urbanization." *Science* 132 (September, 1960), 891.

Szyliowicz, J. S. *Political Change in Rural Turkey: Erdemli.* The Hague, 1966.

Taeuber, I. B. "Population and Modernization in Turkey." *Population Index,* 24 (April, 1958), 101–22.

Tankut, G. *Ankara Gecekondu Problemi.* Middle East Technical University, mimeographed. Ankara, 1961.

Tanoğlu, A. "The Recent Emigration of the Bulgarian Turks." *Review of the Geographical Institute of the University of Istanbul,* 2 (1955).

Tekçe, B. *Urbanization and Migration in Turkey 1955–1965.* Doctoral dissertation, Princeton University, 1974.

Tekeli, I. "Gecekondu Plânlama Sorunları ve Yolları." *METU Studies in Development,* 1 (Spring, 1971).

Texter, R. B., et al. *The Social Implications of Industrialization and Urbanization. Five Studies of Urban Populations of Recent Rural Origin in Cities of Southern Asia.* Calcutta, 1956.

Tezcan, M. *Türk Sosyoloji Bibliyografyası, 1928–1968.* Ankara, 1969.

Toro, A. L. "Migración y Marginalidad Urbana en Paises Subdesarrollados." *Demografia y Economia,* 4, 2 (1970), 192–209.

Toschi, U. *La Città: Geografia Urbana.* Torino, 1966.

Tourneau, R. Le. "Social Change in the Muslim Cities of North Africa." *American Journal of Sociology,* 60, 6 (May, 1955).

Trebous, M. *Migration and Development: The Case of Algeria.* OECD, Paris, 1970.

Tümertekin, E. "The Distribution of Sex Ratios with Special Reference to

Internal Migration in Turkey." *Review of the Geographical Institute of Istanbul*, 4 (1958).

Turkiye'de Ic Göçler: Internal Migrations in Turkey. Istanbul, 1968.

Tuna, O. "The Problem of Immigrants from Bulgaria to Turkey." *Revue de la Faculté des Sciences Economique de l'Université d'Istanbul*, 13 (1951–1952).

Tunçdilek, N. *Türkiye Iskân Coğrafiyası*. Istanbul, 1967.

Türk Köyünde Modernleşme Egilimleri Araştırması. State Planning Organization, Ankara, 1970.

Türkay, O. *Türkiye'de Nüfüs Artışı ve Iktisadi Gelişme.* Ankara, 1962.

Türkdoğan, O. *Yoksulluk Kültürü. Gecekonduların Toplumsal Yapısı.* Erzurum, 1974.

Seçilmiş Bazı Yerli ve Göçmen Gruplar Üzerinde Sosyal Değişme Örnekleri. Erzurum, 1971.

Türkiye'de Gecekondu Semineri. A series of papers presented at a conference organized by the Chamber of Map and Survey Engineers, Ankara, February 12–13, 1970.

Turner, J. F. C. "Housing Priorities, Settlement Patterns, and Urban Development in Modernizing Countries." *Journal of the American Institute of Planning*, 34 (November, 1968), 354–63.

"Lima's Barriadas and Corralones: Suburbs versus Slums." *Ekistics*, 112 (March, 1965), 110–20.

Uncontrolled Urban Settlement: Problems and Policies. Paper presented at the U.N. Inter-Regional Seminar on Development Policies and Planning in Relation to Urbanization, University of Pittsburgh, October 24–November 7, 1966.

Tütengil, C. *Köyden Şehire Göç Meselesi.* Brochure number 31, Institute of Economics and Sociology, Istanbul, 1963.

Sosyal bir Yapı Olarak Türkiyede Köy ve Meseleleri. School of Architecture, Istanbul, 1966.

United Nations. *Improvement of Slums and Uncontrolled Settlements.* Department of Economic and Social Affairs, Report of a seminar held in Medellin, Colombia, 1970. New York, 1971.

International Social Development Review, 1 (1968) and 2 (1970).

Inter-Regional Seminar on National Youth Service Programs. Set of unpublished working papers for a conference in Denmark, November, 1968.

Preliminary Report on Long-Term Policies and Programmes for Youth in National Development. Commission for Social Development. Document E/CN. 5/434 (January 7, 1969).

Rehabilitation of Transitional Urban Settlements. Report E/C. 6/115. New York, 1971.

Report of the United Nations Inter-Regional Seminar on Development Policies and Planning in Relation to Urbanization. Document ST/TAO/SER. C/97. New York, 1967.

Report on World Social Situation. Report E/C. 6115. New York, 1957, p. 114.

Report by Secretary General to the United Nations General Assembly. Report A/8037 (August, 1970).

Research Notes No. 1. Research Institute for Social Development. Geneva, June, 1968.

Request by the Turkish Government in 1970, in Accordance with ECOSOC Resolution 1224 (XLII Session). Ankara, 1971.

Yasa, I. *Ankara' da Gecekondu Aileleri.* Ankara, 1966.

"Gecekondu ailesi." *Siyasal Bilgiler Fakültesi Dergisi,* 25. (December, 1970).

"The Impact of Rural Exodus on the Occupational Patterns of Cities (Ankara's Case)." *Siyasal Bilgiler Fakültesi Dergisi,* 22, 2 (1967).

Yener, S. *1960–65 Döneminde Köyden Şehire Göçler.* State Planning Organization, Ankara, 1970.

Yücel, R. T. "Türkiye'de şehirleşme hareketleri ve şehirler." *Türk Cografya Dergisi,* 20 (1960).

Yurt, I., Ergil, G., and Sevil, H. T. *Orman Köylerinin Sosyo-Ekonomik Durumu.* Ankara, 1971.

Yurtören, S. G. *Fertility and Related Attitudes Among Two Social Classes in Ankara.* Master's thesis, Cornell University, 1965.

Weitz, R., ed. *Urbanization and the Developing Countries.* Report of the Sixth Rehovat Conference, New York, 1973.

White, J. W. *Political Implications of Cityward Migration: Japan as an Exploratory Test Case.* Beverly Hills, Calif., 1973.

Wirth, L. "Urbanism as a Way of Life." *American Journal of Sociology,* 44 (1938), 1–24.

Wolf, E. R. *Peasants.* Englewood Cliffs, N.J., 1966.

Peasant Wars of the Twentieth Century. New York, 1969.

Zorbaugh, H. W. *The Gold Coast and the Slum.* Chicago, 1961.

Index

Adana, 6, 11, 59, 60, 61, 64, 66
Agriculture, 17, 19, 21, 109–10,
  181–8, 253 n21 and 23, 256
  n43
Akrabalık (blood relationship), 85,
  86, 115; *see also* Migration,
  patterns of
Alevis, 19, 54, 72, 86, 119–21,
  126–9, 220, 222, 228, 257 n1,
  259 n1, 261 n9, 262 n11; *see
  also* Migrant, religious ties;
  Squatter, political behavior
Algeria, 45; *see also* City, Muslim;
  Migration, beginnings, causes;
  North Africa; Village
Alienation, 36, 43, 246 n69
  in the Celâlettin Paşa settlement,
  124
  in Morocco and Algeria, 45
  of the successful squatter, 114,
  173 (t7.4)
Ankara, 6, 11, 12, 58–61, 64
Anna (Yeniyöl, village of), 177; *see
  also* Village, squatter's influence
Armenians, 48, 51, 53, 252 n15
Armutlu, 179
Asia, 2, 8, 10; *see also* India; United
  Nations, reports
  uncontrolled settlements, 12
  urban population growth, 12
Aşiret (tribe), 118
Assimilation, 43
Atatürk (Mustafa Kemal), 63, 216,
  264 n7

Bachelors, 5, 87, 88 (t3.4), 89
  (t3.5), 90 (t3.6, 3.7), 91 (t3.8,
  3.9), 108 (t4.8), 111, 112, 116
  (t4.11), 135, 186; *see also*
  Migrant; Squatter

aspirations, 159–60 (t6.13–6.16)
  education and literacy, 98–100
  (t4.2), 147–8 (t6.6)
  employment, 100–6 (t4.3, 4.6),
  113 (t4.10)
  life in city, 140–5 (t6.1–6.5)
  and politics, 206–12 (t8.1–8.7),
  216–19 (t8.12, 8.14, 8.15)
  and recreation, 148–9 (t6.7)
  relations with city, 151–8 (t6.12)
  relations with village, 168–70
  (t7.1–7.3), 171, 173–5 (t7.4,
  7.5)
Balán, Jorge, 22, 242 n33
Baltaliman (*Gecekondu* of), 65, 66
  (t2.4), 81; *see also* Gecekondu
  establishment, 81–2
  leadership, 122
  political activities, 199, 226–30
Barriada, 38, 43, 44; *see also* Peru
Başkaya, Mehmet, 229
Başlık, 153; *see also* Squatter,
  changes in concept of family
  and marriage
Beylik, see North Africa
Bidonville, 33, 38, 46, 47, 245 n53,
  248 n83; *see also* Algeria; Integration; Morocco; North
  Africa
Black Sea, *see Gurbetçilik;* Migrant,
  migrant-sending provinces; Migration, beginnings, causes
Brazil, 35, 240 n9
  population growth, 10
  shantytowns, 10–12, 16–17
Buechler, H. C., 41, 249 n86
Bursa, 6, 59–61, 64, 66
Busti, see India
Butterworth, D. S., 246 n62, 67, 248
  n84

285